Film and Ethics

Film and Ethics considers a range of films and texts of film criticism alongside disparate philosophical discourses of ethics by Levinas, Derrida, Foucault, Lacanian psychoanalysts and postmodern theorists.

While an ethics of looking is implicitly posited in most strands of cinema theory, there is no established body of work that might be called ethical film criticism. This book, therefore, redresses the reluctance of many existing works to address cinema from an explicitly ethical perspective.

Readings range across popular Hollywood films such as *Thelma and Louise*, Alfred Hitchcock's canonical corpus, and films from European and World cinemas, including Dreyer's *The Passion of Joan of Arc* and the little-known African film *Bamako*. The book engages with debates concerning censorship and pornography; the ethical implications of 'positive representation'; the ethics of making and viewing images of atrocity and suffering; and the relationship between ethics and aesthetics.

Lisa Downing and Libby Saxton re-invigorate debates in film studies by foregrounding the ethical dimensions of the moving image, and create dialogues between ostensibly incompatible philosophical and political trends of thought, without seeking to reconcile their differences.

Lisa Downing is Professor of French Discourses of Sexuality at the University of Exeter. Her publications include *Patrice Leconte* (2004), *From Perversion to Purity: The Stardom of Catherine Deneuve*, ed. with Sue Harris (2007), and *The Cambridge Introduction to Michel Foucault* (2008).

Libby Saxton is Lecturer in French and Film Studies at Queen Mary, University of London. She is author of *Haunted Images: Film, Ethics, Testimony and the Holocaust* (2008) and co-editor, with Simon Kemp, of *Seeing Things: Vision, Perception and Interpretation in French Studies* (2002).

Film and Ethics

Foreclosed Encounters

Lisa Downing and Libby Saxton

Routledge
Taylor & Francis Group

LONDON AND NEW YORK

British Library Cataloguing in Publication Data
A catalogue record for this book is available from the British Library

Library of Congress Cataloging in Publication Data
Downing, Lisa.
Film and ethics: foreclosed encounters / Lisa Downing and Libby Saxton.
    p. cm.
Includes bibliographical references.
    1. Motion pictures – Moral and ethic aspects. 2. Motion pictures –
Philosophy. I. Saxton, Libby, 1975-II. Title.
        PN1995.5.D63 2009
        791.43'653 – dc22
                    2009007752

ISBN13: 978-0-415-40926-1 (hbk)
ISBN13: 978-0-415-40927-8 (pbk)
ISBN13: 978-0-203-87201-7 (ebk)

Contents

Acknowledgements

An earlier version of the material on *Baise-moi* that appears in Chapter 5 was published as Lisa Downing, '*Baise-moi* or the Ethics of the Desiring Gaze', *Nottingham French Studies*, 45:3, Autumn 2006, 52–65, and is reprinted here by kind permission of *Nottingham French Studies*. An earlier version of the material on Levinas and Lanzmann that appears in Chapter 6 was published as Libby Saxton, 'Fragile Faces: Levinas and Lanzmann', *Film-Philosophy*, 11:2, 2007, 1–14, and is reprinted here by kind permission of *Film-Philosophy*. An earlier version of the material on *Monsieur Hire* that appears in Chapter 8 was published in Lisa Downing, *Patrice Leconte* (Manchester University Press, 2004), 97–104, and is reprinted here by kind permission of Manchester University Press.

Lisa Downing wishes to thank Robert Gillett for inspirational conversations on the ideological differences between *Thelma and Louise* and *Butterfly Kiss*, and Claire Boyle for her helpful comments (and fruitful disagreements) on a draft of the *Butterfly Kiss* material, without which Chapter 2 could not have been written. Dialogue with members of the Critical Sexology Seminar Group and Backlash, especially Alex Dymock, lent crucial activist energies to the material in Chapter 5 on the relationship between theories of pornography and the 'Extreme Images' legislation. Elza Adamowicz and Kiera Vaclavik very kindly invited her to present a paper at the 'Across the Arts' conference held in memory of her former doctoral supervisor, the late Malcolm Bowie, at Queen Mary, University of London in 2007. The material in that paper became Chapter 9 on psychoanalytic ethics, and was written with Malcolm's tremendously creative and innovative applications of psychoanalysis firmly in mind. Other forms of invaluable help and encouragement – both intellectual and personal – were provided by Lucy Bolton, Ben Dennis, Fiona Handyside, Dany Nobus and Helen Vassallo.

Libby Saxton is grateful to Queen Mary, University of London for granting her a semester of sabbatical leave during which much of the material in her chapters was completed. Others to whom she is indebted, variously, for stimulating intellectual exchanges, sound advice and saintly patience are: Claire Boyle, Nemonie Craven, Chris Darke and Anna Morvern.

Both authors owe a debt of thanks to Sarah Cooper, who organized a groundbreaking conference on 'Levinas and Film', at the Institute of Germanic and Romance Studies, London, 2006, where they presented work on film and ethics, and had the rare opportunity to share these seldom-discussed issues with fellow scholars; and Helen Vassallo and Paul Cooke, at whose conference on 'Alienation and Alterity' (University of Exeter, 2007), they were privileged to be invited to present embryonic work that fed in to chapters of this book. Louis Jackson's technical expertise and generous assistance with preparing images for the book are immensely appreciated.

The authors express thanks to each other for the insights gained during the course of this collaboration between two individuals who are fascinated – in both scholarship and life – by very different ethical ideas. During the months of co-writing, Lisa learned the obligation of her responsibility towards the other and Libby learned to follow the truth of her desire!

Introduction

A tremendous amount of moral thinking and feeling is done when reading novels (or watching plays and films, or reading poetry and short stories). In fact it is not an exaggeration to say that for most people, this is the primary way in which they acquire ethical attitudes, especially in contemporary culture.[1]

Critical work in the arts and humanities influenced by those branches of thought known as poststructuralism, have been characterized in recent years by what has been termed a 'turn to ethics'.[2] This post-Second-World-War trend has been brought about by the incorporation into the critical canon of the work of ethical philosophers such as Emmanuel Levinas, the later work of Jacques Derrida (itself borrowing from Levinas's theory), and the ethical dimensions of Lacanian psychoanalysis, feminist thought, postcolonial studies and queer theory.

As the citation from McGinn, which forms the epigraph above, shows, ethics can be thought of as the encounter that occurs between a reader or viewer and a text or work of visual art, as much as a moral or political code in daily life. What McGinn perhaps underplays is the specificity of the role of visual media in contemporary culture (film seems to be an afterthought in his statement). In a society increasingly saturated with images, the visual, rather than the written word, becomes a privileged locus of exploration of the ethical. Ethical criticism has sought to foreground the dimensions of responsibility, self-reflexivity, desire and engagement with otherness, when considering our intellectual (and emotional) attachments to art and culture. However, ethical criticism differs vastly in its attitude towards these questions. Where a Levinasian reading would foreground the responsibility of the self towards the absolute vulnerability of the other, a postmodern Lacanian ethics, as propounded by Slavoj Žižek, would emphasize instead an ethics of the self, in which the ethical gesture would involve fidelity to the real of one's desire, even if this resulted in betrayal or destruction of the other. In either – extreme – scenario, what is at stake is the encounter and the act of interrogating the self about its relationship to the other. As Colin Davis has pointed out, in the context of a Levinasian reading of modern French literature, the ethical turn in criticism needs to take into account the preoccupation with 'alter-icide' (killing the other) visible in postwar cultural production.[3] This is true too of the visual arts, and any ethical enquiry into film will need to engage with the destructive and anti-social, as well the creative and social, energies underpinning and represented in filmic production. If we also take on board ethical philosophical models that admit of negativity within their very framework, the project of ethical criticism becomes even more fraught.

While the poststructuralist ethical turn has influenced literary theory and cultural studies most particularly, film studies has been relatively slow on the uptake. At the same time, however, film scholarship has become increasingly preoccupied by ethical questions, even though this concern with ethics has generally remained implicit. This book aims to redress this reluctance to view the moving image in explicitly ethical terms, to stage the encounter that, as the title suggests, has been *hinted at* in existing criticism, but largely short-circuited, downplayed or foreclosed. Filmmakers have responded in a variety of ways to the challenge of adequately representing identity, difference and the relationship between self and other. Moreover, in tandem with developments in film practice, an ethics of looking is implicitly posited in most strands of theory, from feminist gaze theory, through postcolonial and queer perspectives, to Žižekian accounts of Hollywood cinema. While there is no established body of theory that might be described as 'ethical gaze theory', the idea that ethics is an optics through which we habitually view and conceptualize is a persuasive one.

Summary of key strands in ethical thought

'Ethics' as it is being used in this book, and in the strands of criticism alluded to above, needs to be understood as distinct from (though, without doubt, as a response to) the understanding of ethics that has preoccupied Western moral philosophers from the Greeks up to the present day. Such philosophical models of ethics are informed by, though not reducible to, religious and societal moral discourses. In the analytic tradition, ethics designates the morally practical questions of obligation: What ought I to do in a given situation? What are the limits of my responsibility? How do my actions morally affect the community of which I am a part? Such questions – in both pragmatic and religious contexts – seem to assume that the human being operates from a conscious moral centre, an ethically capable ego. This is the very assumption which continental thought has destabilized and deconstructed.

Contemporary analytical philosophers, such as Martha Nussbaum who has engaged with ethics as a reading as well as living practice, have posited the ethical relationship between reader and text as one of friendship, alliance or community.[4] This positivistic and humanistic model of 'virtue ethics' is at odds with developments in continental thought, which challenge the supremacy of the human subject (as cogito) and insist (especially after Levinas) on the ineffable strangeness of the other whom one could not recognize or assimilate as friend or comrade, but must respect precisely *as* other. This perception is even further from the radical anti-humanistic ethics of a Lacan or a Žižek.

Ethics in its continental sense and in its application for a critical engagement with cultural products can perhaps most profitably be seen as a process of questioning rather than as a positivistic exercise of morality. It must also be dissociated from sentimentality and the knee-jerk neoliberal affect. Michele Aaron articulates this distinction helpfully: 'being moved ... marks [an] experience as moral but not ethical: involuntary emotion is the opposite of reflection and implication'.[5] This conceptualization of ethics frames it as interrogation, and as resistance to affective capitulation to acculturated norms. It is productive to think about what ethics might *do* and where it may be located, rather than what it *is*. Our concept of ethics defines itself in opposition to what Alain Badiou calls 'ethical ideology', i.e. prescriptive moral codes and rules.

The importance of avoiding reifying 'ethics' is itself a part of an ethical project. Levinas's formulation of ethics as 'otherwise than being' – a way of operating beyond ontology and outside of totality (more on this below) – suggests a heuristic modality rather than a positivistic or normative project. Ethics designates a way of responding to the encounter between self and other/s, while suspending the meaning of the subject–object relation, with its implicit dynamic of dominance and subordination. Thus, ethics has been described by Marjorie Garber, Beatrice Hanssen and Rebecca L. Walkowitz as 'a process of formulation and self-questioning that continually rearticulates boundaries, norms, selves and "others"'.[6]

It is worth setting out below in some detail the defining characteristics of the strands of ethical continental thought with which we will engage in this book in our analysis of filmic texts, texts of film criticism, and viewing and filming practices.

Levinas

The writings of Emmanuel Levinas have become a virtually obligatory reference point for contemporary discussions of ethics in the West. Levinas's conception of ethics diverges sharply from those of analytic philosophers and challenges the fundamental premises of traditional moral thought. Early in *Totality and Infinity* (1961), one of his two major philosophical works, Levinas describes ethics as 'a calling into question of my spontaneity by the presence of the Other'.[7] Ethics, then, is framed from the outset as a process of interrogation, rather than a set of rules or theory of the basis for moral choices. The catalyst for this process is a primordial encounter with alterity which disturbs our solitary enjoyment of the world, our illusory position of omnipotence and sovereignty. In the same passage, Levinas emphasizes the 'strangeness' of the Other, 'his irreducibility to the I, to my thoughts and possessions', his 'transcendence', his absolute and irrecuperable alterity.[8] Ethics involves a responsible welcoming of the Other which does not violate its alterity by incorporating it into a pre-existing totality. It is on these grounds that Levinas takes issue with Western philosophy, which in his view 'has most often been an ontology: a reduction of the other to the same', in short, an 'egology'.[9] Levinas seeks to break with this history by repositioning ethics, rather than ontology, as 'first philosophy'.[10] But a series of crucial questions arises here, which threatens to undermine Levinas's project: 'how can the same, produced as egoism, enter into relationship with an other without immediately divesting it of its alterity?'[11] How, for example, can Levinas give an account of the Other without turning that Other into an object of philosophical enquiry and thereby into a projection of the same? Levinas grapples at length with these questions in *Totality and Infinity* and his other key work, *Otherwise than Being or Beyond Essence* (1974), where the difficulty of describing, without betraying, the ethical 'relation without relation' entails a disruption of textuality and a search for new forms of ethical articulation.[12] For Levinas, ethics, the exposure to the Other, incurs an interrogation not only of the self but also of the very language of ethical investigation.

Levinas's writings have been credited with transforming our understanding of ethics in the Western humanities, and many of his key terms – otherness, responsibility, encounter, the face-to-face – have been seamlessly incorporated into contemporary critical discourse. However, this almost ubiquitous acceptance and appropriation may have come at a price. Taking stock of Levinas's legacy, Davis warns against what he sees as a prevalent critical tendency to 'tam[e] ... Levinas's exorbitance', in other words, to bowdlerize and transform Levinas's complex and sometimes unpalatable insights into a 'bland and empty injunction to respect otherness'.[13] While acknowledging its debt to Levinasian thought, this book will not leave it uncontested. We engage with objections to Levinas's claims and contend throughout with the irreconcilable contradictions between his other-oriented ethics and the reorientation towards the self that underpins concurrent traditions of ethical thinking. Chapter 6 explores the relevance of Levinas's insights to the relationships of responsibility between filmmakers, spectators and imaged subjects, arguing that certain films challenge the legitimacy of Levinas's denigration of the gaze as a mechanism of oppression.

Derrida

One of Levinas's most prominent commentators is Jacques Derrida, whose extended essay on *Totality and Infinity*, 'Violence and Metaphysics', published in 1964, played a key role in bringing Levinas's thought to critical attention and shaping its reception in France, the UK and the US. While Derrida has acknowledged the extent of his debt to Levinas, his approach to Levinas's texts is interrogative and deconstructive rather than simply assimilative, in line with the method of reading he advocates. Derrida is more cautious in his use of the term 'ethics' than Levinas and has sometimes seemed reluctant to speak explicitly about the subject. This reticence stems from his suspicion of the philosophical heritage of the term; ethics is part of the Western metaphysical tradition which is one of deconstruction's principal targets. In 'Violence and Metaphysics', Derrida questions the extent to which Levinas's exposition of ethics remains dependent on this tradition and the language of ontology which it simultaneously critiques. At the same time, here and in subsequent readings, Derrida traces a deconstructive gesture in Levinas's writing which breaks with that tradition. Levinas's re-appropriation and redefinition of a term laden with unwelcome metaphysical resonances provides a vital resource for what Simon Critchley calls Derrida's 'double-handed treatment of ethics'.[14] Geoffrey Bennington warns that 'deconstruction cannot propose an ethics'.[15] That is to say, an ethics cannot be seamlessly derived from deconstruction. However, a displaced and displacing sense of the ethical is nonetheless an integral part of its context. Derrida deconstructs ethics, but an ethical residue persists in and orients his writing. Derrida's description of deconstruction as the thinking of 'a relation to what is other' sounds not unlike Levinas's description of ethics.[16] Indeed, ethics has been seen as the 'privileged clue', 'goal' or 'horizon' of Derridean thought.[17] This horizon comes into sharper focus in Derrida's later work, where he turns his attention to concepts of obvious ethical import, including responsibility, duty, justice, the law, the decision, the promise, the gift and hospitality. As we shall see in Chapter 7, Derrida insists that the potential compromise, perversion or betrayal of the ethical relation paradoxically constitute its necessary conditions of possibility.

Lacan and Žižek

Jacques Lacan's seminar on *The Ethics of Psychoanalysis* (1959–60) addresses the question of whether psychoanalysis as a clinical and philosophical discourse can intervene in questions of ethics. Lacan's response places him in direct opposition to the ethics of Levinas, concerned as it is with the status of alterity and the self's responsibility towards its neighbour (a recognisably Judeo-Christian model, paradoxically situated in the largely atheistic context of poststructuralist French thought). For Lacan, qua psychoanalyst, the fundamental category of desire plays a central role in his redefined ethics. Lacan's ethical imperative is: 'do not give up on your desire!' Desire here is understood as a principle of truth that has nothing to do with conventional categories of 'good' or 'bad', which belong in the rational and representational realm of the Symbolic. Rather, desire has everything to do with the Real, the order of the undifferentiated, the ineffable, and therefore of authenticity. Desire in this radical sense seeks neither social approbation nor personal happiness as such. Rather it seeks only fidelity to its uniqueness. Alterity, then, is at stake within Lacanian ethics, but it is the radical strangeness of our own desire, the otherness within — what Lacan terms 'extimacy' — that is of import here.

The category of the Real at certain points in the Lacanian corpus is linked to the realm of human finitude: death. The death-driven aspects of ethics and the Real have been developed by contemporary Lacanians, Alenka Zupančič and, most notably, Slavoj Žižek. In *The Ticklish Subject: The Absent Centre of Political Ontology* (2000), Žižek argues that Lacanian ethics concerns 'those limit-experiences in which the subject finds himself confronted with the death drive at its purest'.[18] An ethical response to the abject encounter with 'self-withdrawal, the absolute contradiction of subjectivity' is to confront it without flinching.[19] This involves, in Žižek's words, a 'subjective destitution'; reduction to an excremental remainder. Ethical subjectivity, then, is an anti-subjectivity. The ethical in Lacan is concerned not with the self as an ego or set of imaginary identifications, but with the self as a principle of negativity.

Lacan's seminar on ethics was used by cultural theorists such as Žižek in the 1980s and 1990s, to elucidate the way in which cultural and artistic products (including popular cultural phenomena such as television and mainstream narrative cinema) often enact and embody the same structures, dilemmas and models as those described in psychoanalytic theory. (Thus, the hard-boiled detective Philip Marlowe exemplifies for Žižek the subject who resists the Real of his desire; as Antigone has exemplified for Lacan the subject who accedes to it and enters her 'living death'.[20]) Žižek's Lacanian writing on film is important for any review of the place of ethical theory in thinking about cinema, and is treated in Chapter 9 of this book.

Feminist ethics

Much Anglo-American feminism, particularly in the early days of the movement(s), was concerned with grass-roots political questions such as civil rights, equal pay and issues regarding women's relationships with their bodies (e.g. contraception and abortion), all of which can be said to engage with a practical ethics. In film studies, 1970s feminist sociologists engaged with the ways in which women were represented on screen as 'positive' or 'negative' stereotypes (more on this in Chapter 2).

British post-Lacanian film theorist Laura Mulvey broke with the tradition of the 'positive images' school of film criticism, introducing to feminist film scholarship the idea, popularized by, among others, Jean-Louis Baudry and Christian Metz, that representations act on the unconscious as well the conscious mental processes. This shows up the limitations of a purely sociological approach. Her seminal article on narrative cinema and visual pleasure (1975) uses the Lacanian concept of scopophilia to describe the relationship between the masculine position of the cinematic viewer and the feminine position of the onscreen object (usually a beautiful film actress), connoting 'to-be-looked-at-ness'. It is possible to revisit this article and the numerous responses, redresses, correctives and derivations it spawned as properly ethical, since it addresses head-on the relationship between subject and other, and a dynamic of pleasurable possession that may be embraced or rejected. Chapter 5 of this book considers the use of feminist ethics in a discussion of the representation of the body and sex acts, to establish how an ethically informed feminist response to pornography might look.

Foucault

Like Lacan's seminar on ethics, Michel Foucault's philosophy has been termed an ethics of the self; as opposed to an ethics of the other, such as we associate with Levinas.[21] John Rajchman has also described Lacan and Foucault as pursuing an 'ethics of Eros', since sexuality is central to ethics in both corpuses. However, Foucault is an anti-Lacanian, questioning the psychoanalytic model of 'desire', which he sees as inevitably linked to the normalizing and pathologizing energies guiding Western models of sexuality (despite Lacan's assertion that desire is not synonymous with a tamed notion of sexuality but with something abject and extreme).

In fact, much of Foucault's corpus can be seen to have ethical undertones – and indeed to raise issues that appear, at least superficially, to touch on an ethics of the other. His early work on madness from the 1960s, for example, argues that the Western Enlightenment scapegoated unreason as inherently different – and inferior – to reason. In the plea on behalf of the irreducible alterity of unreason found in *History of Madness* (1961), we see an almost Levinasian gesture towards the divinity of the other (though the language used does not approximate Levinas's quasi-mystical discourse). And in his work on the penal system and the model of power it generates, *Discipline and Punish* (1975), he considers the means of societal surveillance by which subjects are constructed as 'disciplinary' or docile 'bodies'; subjugated to the ubiquity of modern culture's regimes of practices for bodily control. Yet, it is not until the end of his career that Foucault speculates directly about 'ethics', and this is done in the context of his consideration of the history of sexuality and in particular the means by which subjects of modernity are led to constitute themselves as 'subjects of desire'.

Foucault's *History of Sexuality* comprises three volumes, the first of which, *The Will to Knowledge* (1976), is a historiography of the moment at which sexuality became the object of rational study, the nineteenth century. The second and third (*The Uses of Pleasure* and *The Care for the Self*, both 1984) are histories of ancient practices of the self concerning codes and morals about sexual behaviour, designed to provide a pre-history of the modern 'subject of sex' or 'subject of desire'. As Foucault commented in a late interview on 'The ethics of the concern for self as a practice of freedom':

> I would say that if I am now interested in how the subject constitutes himself in an active fashion, by the practices of self, these practices are nevertheless not something invented by the individual himself. They are

models that he finds in his culture and are proposed, suggested, imposed upon him by his culture, his society, and his cultural group.[22]

Foucault's late ethics is thereby interested in the difficult negotiation between the types of disciplinary training that make certain kinds of body and subject appear, and the (limited) freedom subjects may have for pleasurable self-construction through experiments with new forms of relationality, erotic pleasure and self-care.

Foucault makes it clear that he wants to imagine an ethics that would be appropriate for our historical moment and cultural values, but that would think of more imaginative ways of being, and of being together, than are currently the norm: 'I think that there are more secrets, more possible freedoms, and more inventions in our future than we can imagine in humanism'.[23] Foucault identifies this ethical suspicion of universal humanism as one of the concerns underlying his entire corpus. It was via the lures of humanism, he claims, that 'we' constituted ourselves as subjects through the exclusion of others: the insane, the criminal, the pervert. Foucault wonders in his last works whether there may be a form of ethics of the self that would not work to construct 'other' certain subjects as 'abnormal'; and that would be compatible with a mode of democratic political life.

Foucault's writing can be said to engage an ethics of Eros in more than one way. As well as re-imagining self, state, freedom, bodies and power through Eros, Foucault's ethical writing, in its curiosity and passion, 're-eroticized the activity of philosophical or critical thought for our times'.[24] In sketching his history of the ways in which subjects are taught to conceptualize themselves as 'subjects of desire', and in looking for pockets of ethical resistance via 'technologies of the self' to the institutionalized disciplining of sexual subjects, Foucault's *History of Sexuality*, and his reflections about the processes of writing it, laid important groundwork for late-twentieth and early-twenty-first-century currents of thought. In particular, it influenced the academic and political field of enquiry concerned explicitly with interrogating the truth of sexual knowledge, namely queer theory. In Chapter 8 of this book, the ethical implications of Foucault's theories for considering the power relations implicit in cinematic viewing, and forms of corporeal representation, are discussed.

Badiou

Badiou's *Ethics: An Essay on the Understanding of Evil* (1998) constitutes an attack both on humanistic concepts of ethics and on the kinds of ethical premise associated with Levinas's privileging of the Other. Both of these he terms '"ethical" ideology' and he associates them with sentimental ideologies of contemporary liberalism. Badiou's account discusses two realms of experience: 'knowledge' and 'truth'. The former is everyday, factual and attainable. The second is transcendental, ineffable and only approached via the 'subject of truth'; an ethical subject who is a 'militant' of the truth; who 'holds true' to a principle. A properly ethical act, then, for Badiou, is that which 'helps to preserve or en-*courage* a subjective fidelity'.[25] It is a selfless pursuit of the truth, which inevitably flees and evades human life. The Badiousian ethical can be summarized by the imperative 'keep going!' or 'continue!'; designating the necessity to avoid the 'forms of corruption or exhaustion that can beset a fidelity to truth'.[26] These forms of corruption (or 'evil') are threefold: betrayal, delusion and terror. The first (betrayal) describes the lure of temptation that might beset the subject of truth and send him or her off course. The second (delusion) designates the elision of the universal nature of the genuine event and its collapse onto the specific address located in a particular community. Nazi propaganda and politics exemplify this form of corruption for Badiou. The third (terror) evokes the hubris of one who sacrifices the search for truth to the temptation to impose order and meaning on events (i.e. to put knowledge in the place of truth). Stalinism is given as a political example of this.

Badiou's ethics is something close to a Sartrean 'project'. It argues that 'there can be no "ethics in general", no general principle of human *rights* for the simple reason that what is universally human is always rooted in particular truths, particular configurations of active thought'.[27] Against the humanism of a more conventional ethics, Badiou draws on the anti-humanist poststructuralist perspectives of Foucault and Lacan described above, stating powerfully and uncompromisingly that 'all ethical predication based on recognition of the other should be purely and simply abandoned'.[28] Badiou proposes an ethics not of the other but of *the Same* since differences *are*, but the Same is what may *come to be*. This generic Same must avoid translating truth into knowledge and the other corruptions, but in its ethical form, may transform universal truth into a good that is valid for all, while attending to and guarding against local and specific bigotry. It is not, however, a defensive ethics, responding to pre-existing situations of inequality, but a constructive ethics of truth; in which the *event* stages the encounter between the Same and the truth; not between the one and the other. Badiou's text is difficult to situate accurately in discourses of ethics. It is a seemingly anti-ethical ethics; an anti-postmodern, absolutist rant against moral relativism which can appear strangely fundamentalist. However, at the same time, it also clearly engages with postmodernist thinking, for example Žižek's theories. In Chapter 10, a whimsical reading of Quentin Tarantino's *Kill Bill* (2003 and 2004) through the lens of the Badiousian idea of the 'subject of truth' is undertaken, in counterpoint with a consideration of postmodern and post-human theories that engage with ethics (by such names as Zygmunt Bauman and Jean Baudrillard).

***

Taking account of the importance of the – often contradictory – ideas of the ethical sketched above, this book seeks not only to make ethics more explicit as a concern for cinema theory, but also to challenge assumptions regarding the meaning of the term. No one philosopher's definition or model of ethics is given 'authority' status, though the work of Levinas, Lacan and Derrida will be particularly significant reference points, given the influence they have had on contemporary critical discourse. Our aim in taking these philosophers to the cinema is not to find straightforward filmic illustrations and validations of their philosophies, as this would do violence to the specificity of the filmic medium, but to place film and thought in dialogue with each other. This allows us to explore how films might pose similar ethical questions to theory, but in a visual register which generates an ethicized engagement that is materially and experientially different from that produced by the reading encounter.

Just as we recognize the importance of avoiding reducing film to a mere illustration of philosophy, so we are aware that ethical criticism has been accused of evacuating the political significance of the phenomena it analyses, and this also requires a pre-emptive defence. This charge of political indifference rests on a false dichotomy which assumes that politics and ethics can be neatly distinguished one from the other. All the philosophers discussed in the book have made philosophically informed commentaries on, and interventions into, debates and events of political import. Levinas's discussions of war in general and the Israeli–Palestinian conflict in particular; Derrida's writings on Marxism, democracy, Europe, apartheid and immigration; Foucault's patients' and prisoners' rights activism; Žižek's theorization of 9/11; Badiou's references to Nazism and Stalinism all suggest that at least some terrain is inevitably shared between ethics and the political. Levinas and Derrida in particular have grappled with the question of how to conceive of an ethical politics, one which respects, rather than reduces, the alterity and transcendence of the other – in short, a politics that begins with ethics. Levinasian ethics opposes totalizing forms of politics which lead to war and genocide with a politics rooted in our responsibility to alterity, deriving from an encounter with the Other which is fundamentally peaceful in nature.[29] Rather than trapping the subject within an exclusive duality, this encounter makes the subject aware of the presence of the third party, of other others, positioning him or her within a political context and alerting him or her to the exigency of justice.[30] Derrida investigates these issues further in *Adieu to Emmanuel Levinas* (1997), where he questions the relationship between a Levinasian '*ethics* of hospitality (an ethics *as* hospitality) and a *law* or *politics* of hospitality'.[31] Derrida suggests that while the latter cannot be straightforwardly deduced from the former, this impossibility or 'hiatus' is instructive in itself since it demands that we rethink law and politics. For Derrida, rather than sidestepping the political, Levinas's account of ethics implies the need to take political decisions and responsibilities 'without the assurance of an ontological foundation'.[32] Ethics becomes unethical if it does not expose itself to the possibility of betrayal and contamination inherent in political and juridical discourse, in the attempt to establish laws and rights. Derrida's is only one particular take on the relationship between ethics and politics, and one which would be contested by the ethicists of the self. Nevertheless, the recognition that ethics and politics are mutually implicated and enabling, yet irreducible to one another, informs our investigations in this book; investigations which we sometimes refer to as 'ethico-political'.

Our model of ethics is deliberately not totalizing. It is not a first philosophy, a master-narrative or a meta-paradigm which seeks to exceed other critical approaches or to reduce all reflection on cinema to ethical concerns. Rather we aim to articulate how ethics may be integral to film practice, the phenomenology of cinema, and to much film theory. We also develop a discussion of the inter-relatedness of politics and ethics by locating the ethical in branches of film theory (feminist, queer, postcolonial) that are more usually thought of as political. Rather than devising a system of values in which films can be classified as 'ethical' or 'unethical', we contend that the ethical is the *context* in which all filmmaking takes place, since the creation and reception of a work of art always already engage desire and responsibility (for both artist and audience). Whenever we negotiate between desire and responsibility, we place ourselves in the arena of ethics.

Existing ethical perspectives in film theory

As already stated, film studies has had surprisingly little to say about ethics, at least in the philosophical sense in which the term is used here. Ethics as a legalistic category has, however, been discussed in relation to documentary. There is a significant body of work on the rights of documentary subjects which turns on issues of responsibility and informed consent.[33] However, in the 1980s and 1990s, two American film scholars, Vivian Sobchack and Bill Nichols, began to look beyond these strictly juridical concerns in their work on ethical space in documentary. In a phenomenological reading of unsimulated representations of death in non-fiction film, Sobchack observed that the event of death charges both filmmaker and spectator with ethical responsibility for their acts of filming and viewing. She explored how the filmmaker's relation to the death filmed is inscribed on the screen, where it is open to ethical scrutiny by the viewer, whose own look in turn becomes an object of ethical judgement. 'Responsibility for the representation of death', she surmised, 'lies with both filmmaker and spectator – and in the ethical relationship constituted between the vision of each'.[34] Nichols developed several of Sobchack's propositions in a study of what he called 'axiographics' in documentary: 'the attempt to explore the implantation of values in the configuration of space, in the constitution of a gaze, and in the relation of observer to observed'.[35] Nichols argued, contentiously, that the difference between fiction and documentary is similar to that between 'an erotics and an ethics'.[36] In his account, the gendering and eroticization of the gaze identified by Mulvey in classic narrative film does not translate directly into documentary, where the object of desire is the historical world and the real social actors which inhabit it, and which therefore calls instead for an ethical interpretation. Sobchack's and Nichols's interventions highlighted the centrality of ethical issues in non-fiction film practice and criticism and paved the way for new interdisciplinary endeavours. However, they used the term 'ethics' in a general sense which remains bound up with traditional ideas of moral judgement, rather than engaging with the poststructuralist reconceptualizations of ethical concepts discussed in this book. Chapter 1 contextualizes these approaches to documentary filmmaking within a longer tradition of philosophical speculation on the morality of representation.

More recently, certain scholars have reviewed films in the light of ethical discourses in philosophy, and Levinas's thought has been a privileged point of reference in this context. Once again, this line of enquiry has most often been pursued with respect to documentary corpuses. Sarah Cooper's *Selfless Cinema? Ethics and French Documentary* (2006) demonstrates how Levinas's concept of the 'visage', or face, can be used to elucidate the place accorded to alterity in a spectrum of postwar French non-fiction films. Addressing the common supposition in documentary theory that film sets up a contract with its viewers according to which it will gratify their desire for knowledge, Michael Renov uses Levinas's thought to move beyond this limiting preoccupation with epistemology. In two chapters of *The Subject of Documentary* (2004), he suggests that a Levinasian approach would prioritize ethics over knowledge and ontology.[37]

The fact that most discussions of film and ethics to date have focused on documentary has perpetuated the misleading assumption that ethical issues are somehow less important or urgent in narrative cinema. Increasingly, however, classic and contemporary narrative film is also being reconsidered in the light of ethical discourses in philosophy and psychoanalysis. A number of recent titles in film studies address ethical questions as they arise in the work of given directors, without making broader claims for the significance of ethical thought for film studies – or vice versa. One director who has generated a wealth of ethical critical attention is Lars von Trier; unsurprisingly perhaps, as the *Dogme 95* manifesto is explicitly concerned with troubling the conventions of narrative film and the activity of spectatorship. *The Idiots* (*Idioterne*, 1998) investigates the morality of looking on, as it depicts behaviour that threatens bourgeois social mores and politically correct assumptions about the representation of the mentally ill.[38] Another director whose work has been discussed in this context – less predictably – is Tarantino. In *The Tarantinian Ethics* (2001), for example, Fred Botting and Scott Wilson draw on the insights of Lacanian psychoanalysis and Levinasian philosophy to analyze the unpredictable, accidental encounters with the Other staged in Tarantino's films. Ethical perspectives are also at stake in Robert Samuels's *Hitchcock's Bi-textuality: Lacan, Feminisms and Queer Theory* (1998). Samuels draws on Lacanian ethics and recent theories of feminine and queer subjectivity to reread a series of canonical Hitchcock films against the heterosexual grain. Lisa Downing's book on Patrice Leconte (2004) devotes a chapter to theorizing the possibility of applying discourses of postmodern ethics (Levinas, Bauman, Žižek) to the type of popular narrative film exemplified by that director's corpus. In *Haunted Images: Film, Ethics, Testimony and the Holocaust* (2008), Libby Saxton rereads films by directors such as Claude Lanzmann and Jean-Luc Godard in the context of recent debates between French filmmakers, philosophers and historians about ethics, representability and documentary images of the Nazi camps.

Genre has also been interrogated for its potential to yield specific ethical responses. Peter French's *Cowboy Metaphysics: Ethics and Death in Westerns* (1997), for example, explores the way in which the Western offers a view of death as annihilation, as the absolute limit of life, and thereby proposes an ethical model of finitude that challenges the Judeo-Christian ethics of behaviour and redemption, life and afterlife. The cowboy is the figure whose intimate connection to his own end, and knowledge of it as a limit-point, makes any act of protection or sacrifice a pure act in and of itself, rather than a guarantee of salvation after death. In a discussion of the genre of the action film, in the issue of *Film-Philosophy* devoted to Levinas, Reni Celeste posits that action is what promises to free film from the fixity of the photographic image, and move it away from the iconography that Levinas decries as unethical.[39] However, in the ensuing argument, it emerges that the action film is both tragic and pleasurable (according to a Nietzschean perspective), such that it fails entirely to deliver on the promise of an ethical movement that propels us away from the frozen nightmare of the artwork. In the lectures collected in *Cities of Words: Pedagogical Letters on a Register of the Moral Life* (2004), Stanley Cavell argues that Hollywood comedies of remarriage from the 1930s and 1940s dramatize a dimension of moral thinking concerned with perfectionism, or the utopian aspiration to a just society. Following the evolution of this concern through the work of philosophers and literary figures such as Plato, Aristotle, Kant, Nietzsche, Freud and Shakespeare, Cavell finds it reconfigured in the remarriage genre, where the crisis faced by the principal couple reveals the split between an imperfect present and an imagined just community, prompting a transformation of interpersonal relations.

While each of these publications has made a valuable contribution to this nascent field, they have limited their ethical readings to a small corpus of films from a single national cinema, to a specific genre or theme, or to the work of an individual director. Joseph Kupfer's *Visions of Virtue in Popular Film* (1999) has ranged more widely across these categories, in attempting to analyze 'popular films with a decidedly moral content'.[40] The kind of method exemplified by Kupfer is described, after Alasdair MacIntyre's Aristotelian model in *After Virtue: A Study in Moral Theory* (1981), as 'virtue theory'. This examines the conduct of a 'self responsible for action' and measures the extent to which this self embodies socially prescribed virtues.[41] A significant problem with this approach from our point of view is that it assumes a 'relatively unified conception of the self'[42] which is at odds with poststructuralist models of subjectivity deriving from Lacan, Foucault, Derrida, amongst others, that underpin our argument.

Michele Aaron, whose theoretical framework more closely approximates our own, has devoted a single chapter of *Spectatorship: The Power of Looking On* (2007) to the ethical dynamics of the contractual alliances between spectators and films. Via readings of an eclectic range of narrative films, she argues that looking in cinema is never innocent or neutral but always complicit and thus ethically implicated. Contending that narrative cinema has historically avoided ethical reflection through its moral frameworks and fictional basis, Aaron attempts to demonstrate how certain films actively foreground and investigate the processes through which agency and responsibility are ascribed to spectators.

This brief survey shows that what remains missing from existing work on film and ethics is a study which provides a systematic evaluation of existing scholarship; broadens the scope of inquiry to include a wider range of both theoretical and filmic texts; and explores cinema's potential to constitute a genuinely ethical space of experience. Our book aims to fill this critical lacuna: it both describes the key issues in the field and suggests directions for future research.

***

Film and Ethics: Foreclosed Encounters is divided into two sections. The first section deals with representation and spectatorship. On the one hand, we explore ethical issues arising from the form and content of the filmed image. We begin by showing how the relationship between ethics and aesthetics has a long history in post-Enlightenment philosophy that is often overlooked in discussions of cinematic representation. We then move to a critique of the notion of 'positive representations' (of gendered, sexual and ethnic identities) in film. The last two chapters in this section address the ways in which spectators view and theorists conceive of spectatorship. We do this via case studies of pornography and the ethics of censorship, and viewers' ambivalent investments in images of others' suffering. Section 2 explores the ways in which postwar continental philosophy (Levinas, Derrida, Foucault, Lacan, Žižek, postmodern theory) helps us to conceptualize the phenomenology of cinema along ethical lines. Both sections consist of a co-authored exposition, followed by five single-authored chapters, offering a range of critical perspectives on the subject.

The co-authorship of this book facilitates the interrogatory approach that we believe to be most appropriate to our subject-matter. The single-authored chapters within the two sections adopt sometimes contrasting perspectives, while incorporating reflection on the points of contact which emerge between them. The dual authorship of the book enables us to address a broader range of critical perspectives, since the authors have expertise in distinct areas, as reflected in previously published works in the field of film and ethics. While Libby Saxton has written on documentary and narrative post-Holocaust filmmaking with reference to Levinas, Derrida and theoretical debates about the ethics of representing and viewing atrocities, Lisa Downing has published mainly on the ethics of gendered, sexed and erotic representations in narrative films using psychoanalytic and queer frameworks, and readings of Levinas against the grain. The book brings together approaches to narrative and documentary filmmaking; issues of viewing and theorizing; and the ethics of 'self' and 'other'. Our distinct approaches are reflected in the conceptions of ethics that underpin the readings in our individual chapters. Where an ethics of otherness and responsibility informs much of Saxton's theorization, Downing often locates the ethical in the sometimes anti-social and self-oriented energies of radical philosophies influenced by psychoanalysis and queer. The book thereby offers not only an introduction to, and critical reflection on, the relationship between ethical thought and film, but also stages a set of encounters between apparently opposing or contradictory perspectives and refuses to flatten out the difficulty of ethical engagement with difference.

Notes

1 McGinn, *Ethics, Evil and Fiction*, 174–5.
2 See: Garber, Hanssen and Walkowitz (eds), *The Turn to Ethics*.
3 Davis, *Ethical Issues in Twentieth-Century French Fiction*, 11.
4 See, for example: Nussbaum, *Love's Knowledge* and 'Non-Relative Virtues'.
5 Aaron, *Spectatorship*, 116.
6 Garber, Hanssen and Walkowitz (eds), *The Turn to Ethics*, viii.
7 Levinas, *Totality and Infinity*, 43.
8 Levinas, *Totality and Infinity*, 43.
9 Levinas, *Totality and Infinity*, 43, 44.
10 Levinas, *Totality and Infinity*, 304.
11 Levinas, *Totality and Infinity*, 38.
12 Levinas, *Totality and Infinity*, 80.
13 Davis, 'Levinas at 100', 98, 97.
14 Critchley, *The Ethics of Deconstruction*, 13–20.
15 Bennington, 'Deconstruction and Ethics', 64.
16 Derrida, 'The Deconstruction of Actuality: An Interview with Jacques Derrida', 31.
17 Bennington, 'Deconstruction and Ethics', 64; Critchley, *The Ethics of Deconstruction*, 2.
18 Žižek, *The Ticklish Subject*, 160.
19 Žižek, *The Ticklish Subject*, 154.
20 See Žižek, *Looking Awry: An Introduction to Jacques Lacan Through Popular Culture*, 48–66.
21 An essay which makes explicit this distinction is Barry Smart's 'Foucault, Levinas and the Subject of Responsibility'.
22 Foucault, *Essential Works*, vol. 1, 291.
23 Foucault, *Technologies of the Self*, 15.
24 Rajchman, *Truth and Eros*, 1.
25 Badiou, *Ethics*, translator's Introduction, xi.

26 Badiou, *Ethics*, translator's Introduction, xi.

27 Badiou, *Ethics*, translator's Introduction, xiv.

28 Badiou, *Ethics*, translator's Introduction, xv.

29 For Levinas's critique of totalizing politics see, for example, *Totality and Infinity*, 21–22 and 'Ethics and Politics', 289–97. Critchley argues that 'politics provides the continual horizon of Levinasian ethics, and that the problem of politics is that of delineating a form of political life that will repeatedly interrupt all attempts at totalization' (*The Ethics of Deconstruction*, 223).

30 See, for example, Levinas, *Totality and Infinity*, 212–14, and *Otherwise than Being or Beyond Essence*, 16.

31 Derrida, *Adieu to Emmanuel Levinas*, 19.

32 Derrida, *Adieu to Emmanuel Levinas*, 21.

33 See, for example, Calvin Pryluck, 'Ultimately We are All Outsiders: The Ethics of Documentary Filming'.

34 Sobchack, 'Inscribing Ethical Space: Ten Propositions on Death, Representation, and Documentary', 244.

35 Nichols, *Representing Reality*, 78.

36 Nichols, *Representing Reality*, 76.

37 Renov, *The Subject of Documentary*, 148–67.

38 For (very different) discussions of von Trier's films in the light of ethical criticism, see, for example: Aaron, *Spectatorship*, 98–109, and Nobus, 'The Politics of Gift-Giving and the Provocation of Lars von Trier's *Dogville*'.

39 Celeste, 'The Frozen Screen: Levinas and the Action Film'.

40 Kupfer, *Visions of Virtue*, 1.

41 Kupfer, *Visions of Virtue*, 3.

42 Kupfer, *Visions of Virtue*, 31.

Section 1

Introduction to Section 1

Representation and spectatorship

Perhaps the most obvious way of thinking about the ethical in film is to consider representations of agents facing ethical dilemmas on screen. The most popular forms of film recurrently stage battles between 'good' and 'evil' or virtue and vice. Many Hollywood narratives, regardless of genre, inscribe themselves within a moral framework in which virtue often manifests as self-sacrifice for the greater good. An obvious example is the denouement of *Casablanca* (Michael Curtiz, 1942), in which the protagonist chooses duty to the ideal of democracy over the personal aims of romantic love and desire. The emphasis on self-sacrifice is recognizable as an inheritance of the Judaeo-Christian tradition, which is more explicitly evoked in films such as the theological thriller *The Exorcist* (William Friedkin, 1973), in which good and evil are not metaphorized, but theological absolutes.

Self-sacrifice is often represented alongside other traditional virtues, including courage, loyalty and wisdom. Dominant forms of narrative film typically present us with a hero who embarks upon a quest which is coded as moral, in the course of which he is called upon to display these virtues. In the introduction, we made mention of Kupfer's *Visions of Virtue* as a work which deals directly with such moral protagonists. As well as the reservations we expressed there concerning his conception of a unified subject, a further problem with Kupfer's application of 'virtue theory' to film is its tendency to elide the differences between real and represented agents. It ignores the specificity of the filmic medium and the ways in which the apparatus manipulates and conditions our responses to the hero's actions. In classical Hollywood cinema, the agent embodying the role of 'hero' is typically a straight, white man. Criticism such as Kupfer's does nothing to dispel the myth of neutrality contained within the model of the universal subject proposed by humanism (oft deconstructed by feminist, queer and postcolonial theory). Kupfer's account exemplifies the danger of ethical theory without sensitivity to the politics of identity. With one exception, the agents of virtue he discusses are white males, the nuclear family and a heterosexual couple.

Certain recent films have explored what happens to the moral structure defined above when the 'hero' figure, or the focus of our identification, has a different identity. This moves us properly from the concerns of 'virtue theory' into the realm of the ethico-political, and from the universal self to plural subjects whose differences are foregrounded. When women and members of ethnic and sexual minority groups occupy the role traditionally allotted to the male hero of the moral quest or dilemma, the narrative implicitly affirms this sensitivity to difference. The question of positive representation is at stake here.

The kind of sensitivity to difference to which ideas of positive representation appeal – often pejoratively labeled 'political correctness' – would be anathema to an anti-humanist philosopher such as Badiou, who calls such discourses '"ethical" ideology' to distinguish them from a search for 'truth'. However, what Badiou overlooks is that certain strands within feminist, queer and postcolonial thought self-reflexively problematize the reification of identity and resist the solidification of political impulses into ethical ideology. Moreover, Badiou's strategic attempt to recuperate the category of the universal as an alternative to both neoliberal discourses of tolerance and the 'ethics of otherness' exemplified by Levinas, may be premature. It runs the risk of assuming that the work these strands of thought and politics need to do to highlight real instances of oppression has already been done, and that we are thereby in a position to consider them obsolete and abandon them. Recognition of the necessity of this work is reflected in the structure of this book. Before moving on to a consideration of such radical refusals of commonsense notions of ethics, we need to interrogate the potential of representational ethics and identity politics. This will also involve examining their own points of resistance to categories of identity, as found in 'queer' and in deconstructive strands of feminism and postcolonial theory.

Chapters 2 and 3 demonstrate that, in order to think through these questions of identity and representation, it is essential to take account of the registers into which cinema translates power relations. This is to avoid the pitfalls of reflection theory and its assumption of the possibility of straightforward mimetic replication of social reality. These registers include the manipulation of generic and narrative codes, the organization of cinematic space (how our attention is directed to certain characters or objects through their positioning within the field of vision), the ascription of optical and figural point of view to a given character, and the means of spectatorial position. More generally, we argue that any formal decision (e.g. a fixed camera, a tracking shot, or a cut) functions as an imprint of the film's ethical valences. If we accept that filmmaking takes place in the realm of the ethical since these decisions involve a negotiation between desire and responsibility, as argued in the introduction, then every aesthetic decision has an ethical dimension.

Certain types of shot carry very obvious ethical implications, e.g. the closing shot of *It's a Wonderful Life* (Frank Capra, 1947), where the camera homes in to frame the couple and their child, thereby re-establishing the film's family values that had been temporarily threatened in the course of the narrative. In other cases, a normative moral message can be subversively undermined by a formal decision, as discussed in several chapters of this book. Other forms of shot that appear neutral, however, must also be understood to reflect an ethical perspective. The apparent neutrality of the camera does not necessarily imply moral indifference or the absence of any ethical position. For example, filming an act of violence from a fixed, see-mingly objective, point of view (as in the rape scene of *Irréversible*, Gaspar Noé, 2002 or the suicide scene of *Caché*, Michael Haneke, 2005) may be a means of disorienting the viewer rather than indicating indifference to or complicity with the event. Such instances produce moments of ethical ambiguity, as witnessed by ongoing critical debates about the significance of these scenes. The camera refuses to inscribe a moral perspective or offer a prescription of appropriate spectator response. In certain cases, there may in fact be a moral perspective offered on the event, but it is communicated through cinematic means other than camerawork. In one scene of *Code inconnu* (*Code Unknown*, Haneke, 2001), for example, the apparent objectivity of a static shot of an underground train carriage is undermined by the narrative privileging of interest in one of the passengers. While information about the histories of the second-generation North African immigrant passengers is withheld, we are co-opted into sympathizing with the white middle-class woman (Juliette Binoche) who is insulted by them, both because we have been given the information about her back story, and because of Binoche's star status that (however unconsciously) compels our complicity.

The points made above regarding the relationship between form and content may apply to both documentary and fiction films. However, documentary theorists have argued that distinctive ethical questions are raised by filming documentary subjects as opposed to actors playing fictional characters. While our analyses are informed by this critical assertion, they will also test its validity as a universal claim. We acknowledge that in documentary, the shot can be seen as a more direct imprint of the filmmaker's relationship to his or her subjects, whereas in fiction film the filmmaker's ethico-political position cannot be directly inferred in this way. However, the reification of these distinctions has led to a tendency to downplay the extent to which fiction film also directly embodies ethical perspectives. We would make the more nuanced claim that whereas in documentary, the ethical perspective reflected is more likely to be that of the director, in fiction film the diegetic world is apt to construct an ethical framework that may or may not directly align with the director's ethico-political position. Moreover, these distinctions are further complicated by modes of documentary consumption (the assumptions with which we come to a film). The ethical values embedded in documentary space are discussed in relation to wider historical debates about ethics and aesthetics in Chapter 1.

The fact that ethical meaning does not reside purely in the flow of images but emerges more urgently in the course of the reception and circulation of these images – in the multifarious encounters between audiences and films – raises questions about the ethics of the act of viewing: who is looking at whom, and how, and what kind of relations are established or dismantled in this encounter? Explicitly or implicitly, such questions have remained a perennial preoccupation of theoretical accounts of spectatorship, from early sociological studies of film audiences, through psychoanalytic accounts of spectatorial identification and desire, to more recent analyses of spectatorial heterogeneity. Current debates about spectatorship revolve around the spectatorial differences (of gender, sexuality, class, race and ethnicity) that disrupt the fixity of earlier models of viewing relations. Drawing on the insights of queer theory and postcolonial theory, film theorists have asked whether viewing positions (and the ideologies they presuppose) are determined in advance by perspectives already inscribed in the image, or whether they can instead be subverted by resistant viewing practices which refuse to see 'straight' and instead 'look awry'. In its critique of homogenous categorization, such work is insistently inflected by ethico-political concerns with difference and alterity, with marginalized voices and stigmatized communities.

In spite of the many discussions of plurality in spectatorship theory, the dynamics of spectatorship have yet to be fully unpacked in explicitly ethical terms. This is perhaps surprising, given that cinema was, in the early days of the medium, accused of being immoral due to the fascination it exerted over its viewers. In Chapters 4 and 5, we examine two types of spectacle that continue to be construed as particularly morally problematic: images of atrocity and suffering, and so-called 'pornographic' images. The chapters tackle comparable questions from differing perspectives. Where looking at representations of suffering can be seen to charge the viewer with responsibility, especially where the suffering on screen is 'real', i.e. footage of war, genocide or murder, sometimes intercut with fictional scenes in a narrative film (as in the case study of *Persona* discussed in Chapter 4), ethical debates turn on the question of the spectator's implication in the suffering watched, and ask what the limits of spectatorial responsibility are. The discussion of the category of images labelled pornography in Chapter 5, on the other hand, addresses the complex question of rights when it comes to viewing spectacles that are interpreted as pleasurable by some; distasteful or ethically repugnant by others. The debate engages both legal questions concerning the production, circulation and possession of pornography, on the one hand, as well as a more philosophical set of concerns, on the other, regarding the troubled status of 'reality' in pornography. Also at stake is porn's capacity – in its filmed forms – to alter and play with its meanings through the kinds of cinematic manipulation of genre and point of view that we have discussed with regard to narrative and documentary films. The fact that Saxton's chapter addresses an ethics of responsibility, while Downing's problematizes discourses that would seek to render reprehensible the pleasure of looking – to restate the ethical importance of having the right to look – typifies, perhaps, the different models of ethics with which we are, individually, most concerned. In both chapters, however, the case studies chosen show that often the most apparently pernicious representations are the ones that can enlist the viewer in particularly nuanced ethical reflection. When we inject the factor of guilty pleasure into the experience of viewing the morally reviled, we are faced with the often disavowed messiness and ambivalence of ethical response.

Chapter 1

'Tracking shots are a question of morality'

Ethics, aesthetics, documentary

Libby Saxton

Probably the best-known critical statement about film and ethics is Jean-Luc Godard's quip in 1959 that 'le travelling est affaire de morale' ('tracking shots are a question of morality'). Asked during a round-table discussion of *Hiroshima mon amour* (Alain Resnais, 1959) whether the unease generated by the film was moral or aesthetic, Godard provocatively reformulated a remark made by Luc Moullet in defence of the films of Samuel Fuller: 'la morale est affaire de travellings' ('morality is a question of tracking shots').[1] Both these claims posit a connection between ethics and aesthetics; more specifically, they suggest that moral significance is generated by the formal organization of pro-filmic reality through *mise-en-scène*, rather than intrinsic to that reality. While Moullet's comment carries the reactionary implication that morality is *only* a question of tracking shots, Godard's version implies that an ethical hermeneutics might destabilize traditional distinctions between form and content. In Godard's account, the tracking shot functions as a synecdoche for

Figure 1 Être et avoir

cinematic form and *mise-en-scène*. Such affirmations of the moral and, by implication, political significance of *mise-en-scène* may be seen as strategic at a time when cinema's status as a serious art form was still contested, and underpinned the *mise-en-scène* criticism pioneered in the 1950s in the French journal *Cahiers du cinéma*. Yet although Godard's provocation retains little of its original polemical force today – ironically, it has been reduced to a cliché – much contemporary film criticism remains indebted to his insight. 'To write about cinema, today, is to inherit … [an] *idée fixe*: tracking shots are a question of morality', observed one French critic in 1998 of a formulation which has also found resonance in contexts outside France.[2] For Godard's remark raises a question of continuing pertinence in film studies: to what extent does aesthetic form, or style, determine ethical meaning?

While this question has been addressed from a variety of perspectives in film theory and criticism, it needs to be understood within the context of a Western tradition of aesthetic inquiry which predates the invention of cinema. Moullet and Godard were heirs to a legacy of philosophical conjecture about the relation between aesthetics and ethics, or the beautiful and the good, which stretches back to the ancient Greeks. In dialogues such as the *Phaedrus*, the *Philebus* and the *Symposium*, Plato suggested that our appreciation of beauty can lead to knowledge of moral goodness, even though he had misgivings about mimesis and famously excluded poets and painters from his ideal republic. Aristotle responded in the *Nicomachean Ethics* by defending imitation and art as conducive to moral formation. These connections were reconsidered by Enlightenment philosophers such as Immanuel Kant, whose views on the moral value of aesthetic experience retain an influence today and occupy a prominent, if embattled, position in Continental thought. Implicitly, in asserting that tracking shots were constitutive of morality, Moullet and Godard were simultaneously reclaiming and contesting this legacy. On the one hand, they were staking out a place for cinema and cinephilia in the history of Western aesthetics; on the other, they were proposing that we require a new account of the alliance between beauty and goodness to understand the affective and cognitive experiences offered by film.

This chapter begins with a brief look back at theories of aesthetics which emerged in the eighteenth and nineteenth centuries. It then turns to two attempts to rethink the relationship between ethics and aesthetics in the light of the specific properties of cinematic technology, one in French cinephilic criticism and the other in North American documentary theory. The rest of the chapter aims to elucidate a particular conjunction of aesthetic concerns and ethical vision though analysis of a documentary at the centre of recent debates about filmmakers' responsibilities toward their subjects. It is important to emphasize at the outset that this chapter deals with only two of many approaches to film form that are explicitly ethical in their orientation and to acknowledge the limitations of those considered. Despite its declared interest in questions of morality, the *mise-en-scène* criticism promoted by Moullet and Godard in the mid-twentieth century has been condemned for its romantic, pre-structuralist view of art and politically reactionary formalism. Such approaches provide at best suggestive points of departure for ethical criticism, rather than fully developed interpretative frameworks. Moreover, the models of ethics discussed in this chapter either predate poststructuralism, or, in the case of one documentary theorist, reject it as having minimal regard for ethical experience (an allegation which is refuted throughout this book).[3] Poststructuralist critics have challenged some of the fundamental beliefs of the Enlightenment philosophers alluded to here: their faith in universal humanity, a transcendental, unified subject and emancipatory grand narratives of science and reason. Subsequent chapters of this book highlight the problems with a Kantian view of the moral agent as rational, autonomous and universal and examine alternative models of ethical subjectivity.

The good, the bad and the beautiful: Kant, Schiller and Hegel

In *Critique of Judgement* (1790) Kant argues that 'the beautiful is a symbol of the morally good'.[4] Kant does not mean that beautiful objects are of intrinsic moral worth. On the contrary, he insists that aesthetics and ethics are entirely separate domains, but explains that there is an 'analogy' between the ways in which we judge aesthetic and moral value.[5] The four moments of the beautiful described in this text bear a structural resemblance to the theory of moral action he had previously outlined in *Groundwork of the Metaphysics of Morals* (1785). Kant maintains that judgements of what is beautiful, just like judgements of what is good, are disinterested, even if they coincide with personal inclination, and universally valid or normative in status. Furthermore, both are autonomous, or freely made, rather than dictated by external laws. Just as a moral act is the result of a free individual choice made in accordance with duty, so an experience of beauty is the consequence of the 'free-play' of the imagination and understanding which organize the sensuous components of an object into a 'purposive' form.[6] In Kant's account, these structural similarities mean that aesthetic experience can act as a 'propaedeutic' for morality; beauty can prepare us for moral action by revealing its structure symbolically through sensible form.[7]

Kant's preoccupation with form is pertinent in the context of the claims about filmic *mise-en-scène* mentioned above, which identify the ethical with the formal choices made in reshaping the world through cinematic technology. For Kant, it is a beautiful object's seemingly harmonious form, which is constructed subjectively in the freedom of the imagination, rather than some property of the object itself, that absorbs us, affords us pleasure and thereby enhances our moral awareness. Kant's formalism is challenged by Friedrich Schiller in his *Letters on the Aesthetic Education of Man* (1794–95), where he contends that the experience of abstract form alone is insufficient to acquaint us with the good. According to Schiller, if beauty is to function as a symbol of morality, ameliorative content is as important as unity of form.[8] The *sinnliche Trieb* ('sensuous drive', linked to sensibility, matter and nature) and the *Formtrieb* ('formal drive', linked to reason) are not opposed, as Kant tends to suggest. Instead of 'clearing form of content' in the manner of Kant, a balance must be established between the two such that 'matter will have some say, and not merely in a role subordinate to form, but also co-ordinate with it and independently of it'.[9] The practical implications of this theory are explored in Schiller's plays, which thematize virtues such as justice and self-sacrifice in the attempt to generate moral reactions.

Schiller's ideas about the relation between form and content were taken up and developed by G. W. F. Hegel in his *Lectures on Aesthetics* (1835). Hegel agrees with Schiller's contention that the aesthetic offers a way of resolving the contradictions between reason and feeling, duty and inclination which Kant had been unable to overcome. Central to Hegel's typology of art is the correspondence between the 'Idea', a term which refers to this reconciliation of opposites, and the sensuous, concrete shape into which it is transformed by the artist. Hegel argues that the appropriateness of the medium of expression to the message expressed is a crucial criterion of aesthetic merit: 'the Idea, and its plastic mould as concrete reality, are to be made completely adequate to one another. When reduced to such form the Idea, as a reality moulded in conformity with the conception of the Idea, is the *Ideal*.'[10] In Hegel's view, different stages in the history of art are characterized by distinctive relations between form and content. The ideal harmony of the Idea with its mode of expression is embodied in Greek ('classical') art, while post-Greek ('romantic') art marks a decline since its content – which Hegel identifies as the Christian God and inner intellectual realities – cannot be fully represented in sensuous forms.[11] Through the harmonization of form and content, art can reunify modern oppositions between the realms of the intellect and sensuality. For Hegel, art is thus an end in itself, rather than merely a vehicle for moral instruction; its vocation, like that of philosophy, is to uncover the truth.

Kant's, Schiller's and Hegel's names rarely crop up explicitly in contemporary debates about the capacity of film to shape our ethical attitudes towards ourselves and others. Nevertheless, their accounts of aesthetic experience have influenced key currents in film theory, criticism and practice, particularly in the European tradition. Kantian aesthetics, for example, were an important source of inspiration for Weimar film theorists like Béla Balázs and Siegfried Kracauer.[12] More generally, in spite of the sustained critical scrutiny to which poststructuralist thinkers subjected the foundations of Enlightenment philosophy in the second half of the twentieth century, Kant, Schiller and Hegel remain inescapable points of reference in discussions of the morality (or immorality) of art (Kant's *Critique of Judgement*, for example, is an important point of orientation in Lacan's seminar on ethics, where he prioritizes the beautiful and the death-driven over the good). Stephen Boos underlines the pertinence of their work to current thinking on ethics and aesthetics:

The attempt to rethink the relationship between the ethical and the aesthetic requires a return to Kant, Schiller, and Hegel, since it is largely through their efforts that the modern notion of the aesthetic as the reconciling unity of spirit and nature, duty and inclination, and reason and feeling was first invented.[13]

The task facing film theorists who engage with these philosophers is to develop an account of the ways in which modern media technologies alter the dynamics of sensuous perception. In the context of this chapter, what is at stake is the extent to which cinematic technology modifies the ethical values we ascribe to aesthetic experience. Film's privileged bond with reality – its indexical aspect – poses fresh questions about the ethics of representation. The next two sections explore how eighteenth- and nineteenth-century insights into the moral dimensions of aesthetic experience have been translated into terms more appropriate to the properties of the filmic medium and transformed in the process.

The ethics of *mise-en-scène*

I suggested above that there is a Kantian dimension to Moullet's and Godard's insistence on the moral charge of tracking shots. Kant's proposition that we derive pleasure and moral insight only from the *form* of an object, rather than the content it expresses, resonates with the film critics' ascription of moral meaning to *mise-en-scène*. Yet, read in context, Godard's remark implies that the morality of technique is determined by its relation to the subject-matter. In *Hiroshima mon amour*, the film under discussion, Resnais attempts to devise a form adequate to the fall-out of the nuclear bomb dropped on Hiroshima, which may not be representable through traditional narrative schema. Tracking shots are one of a number of devices used in the film to cultivate uncertainty about spatial and temporal relations and thereby attest to the cognitive challenges posed by such an event. In the light of Resnais's quest for a representational mode befitting the film's traumatic subject, Godard's dictum can be understood as affirming the integration of form and content as a necessary condition for ethical representation. For Godard, then, beauty can be a symbol of morality, but only where ethical content is moulded into an appropriate sensible form, a position which aligns him more closely with Schiller and Hegel, in their attempts to reconcile the opposition between reason and feeling, mould and matter, than with Kant in his formalism.

Godard's views on the morality of form are informed by a conviction that it is unethical to aestheticize atrocities such as the Holocaust. Antoine de Baecque notes: 'Godard was one of the first to want to advance an ethics of representation of the extermination, refusing all aestheticism in this regard.'[14] Godard's argument and Moullet's dictum are taken up two years later in a brief but controversial essay by Jacques Rivette entitled 'Of Abjection' (1961), which attacks Gillo Pontecorvo's *mise-en-scène* of

Auschwitz in *Kapo* (1960). Rivette argues, contentiously, that fictional reconstructions of the camps such as Pontecorvo's diminish their horror and 'fall within the province of voyeurism and pornography'.[15] For Rivette, the problems with Pontecorvo's approach are most vividly demonstrated by one particular shot: a forward track which reframes the lifeless body of Terese (Emmanuelle Riva) in a more harmonious, balanced composition as it hangs from the electrified barbed wire fence against which she has thrown herself in a final act of despair. What repels Rivette about this shot is its aspiration to a traditional ideal of formal beauty which betrays its content. The aesthetic pleasure we derive from the reframing is an inappropriate and palliative response to the agony of Terese's death. Rivette contrasts *Kapo*'s 'abject' aesthetics with the formal approach adopted in *Nuit et brouillard* (*Night and Fog*, Alain Resnais, 1955), where an innovative, contrapuntal interlacing of black-and-white archive images, newly shot colour footage, voice-over and musical score creates a dissonant aesthetics Rivette views as more in keeping with the reality of the camps. Rivette's polemic provides a template for critics such as Serge Daney, who claims 'le travelling de *Kapo*' as 'the indisputable axiom' (or, in Nezick's phrase, the 'moral *a priori*'), which has governed his critical practice.[16] Rivette's and Daney's reduction of *Kapo* to a single camera movement and fixation on this single detail and have been seen as fetishistic.[17] In spite of this criticism of their methodology, however, what is relevant here is that their interventions echo Hegel's view that the artist's raw material and its plastic mould must be adequate to one another, or, in Schiller's terms, that matter must 'co-ordinate' with form, rather than being 'subordinated' to it as in 'le travelling de *Kapo*'. At the same time, the films celebrated by these critics challenge Hegel's notion that the relationship between form and content should be 'harmonious'. Both *Nuit et brouillard* and *Hiroshima mon amour* display internal discords and cultivate awareness of the disjunctions between the realities they depict and the aesthetic forms they impose on them. Furthermore, Godard's and Rivette's interventions question not only Kant's affirmation of the ethical value of abstract form emptied of content but also his fundamental analogy between beauty and goodness. Whereas Kant's argument implies that immoral artworks cannot be beautiful and that depictions of the offensive will be morally pernicious, for Godard and Rivette subject-matter we judge to be ugly can also be a symbol of the morally good. This is clear from Rivette's divergent responses to *Kapo* and *Nuit et brouillard*. Although both films are replete with images of death and physical and psychological suffering, the former is rejected for its false beautification of these realities, whilst the latter is praised for refusing to transform their chaos and horror into a more pleasing sensible form.

Nevertheless, in spite of their differences over the value of beauty and form, Kantian thought and this strand of French film criticism are underpinned by related concepts of ethics. In Kant's account, one of the essential criteria for beauty in an artwork is that it allows space for the imagination to play freely. Didactic works cannot be beautiful since they deprive us of the autonomy which characterizes moral agency, our freedom to choose for ourselves the principles by which we live. An ideal of autonomy is also at stake in Godard's remark about the morality of tracking shots. In a discussion of this dictum, Jean-Michel Frodon contrasts two different types of films: those which aim to 'subjugate', 'manipulate', 'oppress' or 'alienate' their audience, 'to make them renounce their free choice', and those which 'open up spaces of liberty, affective and intellectual autonomy'.[18] If Godard's point is that morality is determined by the choices involved in *mise-en-scène*, then one of the principal criteria by which these choices are to be evaluated is the degree of autonomy they grant to viewers. Viewed through a Kantian lens, tracking shots and other formal techniques would serve as a 'propaedeutic' for morality if they afford viewers an experience of the freedom they possess as moral agents, however problematic such a conception of agency may be for twenty-first-century critics. Such autonomy is validated by Rivette's response to Pontecorvo, which accuses 'le travelling de *Kapo*' of heteronomy, an attempt to coerce its viewers into a position where they are subject to an external law, a meaning imposed from the outside which alienates them from their freedom as moral subjects.

Documentary form

Godard, Rivette and Daney take their examples from both fiction films and documentaries without drawing distinctions between the two modes of representation in terms of the production of ethical meaning. Such distinctions are transcended by their conception of cinema as a collection of traces of historical reality. In contrast, these distinctions are of defining significance in another account of the ethics of form which emerged in the field of documentary theory in the United States. In his discussion of 'axiographics', Nichols begins from the same basic premise as Godard: film style is never neutral but a 'bearer of meaning' which is 'intimately attached to a moral point of view'.[19] However, Nichols argues that the nature of this 'attachment' differs in fiction and documentary. Whereas the former mode presents invented characters, the latter involves 'social actors', whose presence places a 'different burden of responsibility' on the filmmaker.[20] Nichols reasons that while fiction films do not necessarily directly attest to the ethical positions of their directors, in documentary 'an indexical bond exists between the image and the ethics which produced it'.[21] He demonstrates how formal characteristics such as the position of the camera and the presence or absence of the filmmaker in or from the shot reveal the particular 'ethical code' commanding his or her behaviour. For example, a shot which shakes as the filmmaker hurries to the aid of a person in danger attests to an ethic of courage, whereas a static long shot of the same subject begs questions about whether she or he may have had a duty to intervene.

Nichols's analysis of the concrete ways in which virtues such as sympathy and courage are embodied in filmic space reorients the debate about the ethics of form away from concepts of aesthetics, beauty and freedom towards issues of responsibility. His understanding of ethics is different from, but not directly at odds with, Godard's conception of 'morale'. Whereas the French critics are concerned with the level of autonomy film accords to its viewers, Nichols emphasizes instead documentary filmmakers' distinctive moral and social obligations to their subjects. Nevertheless, the desiring, epistephilic spectator envisaged by Nichols is capable of making free moral judgements about a filmmaker's choices, just as artistic responsibility is at stake in Godard's dictum. Notions of autonomy and responsibility are closely associated in Kantian moral theory. Although Kant does not use the latter term, he is regarded as a classical exponent of individual accountability, for free, rational moral agents can be held to account for their actions.[22] So while Godard's and Nichols's approaches emerge at different times and places and frame the question of ethics in divergent ways, they can be linked to a common Western tradition of speculation about the morality of art. Nichols's contribution to the debate is to identify the specific responsibilities incumbent upon documentarists, a concern of particular relevance in the rest of this chapter. As becomes clear when his account is compared with those of the French critics, however, Nichols downplays the extent to which fiction films too reflect ethical positions, an issue which will be taken up in subsequent chapters. I turn in the meantime to a documentary which transposes some of these theoretical questions into a filmic register.

Être et avoir

In 2003 a documentary about a primary school in rural Auvergne hit French headlines when the schoolteacher featured in the film, Georges Lopez, launched a law suit against its director, Nicolas Philibert, and producers. Following the box-office success of Être et avoir (2002), the most financially lucrative documentary in France for over a decade, Lopez claimed that Philibert had plagiarized his work and demanded a full share of the profits as 'co-author' of the film. Some of the families whose children appeared in the documentary followed his lead, arguing that certain scenes were staged and that their children should therefore be remunerated as actors. These ultimately unsuccessful claims reignited debate in the French media about the kinds of judicial question that have dominated discussion of documentary ethics in the United States since the 1970s. Do documentary participants ever have a legal right to payment, or is this incompatible with the 'essence' of documentary, as the Association des cinéastes documentaristes claimed?[23] Crucial to the legal rulings was the fact that Lopez and the children's families had consented to Philibert's use of their images. Yet, as Nichols points out, the principle of 'informed consent', a common litmus test in such cases, is not cut-and-dried, since filmmakers can never inform their subjects in advance of the future consequences of a film.[24] As explained in the introduction, however, our primary concern in this book is not with concepts of right and consent but with ethical issues which exceed purely legal determination.

Être et avoir depicts a school in the village of Saint-Étienne-sur-Usson where 13 children aged from 4 to 10 are taught in different age-groups in a single classroom. The film seeks out the singular and remarkable in the ostensibly banal and quotidian, yet its themes have a universal dimension. Critics have tended to view the film as nostalgic and 'heart-warming'; it has been described as 'a utopia predicated on circularity and stability'.[25] Looking closely at the relation between its subject-matter and mode of representation, and the connections between its aesthetic and ethical dimensions, I want to argue that the film is about the present rather than escaping into the security of an imagined past or future ideal. Through its form as much as its content, it hints at the uncertainty and anguish which characterize childhood experience and questions the meanings we habitually ascribe to it. Documentary's traditional role as purveyor of knowledge about other people is also subject to interrogation. The film is concerned not only with the interactions between children and teachers but also with the power dynamics between filmmakers, participants and viewers. It asks us to consider how the camera reshapes reality and what responsibilities this entails for those who make, appear in and watch it.

Certain moral themes are intrinsic to Philibert's subject-matter. *Être et avoir* addresses perennial concerns about the responsibilities of state institutions towards children, shown to overlap with those of the family in scenes where Lopez assumes the role of surrogate parent. On another level, the film investigates the processes through which we become moral subjects. Moral education is foregrounded as a central component of the children's learning experience; in the incidents shown, they discover more about codes of social behaviour and relationships than the subjects on the curriculum. The one exception to this is French, for moral learning is inextricably bound up with the acquisition of language, another key preoccupation of the film, as indicated by the titular allusion via auxiliary verbs to grammar lessons. While Lopez's exchanges with his pupils aim to promote Christian virtues such as obedience, self-discipline and tolerance, the film is less interested in exemplary comportment than in moments when moral frameworks are tested or destabilized. As Vincent Malausa points out, *Être et avoir* contains few images of friendship or play, a dearth which is surprising in view of its subject.[26] Those included tend to end in disappointment, as when the tiny Létitia asks each of the children in turn whether they are her friends, only to be rebuffed by a resounding 'non!' from Johann. The film recurrently lingers on behaviour which challenges established norms of 'good' and 'bad', such as Jojo's irrepressible curiosity and Nathalie's introversion. It highlights the difficulty of mastering language, according central roles to the virtually mute Nathalie and the painfully shy Olivier. At the level of content, then, the film assumes a meta-ethical dimension; it deals as much with the nature of moral systems as with first-order questions about virtues and duties.

But equally integral to the film's ethical vision is its deceptively simple form. *Être et avoir* was shot on Super 16 by a small crew who spent ten weeks over the course of seven months in the school, getting to know the class and experimenting with different methods of filming. In interviews, Philibert, who receives the credit for camera and editing as well as direction, explains that his use of natural lighting and positioning of the camera (away from the classroom's thoroughfares) were motivated by the desire to cause minimal disruption.[27] Other decisions, however, were not fully determined by pragmatic concerns of this kind. Long takes are preferred to fast cuts and the camera zooms in to frame individual children in close-up as they work, remaining still for extended periods, rather than following the currents of activity and conversation which flow through the classroom. These techniques enable Philibert to capture unguarded moments of absorption and distraction – Alizé painstakingly arranging her rubbers; Jojo repeatedly losing concentration in his colouring task – and establish intimacy and complicity between child and viewer. At the same time, sound recurrently draws our attention to off-screen space, which is established as the domain of the teacher, whose disembodied voice functions as a signifier of his authority. This power hierarchy becomes more evident during prolonged takes showing children at moments of vulnerability: for example, Johann struggling in vain to read the word in front of him or Olivier on the verge of tears when asked about his father's illness. Due as much to the manner in which they are shot as to what they depict, these scenes heighten our awareness of documentary's potential to exploit its participants. The interventional nature of Philibert's project is further foregrounded by constant reminders that the presence of the camera transforms reality. There are numerous shots in which the children, their parents or Lopez betray their awareness of the camera and crew, either by glancing at them surreptitiously or by visibly modifying their behaviour for the benefit of a future audience. In this way, the film confronts us with one of the epistemological conundrums posed by documentary: what is the ontological status of the 'reality' captured? In line with his interrogative approach to moral subjectivity, Philibert allows questions about directorial responsibility to resonate rather than foreclosing them (by filming such scenes differently or simply excluding them).

How do the codes prioritized at the level of form relate to the ethical issues addressed at the level of content? One way of approaching this question is to compare the role of Lopez to that of Philibert, a comparison invited by the director, who refers to the teacher as his on screen 'double'.[28] As Philibert points out, a close association between actor and director is more often found in fiction films (we might think of François Truffaut and Jean-Pierre Léaud, Michelangelo Antonioni and Monica Vitti or John Cassavetes

and Gena Rowlands), where directors have control over their actors' performances. Lopez and Philibert share certain obvious characteristics and qualities;
they are men of a similar age who exhibit unusual degrees of professional
dedication, patience and curiosity about the world. But the more compelling
question raised by Philibert's parallel is whether his filmmaking and Lopez's
tuition are informed by compatible ethical codes. Reflecting on this connection, Philibert notes that both filmmakers and teachers are required to
judge the most appropriate distance from which to film/address their subjects/
students.[29] Documentary has traditionally been understood to share a common
objective with teaching: the transmission of knowledge. As Nichols observes,
documentary convention 'posits an organizing agency that possesses information and knowledge, a text that conveys it, and a subject who will gain
it.'[30] This convention aligns documentary closely with didactic pedagogical
models. Predicated upon it is the persistent assumption that documentary is
somehow inherently more virtuous than fiction film, which has been deni-
grated since cinema's invention as a source of fascination and entertainment rather
than instruction, much like the novel before it. Yet in different ways both
Lopez and Philibert distance themselves from these didactic paradigms. Lopez
is repeatedly shown helping the children to discover answers for themselves and
resolving disputes through reasoning and discussion. Similarly, Philibert refuses
to cast himself as an omniscient agent or his subjects as objects of knowledge
for the viewer. *Être et avoir* is a documentary about the transmission of
knowledge which rejects the idea that this is what documentary ought to do.

Discussing *Être et avoir*, Philibert conceptualizes his relationship to his
subjects as follows:

> I don't make films 'about', I make films 'with'. This nuance is very
> important. It means that I don't make documentaries with an expert eye
> with the desire to give a speech about the reality I'm filming. ... It's not
> my intention to provide the viewer with lots of facts. I try to create an
> encounter between the viewer and the people on the screen.[31]

Philibert's remarks beg the question of whether it is possible to make films
'with', as opposed to 'about', others, strictly speaking, without involving
them directly in the filming and editing process. In *Être et avoir*, Lopez and
the children never get behind the camera or make editorial decisions (which
was one of the reasons why the courts refused to recognize them as co-
authors), just as Philibert and his crew never appear in the shot. Nevertheless, Philibert's choice of preposition invites us to view the film as a work
of collaboration rather than observation (in this sense his approach has
something in common with fiction direction, although his subjects have
greater freedom of action than actors). In line with this reading, his formal
choices involve the viewers as well as the participants in the production of
meaning. The film's style is more often suggestive than assertive, elliptical

than explanatory, mimetic than didactic. This ambivalence is intensified in images which are empty of human presence, such as the lingering shots of nature which mark the changing seasons, or those of the classroom before and after lessons, where we follow the laborious progress of tortoises across the floor. Philibert's long takes cultivate uncertainty and, in the absence of a voice-over to explain their significance, their meaning often remains indeterminate. What I want to emphasize here is the autonomy this grants to viewers, for it is this aspect of the film's aesthetics which might properly be called 'moral' in the particular senses proposed by Kant, and later Godard and Rivette.

For Malausa, *Être et avoir* is permeated by an 'impression of vague, free-floating malaise', 'an atmosphere of latent violence', 'an indefinite menace'.[32] Malausa's reading astutely draws attention to the way Philibert's camerawork and montage introduce a muted sense of anxiety and foreboding into ostensibly pacific scenarios or images of natural beauty. Towards the end of the film, while the class are enjoying a picnic in the countryside, Alizé goes missing. A sequence showing Lopez and the older boys searching for her in a field concludes with a long stationary shot of the head-high barley swaying in the breeze. Eventually, off-screen voices signal that Alizé has been found, but the camera continues to focus on the restlessly moving field, and we are neither shown the child's return nor given an explanation for her absence. The image of the gently undulating gold-green stems is harmonious and pleasing, but, in conjunction with the withheld image of Alizé, it acquires an ambiguity which solicits a creative act of interpretation from the viewer. Like the discomfort prompted by the acclaimed tracking shots of *Hiroshima mon amour*, the diffuse unease engendered by Philibert's camerawork can be understood, following Godard, as ethical as well as aesthetic in nature. The polysemous, indefinite, sometimes undecidable images offered by the film act as catalysts for the 'free-play' of the imagination which, according to Kant, breeds awareness of our moral freedom. Through its refusal of didacticism, rejection of spurious drama and exploitation of off-screen sound space, the film leaves space for autonomous spectatorial activity where imagination facilitates critical evaluation. At the same time, as I have shown, the content plays an equally significant role in destabilizing fixed meanings and providing an experience of indeterminacy, corroborating Schiller's reservations about Kant's formalism. Moreover, just as the cinematic apparatus limits the autonomy and disinterestedness that characterize Kantian moral and aesthetic judgements, so the film's depiction of the complexities and ambiguities of moral formation thoroughly problematize the notion of a unified self capable of making free decisions that constitutes the foundation of the philosopher's moral theory. If Philibert's images can be viewed, following Nichols, as indexical imprints of the ethics which produced them, they invite the viewer to scrutinize this ethics without buying into a myth of centred subjectivity.

Some concluding remarks

Taking its cue from Godard, this chapter has examined the constitutive role played by film form in the production of ethical meaning, focusing in particular on the values embedded in documentary representation. The ethical implications of *Être et avoir* are not fully determined by its content. Philibert's formal choices cannot be explained by purely aesthetic considerations but articulate moral perspectives which can be appraised by the viewer. In assessing the relationship between ethics and aesthetics, I have drawn attention to the extent to which seminal accounts of the morality of *mise-en-scène* and documentary space are indebted to classic philosophical debates about beauty and goodness, while suggesting that the latter provide under-tapped resources for film theory and criticism. *Être et avoir* neither validates Kantian moral theory nor presents us with exemplary moral agents in the Kantian mould. Philibert's rejection of positivistic and universalizing moral projects of this kind underlines the need to place cinema in dialogue with more recent accounts of ethics, as we do in later chapters of this book. Nevertheless, I have attempted to show that his film foregrounds questions about directorial responsibility and spectatorial autonomy which can be more effectively explored through theories of aesthetics than, for example, legal theory, even if the Enlightenment philosophers discussed here are unlikely to have been able to envisage such an application of their thought.

Notes

1 Godard in Domarchi et al., 'Hiroshima, notre amour', 5; Moullet, 'Sam Fuller sur les brisées de Marlowe', 14. For a discussion of Moullet's and Godard's formulations see de Baecque, *La Cinéphilie: invention d'un regard*, 206–9.

2 Nezick, 'Le Travelling de *Kapo* ou le paradoxe de la morale', 161. See, for example, Rhodes, *Stupendous, Miserable City*, 70; Bukatman, 'Zooming Out: The End of Off-Screen Space', 271; Mayne, *Claire Denis*, 103.

3 Nichols, *Representing Reality*, 102.

4 Kant, *Critique of Judgement*, 228.

5 Kant, *Critique of Judgement*, 229.

6 Kant, *Critique of Judgement*, for example, 229, 243.

7 Kant, *Critique of Judgement*, 232.

8 Schiller, *On the Aesthetic Education of Man*, Fourth Letter, for example, 19.

9 Schiller, *On the Aesthetic Education of Man*, Thirteenth Letter, 85–7.

10 Hegel, *Introductory Lectures on Aesthetics*, 80.

11 Hegel, *Introductory Lectures on Aesthetics*, 84–8.

12 For a discussion of Kant's and Hegel's influence on currents in European film theory, see Aitken, *European Film Theory and Cinema*. See Cavell, *Cities of Words*, especially 119–44, for a recent evaluation of the connections between Kantian moral theory and a specific Hollywood genre. The impact of Schiller's aesthetic theory on film theory has been more limited. Attempts to redress this include Höyng, 'Schiller Goes to the Movies'.

13 Boos, 'Rethinking the Aesthetic', 15. For a broader overview of debates at the intersections of aesthetics and moral philosophy, see Schellekens, *Aesthetics and Morality*.

14 De Baecque, *La Cinéphilie: invention d'un regard*, 206 (my own translation).

15 Rivette, 'De l'abjection', 54 (my own translation).
16 Daney, 'Le Travelling de *Kapo*', 6. Nezick, 'Le Travelling de *Kapo* ou le paradoxe de la morale', 161. Nezick points out that Daney subsequently questioned and revised this 'axiom', a fact which is often overlooked in accounts of his position (163–64).
17 See, for example, Chion, 'Le détail qui tue la critique de cinéma'.
18 Frodon, 'Chemins qui se croisent', in Frodon (ed.), *Le Cinéma et la Shoah*, 11–26 (18) (my own translation).
19 Nichols, *Representing Reality*, 80.
20 Nichols, *Introduction to Documentary*, 6.
21 Nichols, *Representing Reality*, 77.
22 See, for example, Kant, *Religion Within the Limits of Reason Alone*, Books I and II.
23 See M.G., 'Réactions: Questions sur la liberté de création'.
24 Nichols, *Introduction to Documentary*, 10–1.
25 Powrie, 'Unfamiliar Places: "Heterospection" and Recent French Films on Children', 345.
26 Malausa, 'Histoires de fantômes', 79 (my own translation).
27 Philibert, 'J'ai choisi l'instituteur, une sorte de double', 80; 'Nicolas Philibert in Conversation', interview on Tartan DVD of *Être et avoir* (2003).
28 Philibert, 'J'ai choisi l'instituteur, une sorte de double', 81.
29 Philibert, 'J'ai choisi l'instituteur, une sorte de double', 81.
30 Nichols, *Representing Reality*, 31.
31 Philibert, 'Nicolas Philibert in Conversation'.
32 Malausa, 'Histoires de fantômes', 80 (my own translation).

Chapter 2

Testing positive

Gender, sexuality, representation

Lisa Downing

While the previous chapter discussed the ethical import of the technical, formal and aesthetic decisions made by a documentary filmmaker, and grappled with the implications of the Enlightenment history of thinking on ethics and aesthetics for a consideration of filmic production, this chapter turns to the vexed issue of positive representations in narrative filmmaking. It therefore looks at a particular intersection of the political and the ethical in film. It analyzes in detail how the relationship between content and form works in the creation of representations of female and gay characters, and discusses the problems inherent in the terms 'positive/negative representation' for a nuanced ethical understanding.

Unlike Kupfer, in his *Visions of Virtue* (discussed in the Introduction), I am not interested in comparing the fictional film characters discussed according to a hierarchy of absolute virtues. Instead, I explore how what we have been calling ethico-political meaning resides not only in what a director chooses to show characters doing, or what moral characteristics those fictional personages are meant to represent, but also in how the image is framed and shot, and which generic conventions it engages, distorts or challenges. Following on from the analyses in the previous chapter, we shall see that narrative film too

Figure 2 Thelma and Louise

constructs meaning via form as much as via content, and that sometimes ethical meanings and political intentions are undercut rather than enhanced by filmmaking practices and the ideological conditions within which they take place.

The concept of 'positive representation' derives from debates in early feminist film criticism of the 1970s in the sociologically informed so-called 'images of women' tradition, and later in identity-politics-driven gay and lesbian studies. The former strand of scholarship is exemplified by Molly Haskell's *From Reverence to Rape: The Treatment of Women in the Movies* (1973) and by a work that appeared in the same year, Marjorie Rosen's *Popcorn Venus: Women, Movies and the American Dream*. Both undertake a catalogue of stereotypes and functions of the woman in Hollywood film, focusing particularly in Haskell's book on how women on screen are often no more than thinly veiled stereotypes (vamp, virgin, hooker, femme fatale, gold digger), and in Rosen's on how Hollywood worked to 'squash feminine self determination' in the motivations and endings it offered women in film. According to Rosen, Hollywood heroines aspire to '"winning the love of another" above any other aim such as cultivating their work or "an independent future"'.[1] Both books are primarily descriptive and politically idealistic, rather than advancing a theoretical position, and they do not problematize the relationship between political reality and cinematic representation very thoroughly.[2]

Such work on the representation of women was crucial inspiration for a body of scholarship that sought to render visible the previously unremarked upon stereotypes of other minorities in film. Works such as Vito Russo's *The Celluloid Closet: Homosexuality in the Movies* (1981, revised 1987) and Andrea Weiss's *Vampires and Violets: Lesbians in Film* (1993) have drawn attention to the negative representations – or the erasure of representation – of gay and lesbian characters. Russo highlights the long-standing cinematic cliché of portraying gay men as asexual 'sissies' and lesbian characters as monstrous and murderous; the latter being a thematic upon which Weiss expands, while being careful not to suggest that the supplanting of these socially disruptive characters with more 'positive' or 'appropriate' representations would provide 'the answer'. She writes that the 'application of a true or false test to the image suggests that it is sufficient simply to replace the stereotype with a more satisfactory image ... It ignores larger problems of representation, by calling for the removal of the offending image but not questioning the ideological processes that gave rise to it in the first place'.[3]

What, then, *is* a positive representation of a woman or a lesbian, and how is asking this question an ethical undertaking? Like Weiss, quoted above, we might want to be suspicious of the idea that replacing 'negative' with 'positive' representations impacts in any way upon the realities of social attitudes; and be aware that such a sanitizing move can risk further erasing the visibility of deleterious cultural attitudes towards certain groups. Moreover, 'positive' is itself a politically and ethically fraught label, as it carries an implicit value judgement within it, that will always be subjective and culturally specific but that, in the mesmerizing space of the pro-filmic, can convey the impression of neutrality. In the context of a society that valorizes economic success, particularly in the commercial sphere, a film such as *Working Girl* (Mike Nichols, 1988) might be thought of as offering a 'positive' representation of women, since the lead eponymous character played by Melanie Griffith – a secretary who takes on her boss's job – is shown to be as successful as her male counterparts in the Manhattan financial world. However, such a face-value assessment of the representation as feminist completely ignores the political ideologies that are being taken for granted in such an endorsement. Most obviously, this signals complete blindness to anti-capitalist critiques. Readings that valorize a represented woman's 'power' on the basis solely of socio-economic class are evidently partial and problematic. The difficulty of the idea of 'testing positive', then, is that it risks accepting unquestioningly, rather than critically examining, the ideologies underpinning the containing culture of a film's production.

Similarly, however, apparently radical or non-mainstream critical perspectives can also exhibit blind spots. *Thelma and Louise* (Ridley Scott, 1991) is a very good example of a film that seemingly offers straightforwardly 'liberating' female role models, but can be examined as undermining its attempt to create 'positive' images in numerous ways. In the first half of this chapter I will explore how the logic of this filmic narrative undermines the apparent liberationist discourse it espouses, and then ask whether its ambivalent ending calls into question the possibility and/or the ethical value of redemptive narrative *tout court*. It is also productive to interrogate apparently negative representations in order to tap into their ability to show up the workings of the ideologies that create them, and thereby expose ethically and socially problematic perceptions. Michael Winterbottom's portrayal of a murderous lesbian in *Butterfly Kiss* (1995) is read in this way in the second half of the chapter.

Girls on film: *Thelma and Louise*

Thelma and Louise has received considerable critical attention as a groundbreaking feminist film. It offered strong female acting roles to Geena Davis and Susan Sarandon, and was scripted by a female screenwriter, Callie Khouri.[4] At the most basic level, the film undertakes to demonstrate the liberation from heterosexual domestic drudgery of a young stay-at-home wife, Thelma (Davis), when she embarks on a 'girls' holiday' with her more independent, confident, working friend Louise (Sarandon). Along the way, Thelma is radically divested of innocence by means of violence and betrayal by men (in the form of rape and theft), and by her subsequent collusion in Louise's murder of her rapist, and her own perpetration of an armed robbery.

The film uses numerous stereotypical visual techniques to demonstrate the contrast between the worldly Louise and the sheltered Thelma, and then manipulates the visual codes it establishes in order to show the stripping away of Thelma's innocence and her assumption of agency. The well-worn association between a woman's dress and her character, on which much analysis of representations of women in film focuses, is central to the encoding of political meaning in *Thelma and Louise*. When Louise drives up in her convertible to collect Thelma for their trip, she is dressed in a shirt and jeans, sporting sunglasses and with her hair held back by a scarf. The semiotics of her clothing convey practicality, independence and coolness. Geena Davis, meanwhile, wears a white dress with a full peasant skirt and has tumbling, pre-Raphaelite locks. (We have seen her with her hair set in curlers in an earlier sequence, emphasizing Thelma's constructed girlish femininity.) Thus, the pair could not be more strongly visually contrasted at the film's outset.

Similarly, their behaviour around men is clearly intended to indicate the different versions of female 'types' they are designed to exemplify. When in a diner, Harlan (Timothy Carhart) makes an approach to the women, Louise is standoffish, whilst Thelma, her actions fuelled by alcohol (in which, we learn from the dialogue, she does not usually indulge), is encouraging and friendly, eventually dancing with him. 'Can't you tell when someone's hitting on you?' asks Louise. Apparently, Thelma can't, and Harlan will end up raping the drunken and incapacitated Thelma, and being shot dead by Louise. After the shooting – the pivotal event around which the characters' fortunes turn, and the catalyst for their transformation – Thelma is at first optimistic, Louise cynical about the way their actions would be interpreted by the police and society. When Thelma asks, 'Shouldn't we go to the cops? Just tell them what happened? All of it? That he was raping me?', Louise responds: 'Just about a hundred people saw you dancing cheek to cheek with him. Who's going to believe you? We don't live in that kind of world, Thelma'. Khouri has the pair evoking in this dialogue the commonplace, still persistent, discourse of the drunken rape victim having 'asked for it' (a premise that had been the subject of Jonathan Kaplan's film, *The Accused*, 1988, three years before the release of *Thelma and Louise*).

However, Thelma's fall from innocence, identical in the film's logic with increased cynicism about, and animosity towards, men is only complete when J.D. (Brad Pitt), the guy with the 'cute butt', to whom Thelma insists they offer a lift, steals Louise's life savings after a night of passion with Thelma. The contrast between the ways the women are filmed in the scene showing Pitt's and Davis's sex, and those scenes which follow it, is striking. The filming of Davis's body might be described as consistent with the techniques discussed by Mulvey and others as exemplifying the male heterosexual gaze endemic to cinema. The camera moves slowly, in close-up, along Davis's thighs, to her crotch and flat stomach. Our vision is aligned with Brad Pitt's eye line; his face just visible in the shot, as his kisses move up her reclining body. The scene may thus be read to present the man's viewpoint (even though Thelma's enjoyment is obvious in the scene and in her discussion of the sex afterwards with Louise). If this might be thought of as typically objectifying shot of the female body, the next scene with which we are presented offers a deliberate alternative (in a film whose whole aesthetic structure is based on visual contrast). We cut from the sex scene straight to a shot of Louise: alone, thoughtful, framed by a window. Thelma, then, in her earlier, naïve incarnation, exemplifies corporeality, Louise cerebrality.

However, once Thelma is made aware of J.D's theft of their money, her attitude and appearance change, and equality rather than difference begins to characterize the filming of Thelma and Louise. When Thelma robs a shop, in order to pay back Louise's money, we watch her actions, not in the real time of the robbery, but in black and white CCTV footage. Thelma is confident, cool and in command in the grainy images on the screen. In sunglasses and holding a gun, she has moved from simple object of the gaze to agent, as metaphorized by the way the robbery is filmed and presented to the viewer. When the camera pans round from the screen showing the CCTV images, which had previously occupied the entire screen, we are made aware of a room of impressed-looking cops watching on, powerlessly, in the aftermath of the crime. They are sizing her up as an agent, not as a female body, and the male gaze is now mediated by the grainy footage rather than being a set of direct close-ups on her body, as it was in the traditional – almost clichéd – erotic scene with J.D. This different type of framing and apprehension of Thelma exemplifies her progressive distancing from codes of conventional heterosexual femininity. We might argue that the rather typically filmed shots of Thelma's erotic encounter were constructed in that way precisely so as to allow the subsequent ones to provide a (value-laden) counterweight.

As the film draws to a close, the visual distinction between Thelma and Louise has been all but erased. Thelma's hair has been cut; she too wears a denim shirt and jeans, her flowing skirts long gone, and rather than being the object of the gaze, she now shares the gaze with Louise in a woman-only mirroring pair. There are many sequences of the women speeding along in their open-top car. These alternate between long shots of the car, made small in the vast landscape, and close-ups on the women's faces in profile, as they lean in towards each other. This looking sideways, turning away from the camera, rather than being shot face-on, seems to mark a rupture in the filming style. Rather than presenting the woman as spectacle, open to the gaze, it suggests the self-contained, intersubjective intimacy of the pair. During one such sequence of images, Shel Silverstein's *The Ballad of Lucy Jordan*, that poignant tale of a housewife who, one day, flees from 'a white suburban bedroom in a white suburban town' by some unspecified means (whether suicide, madness, or actual escape), becomes the extra-diegetic soundtrack to Thelma and Louise's forward-flung drive to Mexico; a drive that will end instead with a kiss at the Grand Canyon. Lucy Jordan's extraordinary and ambivalent rejection of domesticity and wifedom at the price of representability, functions as a harbinger of Thelma's and Louise's own end.

Having examined the images of femininity and the discourses of feminism portrayed in *Thelma and Louise*, it is necessary to ask questions about genre, as well as gender, when attempting an ethical analysis of this spectacle. *Thelma and Louise* is, generically speaking, a fairly classic road movie. This has traditionally functioned as a generic vehicle to allow, firstly, lone male rebels (e.g. *Easy Rider*, Dennis Hopper, 1969) and, later, female comrades to escape the fixity of domesticity, convention, and heterosexual coupledom. The road movie heroine or hero is often an unlikely one, such as the ageing, lawn-mower-riding protagonist of David Lynch's *The Straight Story* (1999), crossing the country in search of his estranged brother. Unlike many other Hollywood genres, the road movie actively privileges alternative lifestyles, making it an attractive genre for feminist and queer projects. (The high camp style of *The Adventures of Priscilla, Queen of the Desert*, Stephan Elliott, 1994, offers a good example of the road movie very explicitly queered.) This genre, then, is well suited to exploring the subjectivity and adventures of the non-mainstream protagonist, the dissident couple, or the individualist at odds with the norms of society. Yet it has been pointed out that this rejection of norms is usually only allowed to occur within limited parameters. Roadsters are often criminals (as in classics such as *Bonnie and Clyde* (Arthur Penn, 1967) and postmodern parodies such as *Kiss or Kill* (Bill Bennett, 1997) and *Baise-Moi* (Virginie Despentes and Coralie Trinh-Thi, 2000), about which more in Chapter 5), and their criminal acts are usually punished by imprisonment or death. However, it can be argued that the road movie formula tends towards the reactionary and conventional in its very representational nature, over and above these individual cases of punitive and conservative denouements. The promise of deliverance from the everyday and the transcendence of societal expectations that underlies the traditional road movie ideology is, I would argue, *intrinsically* problematic in its assumption of the possibility of liberation through 'self-expression' and escape.

The major way in which the road movie espouses a belief in liberation, which it conveys, sometimes movingly and powerfully to its audience, is via the specific use it makes of setting and space. In an article on the road movie aimed at a readership of scriptwriters, Lucy Scher writes: 'there is an instant iconography around road movies – we know they are going to give us sweeping landscapes counterpointed by the enclosure of the car'.[5] The road movie works, then, by exploiting a visual language which contrasts containment and escape; by suggesting an ideal of sublime freedom to which the roadsters aspire and which they espy from the womb-like safety of their vehicles. In the now iconic closing sequence of *Thelma and Louise*, as the police close in on all sides, the imposing police helicopter dominating the landscape, and the numerous armed police troops in the foreground, dwarfing Thelma and Louise's unprotected convertible, the Grand Canyon represents a suitably vulvic oasis, a feminist promised land of infinite freedom into which we are encouraged to think that Sarandon and Davis will plunge, out of patriarchal discourse. The landscape of the road movie is thus used to suggest visually an ontological ambition. Thelma's and Louise's leap is supposed to be read as a literal leap out of discourse into an experience of the noumenal. However, of course, this promised transcendence is in fact *not* sublime but part of a very codified and specifically American discourse about the possibility of freedom. The promise of the open road is that, at the end of it, one will find some version of the American dream: a whimsically symbolic pro-woman one in the case of *Thelma and Louise*.

I would argue that the representation of Thelma and Louise – while commonsensically 'positive' in all kinds of ways – perpetuates other kinds of damaging ideology and succumbs to a logic that seduces us into a comfortable complicity with the women's plunge into the abyss. It commits that error in thinking to which Foucault draws our attention: the assumption that one can ever escape outside of power. Thelma's and Louise's sublime plunge should mean annihilation, but it is cleverly turned into a celebration of freedom by cinematic means such as the camerawork that freezes the car as it is launched over the precipice, giving the impression that the couple are flying, eternally suspended, refusing to show us their crash to the ground. In addition, the rapturous music that accompanies the closing shots suggests redemption, as does the framing of this embodied ideal of freedom in an exaggeratedly beautiful landscape. Thus, Thelma and Louise are women who do not fulfil the 'negative' passive or domestic stereotypes to which Rosen and Haskell draw our attention, indeed who break out of these roles in all kinds of ways. But the filming of the close of *Thelma and Louise* is disingenuously utopian; it offers a problematic vision of freedom rather than grappling with the thorny issues of women's place within patriarchy or the punishment of social outsiders. This said, I do not ascribe to received wisdom that any film that ends with the female protagonist's death is misogynistic or inherently negative. The disingenuity of *Thelma and Louise* comes in its refusal to show *either* their escape and life together in Mexico, *or* their death. When senior police officer Hal (Harvey Keitel) asks Louise on the telephone 'do you want to get out of this alive?', and she responds 'no', we are offered the promise of an outcome that we are subsequently denied. And in the final moments, as the troops close in on the women, weapons trained on them, Thelma says to Louise 'Let's keep going', assenting implicitly to their death. However, the pair are not allowed an ethically informed choosing of death over the pain of life – a pain acknowledged by the sympathetically portrayed cop Hal, whose final line in the film before Thelma and Louise's leap is 'how many times are they going to be fucked over?'. Critics have tended to read the denouement of *Thelma and Louise* as strategically open-ended, a way of generating the afterlives of the film's meaning, as suggested in the title of Bernie Cook's recent edited book *Thelma and Louise Live!: The Cultural Afterlife of an American Film* (2008), which is taken from a bumper sticker the editor describes having seen that proclaimed the survival of the filmic heroines.[6] Rather, I would argue, the ending is a lie, in which our exposure to the death they have chosen is literally suspended in the freeze frame. We are thereby falsely encouraged to believe that they are 'keeping going' in some more transcendental sense.

A specifically Hollywood-constructed notion of freedom is not for a single moment negated or placed in question in the film. The ethical work that needs to be undertaken to show that one cannot escape outside of power structures in a feel-good way is simply not followed through in this film, and it lies with the critical viewer to restore this ethically indeterminate dimension to a deceptively triumphal spectacle.

The killing of Eu and Mi

Michael Winterbottom's *Butterfly Kiss* is a road movie that has numerous resonances with *Thelma and Louise*. However, one of the most striking features of the UK-made film is its Englishness and specifically its Northern Englishness. The characters Miriam (Amanda Plummer) and Eunice (Saskia Reeves) speak with broad Lancashire accents, marking the film out already from its place in an American generic tradition. The action takes place in the petrol stations and Granada inns on the stretch of motorway and 'A' roads around Preston and Blackpool, economically deprived northern towns. In an early scene, the protagonists stand on the roof of Miriam's mother's council block looking over the surrounding roadscape and Eunice indicates the various compass points before them. Her litany – 'the A588; the A6; the Blackpool tower; and over there the sea' – maps out the boundaries of their territory. When Eunice tells Miriam: 'I've looked up and down all these roads … for someone to love me. You've got to find someone to love you', the terms of Eunice's adventure are established: like many classic road movies, this is a quest for love and for belonging that are perceived to exist at the 'end of the road'. The sentimental, idealistic tone of Eunice's discourse is disrupted by the lack of glamour offered by the working class setting, as well as by the fact that we already know at this point that Eunice is a killer who has bludgeoned several female petrol station workers to death. However, the scene retains poignancy and a strange emotional charge despite our knowledge, created by the soft, eerie extra-diegetic music and by the hypnotic way in which the camera circles around Eunice and Miriam, creating them as the centre of a mobile circle; two illuminated figures set against a nocturnal starry background. This film puts dispossessed, marginalized figures literally at the centre, as a pivot, in order to allow a relativization and reassessment of the 'middle ground' of gender, sex and class, the centre that passes as the neutral and unmarked norm. Thus, one set of discourses is able to contradict, and yet fail completely to cancel out, another.

As is suggested by the unlikely juxtaposition of codes and discourses described above, this is a film that enacts disruption of expectations at every turn, both in its concerns and in its form. Thematically and structurally, the film turns on chaos and contingency, as the couple travel the area on a spree of random murder and car theft; without direction and at the whim of chance. Formally also, disruption is the watchword of the aesthetic. The sequence I have just discussed is unusual in its contemplative stillness. Frenzy is the marker of much of the action. As Eunice stomps around a roadside convenience store looking for a tape which includes a 'song about love', the title of which she has forgotten, the camera cannot keep up with her and literally jostles for a clear shot of her as shelves, turn styles, display units and other bits of set get in the way, disrupting the framing.

Similarly, moving cars are constantly positioned between the viewer and the onscreen protagonists, as seen in the opening sequence in which Eunice determinedly stalks along the hard shoulder as cars, placed between her moving figure and the camera, whizz by her. Fourteen minutes into the film, Eunice and Miriam are seated on the wall of the petrol station facing each other in long shot. The camera is positioned in front of the petrol station, with the road running between it and the women. The spectator's view of Miriam and Eunice, and her ability to make out their conversation, are periodically interrupted by the spectacle and sound of cars speeding past, between the camera and its object. This acts to place a moving barrier between the spectator and the characters. It breaks the direct relation of looker and looked-at and it suggests the constant *possibility* of mobility; as something that promises to disrupt and challenge our relationship with spectacle and the other. Thus, through Eunice's discourse of a quest for belonging, as well as through the relationship between the camera, the road, moving cars and the women, the expectations of a road movie are established, though crucially presented in ways that emphasize dislocation, disruption and distortion.

Identity, and particularly identity as constituted through relationality, is also foregrounded in the film and is accorded a disturbing and unstable status. Eunice's name is shortened to 'Eu' (homophonically: you); Miriam's to 'Mi' (me). Thus, Miriam (me) is the onscreen locus of consciousness in the film. We are made aware of this from the beginning. The adventures of Miriam and Eunice that constitute the main part of the film are presented in the form of full colour flashbacks, intercut with black-and-white documentary-style sequences in which Miriam narrates the story of their love affair and of Eunice's crimes in a police interview. 'Mi', then, is set up using numerous recognizable techniques, including voiceover, as the one with whom the spectator would be encouraged to identify, were this the kind of film that is interested in encouraging straightforward identification. Instead, I would posit that just as it sometimes disturbs identification by the formal means discussed, at other times, as in the nomenclature of the characters (Eu/you and Mi/me), it renders identification overdetermined, such that we cannot identify unproblematically, un-self-consciously. Yet, the film wants to *suggest* this possibility even as it complexifies it. Eunice (you) is the embodiment of alterity in the film, as the tortured, religion-obsessed murderess who wears her burden literally on her body in the forms of chains and piercings. Yet, Eunice constantly mutters furiously as she goes about her business – 'look who it is – it's me', phonetically confusing the subject/object relation between me/Mi and you/Eu (and the viewer and the spectacle); implicating 'me' in her 'you-ness', her othered criminality, and aligning the dissident subject position with the more mainstream one. It is her function in the film precisely to trouble identity, to call it into question constantly, asserting to each woman she meets: 'you're Judith aren't you?', and killing them when they respond in the negative. The name 'Judith' becomes an important signifier in the film, the object of Eunice's ill-fated and single-minded quest. Judith sometimes denotes Eunice's absent lover, and sometimes the Judith of the Bible, who cut off the head of Holifernes, and of whom Eunice keeps a cut-out iconic image in the car. Judith, then, in her two guises is both archetypal femme fatale and sacrificial victim, since Eunice admits to Miriam that she is searching for Judith in order to sacrifice her. Yet, in another tortuous twist, refusing fixed subject/object, active/passive divisions, it is Eunice who ultimately requests the status of sacrificial victim at Miriam's hands, in the moving final sequence of the film in which Miriam drowns her lover in the sea.

Identity and mobility are thus placed into a special relationship in the film. Miriam's housebound mother states: 'I never go anywhere. This is my radius. I never go anywhere. If you don't go out you'll do no evil, will you?', to which Eunice responds: 'evil is in your heart. If you don't go out you'll never get away from it'. Thus identity, while being slippery and unfixed, is also shown to be troublesome in its persistence. In the play of nomenclature and slippage, the film is able to articulate the notion that identity is not self-evident or transparent and yet, simultaneously, suggest the idea that discourses of interpellation – the 'you', and the answering 'look who it is – it's me' – are never fully transcended by Eunice's attempts to escape them through murder; through eroticized punishment (the chains she wears on her body); or through the religious discourse she repeats. The class implications of these elements are very significant. The lures and limits of social mobility and bourgeoisification are gently suggested by Miriam's mother's refusal to go beyond her radius; like those of her generation, she is taught that she must not rise above her last.

The use made of the road in the film enacts at the level of geographical setting what language articulates regarding identity. Being on the road is never quite allowed to be about freedom and escape in the film, but rather literalizes visually the difficulty of making linear progress. Eunice asks in despair at one point, when they have driven their car as far as it will go and have come to a stretch of water: 'how are we going to get across the river?'. She also states: 'I always get lost and I always end up in the woods'. Eunice goes astray, then, in ways that are at once moral, mental and navigational.

Killing another victim equates with making a wrong turn on the road. Eunice is the deliberately problematized subject seeking liberation, who is able to articulate, by dint of her absolute alterity, her mental alienation, the snares and the ultimate impossibility of the project of liberation that the sane are not allowed to speak.

Eunice's discourse is consistently confused and overdetermined in its themes of escape, redemption, love, flight and home. And significantly, her most overdetermined pronouncements tend to be made when she is on the move, on the road. In one scene that takes place in the car, we hear Eunice recite a poem – which she claims was written by Judith – about the difficulty of going home; she sings a hymn of death and transcendence; and then she flirts playfully with Miriam ('Give me a kiss, you pretty little thing!'). This confusing mish-mash of hybrid discourse is voiced in an unprepossessing car, stolen from a murder victim, on a road, in the north of England, to the tunes of postmodern Icelandic pop goddess Björk, singing *There's More to Life than this*. Being on the road, and by extension the notion of quest (for self and for other), does not deliver all it promises, as is announced by each of the different discourses Eunice cites, as well as by Björk's lyrics. Meanwhile, the high angle shots of the motorway and its rolling traffic, with which the sequence opens, suggests inexorable onward motion; journeys with direction. Thus, road movie iconography is used very deliberately at the same time as the discourses which contradict and debunk it. Moreover, as the camera moves lower and tracks alongside the moving cars, the shadow of a large lorry moving in the opposite direction, close to the camera, dwarfs and temporarily hides Miriam's and Eunice's car, relativizing the myth of individual freedom and solitude that the high angle shots suggested. Where the open plains of America's Midwest may offer an illusion of solipsistic individual freedom (mastery of the road), the congested motorways of Winterbottom's North England do not allow for it. As Michael Atkinson writes, in *Butterfly Kiss* there are 'no wide-open American Road-Movie roads, but one dreary Brit dead-end after another'.[7] Significantly, neither the personal nor the social ambitions that the road movie may suggest are achieved: the women zigzag and circle hopelessly within their radius, always on the move, but ultimately getting no further away from where they started than Miriam's mother. The postmodern aesthetic suggested by the incongruous collage of discourses in *Butterfly Kiss*, as well as the juxtaposition of American genre and resolutely English setting, announce a fractured ideology, a hope of transcendence which nevertheless has worn thin and patchy, showing up the horror that lies in its gaps.

It is possible to argue that the twisting of the conventions of the road movie and the use of space discussed above are intimately connected to, and parallel with, this film's representation of the sexuality and marginality of its characters, bearing in mind the homophobic stereotypes that have run through the history of cinema. As Aaron puts it:

within the development of cinema, the queerness of the implied gay or lesbian potential of a character ran concurrent with their murderous motives and with the predictable form of narrative closure: all were killed either by themselves, by others or by accident.[8]

In a discussion of *Butterfly Kiss* and a series of other films about lesbians who kill, all made in 1994 (Peter Jackson's *Heavenly Creatures*; Rafal Zelinsky's *Fun*; Nancy Meckler's *Sister my Sister*), Aaron contends that these films occupy ambivalent ground. They repeat cinematic clichés of dangerous lesbian sexuality, yet they do so in self-deconstructive rather than reifying ways, mainly by creating women-only spaces of reflection, violence, identification and passionate interaction, such as the mirroring pair of Mi and Eu in *Butterfly Kiss*.[9] Indeed, it can be argued that *Butterfly Kiss* is particularly aware of homophobic and misogynistic cultural stereotypes. When, in the love scene between Mi and Eu that takes place in Miriam's mother's bed, Eunice bites Miriam's neck, it is a sly elbow poke at the archetypal cinematic figure of the vampiric lesbian. But here Mi and Eu both dissolve into laughter following the bite. Eunice is certainly seriously deadly and deadly serious at other moments, but deliberately not in the way that conventional representations have led us to expect. The cliché of the vampiric lesbian bite is literalized at the surface and as play, and the danger that Eunice embodies is displaced elsewhere – not against the victim she 'corrupts' but against the world; not as homophobic caricature, but as genuinely disturbing force, disrupting and destroying discourses and bodies in her wake.

Similarly, one might think of the sequence in which Miriam suspects that Eunice has killed a little girl. The child has, in fact, been sleeping in the back of the car and, at a given moment, wakes up and announces her presence, taking Miriam by surprise. Eunice is certainly a murderess in the film, but the film refuses at every turn to allow Miriam or the viewer to anticipate or predict either Eunice's actions or the meaning of them on this basis: while the label of murderess fits her, she is not reducible to it. Just as traditional homophobic representations used the discourse of murder to suggest deviant sexuality, so a queer representation refuses to allow murder, which continues to stand in, trace-like, for dissident sexuality, to signify monolithically or straightforwardly; to be the essence of the character's identity.

Building on this, the denouement of *Butterfly Kiss* is both a gesture in the direction of the cultural tradition of punishing lesbians and other dissident women by death, and a revised response to it. Again, the terms are skewed. Eunice is killed, but it is as a self-designated sacrificial victim. She is assertive and tells Miriam how and when to kill her to assuage her sexualized desire for punishment. Why does Eunice die? Partly because that is what deviant, female characters do in film. Eunice, on some level, is sacrificed as the stigmatized lesbian of cultural representation, perverse, corrupt, deadly and mad. Yet, in the context of the containing film, this ending does not appear politically redundant or reactionary. One might argue that to allow Mi and Eu to live would be to negate the power of the history of representation and to ignore the accrued weight of stereotype. Yet why does she die *in her own way*, at the hand of her lover? To show the elasticity of that same discourse, the possibility of inflecting and adapting the accepted choreographed conventions, in order precisely to draw our attention to those conventions, to make us recall the many un-self-reflexive lesbian onscreen deaths we have witnessed.

Moreover, the death of Eunice works as a double citation and transgression: firstly, it marks the punishment of the lesbian character in film, and secondly it recalls the punishment of the criminal road movie anti-hero, for whom the law is embodied in the closing sequences by the police who attempt to bring the wrongdoers to justice. In *Butterfly Kiss*, significantly, the punishing agency is embodied by Eunice herself. This self-policing has been a constant feature of Eunice's performance, seen in the chains she wears on her body that marked simultaneous ascetic punishment and a source of masochistic pleasure. Embodying, symbolically, lesbian self-loathing, Eunice shows how homophobia has been endemic, internal to cinema. Her radical and visible internalization of its effects, paradoxically re-externalizes it and opens it up for question. This film problematizes at every turn the ethical usefulness of the notion of positive/negative representation. *Butterfly Kiss*, with its difficult, painful and extremely violent content, coupled with its troubling of generic expectations and stereotypes, challenges the polarity of positive/negative representation and of spectatorial identificatory pleasure. As Aneke Smelik writes: 'the question in queer cinema is not simply to get rid of stereotypes (as they are quite resilient), nor how to replace them with positive images (which leave the heterosexist imperative intact), but rather to achieve complexity and diversity'.[10] The very search for positive representation risks eliding a history of misogynistic and homophobic myth: it is, perhaps, for this reason that *Butterfly Kiss* thwarts so devastatingly that search.

This very complex film about mobility and its limits, revealed through the triple foci of class, mental health and sexuality, reveals the awareness of the regenerative and disruptive power of mobilizing discourse, without assuming that mobility will lead straightforwardly to liberation or redemption. The myth of liberation, so central to the road movie, and celebrated as the impossible, inconclusive death-in-life outcome of Thelma's and Louise's adventure, is treated in the same way as the myth of the murderous lesbian in *Butterfly Kiss*. Its cultural resonance is recognized and referenced but it is not straightforwardly repeated. It is undermined and reworked to demonstrate the workings of the naturalized ideology in the traditional narrative. A more productive ethical endeavour for cinema criticism than the project of analysing positive representations, then, might lie in the agenda of showing how representations of individuals and social structures obey or flout generic form. To do so is to make explicit how the history of meaning making in images carries internalized codes of norms and exclusions that can be challenged by dissident representations.

Notes

1 Rosen, *Popcorn Venus*, 105.
2 See: Fabe, *Closely Watched Films*, 207–9.
3 Weiss, *Vampires and Violets*, 63.
4 *Film Quarterly* and *Cinéaste* both published scholarly fora devoted to the film in the year of its release. A monograph, *Thelma and Louise* by Marita Sturken was published by the BFI in 2000, and a collection of essays, *Thelma and Louise Live! The Cultural Afterlife of an American Film*, edited by Bernie Cook, appeared with the University of Texas Press in 2008, in addition to numerous other individual articles and book chapters.
5 Scher, 'Road Movies with a Map' (accessed 29/01/09).
6 Cook, *Thelma and Louise Live!*, 1.
7 Atkinson, 'Michael Winterbottom: Cinema as Heart Attack', 46.
8 Aaron, '"Til Death Us Do Part"', 72.
9 Aaron, '"Til Death Us Do Part"', 74–6.
10 Smelik, 'Art Cinema and Murderous Lesbians', 72.

Chapter 3

The South looks back

Ethics, race, postcolonialism

Libby Saxton

The preceding chapters argued that an exclusive consideration of subject-matter in documentary or plot and characterization in fiction films provides a distorted account of their ethical ramifications. Chapter 2 investigated the ethical implications of the concept of 'positive representation' and showed how progressive intentions may be bolstered or compromised by style, generic positioning and ideological context. Turning from representations of gendered and dissident sexual identities to explorations of cultural identity and neocolonial power, this chapter pursues a parallel critical agenda, reflecting the cross-fertilization between studies of gender, sexuality, race, ethnicity and other axes of difference in cinema. Within film studies, questions of identity have primarily been conceptualized in political terms; research has focused on how cinema perpetuates or challenges the unequal distribution of resources and power between dominant and oppressed or marginalized constituencies. This chapter explores some of the ethical premises which undergird these political considerations. Though analysis of two films which adopt different perspectives on postcolonial injustice and responsibility, I examine the role that cinematic mechanisms of identification

Figure 3 Bamako

and filmic codes such as point of view play in naturalizing or critically exposing relations of mastery and domination between self and other. I argue that it is as much through the manner in which films negotiate the narrative, stylistic and generic conventions of dominant forms of cinema as through the moral agendas which explicitly drive them that they repeat or resist the violence of colonialism's failure to contend ethically with alterity.

Theoretical perspectives: ethics and politics

Borrowing from the methodologies employed by feminist and lesbian and gay criticism from the 1970s onwards, early research into race and ethnicity in cinema was dominated by a preoccupation with the stereotyping of non-white characters in Western films. Exemplary of this trend is Richard Maynard's edited collection *African on Film: Myth and Reality* (1974), a discussion of Hollywood's deleterious misrepresentations of African history, culture and communities. The demythologizing or corrective agenda pursued by such projects has ethical as well as political dimensions. As cultural constructs, racial stereotypes in cinema involve value judgements. Studies such as Maynard's show how stereotypes are entrenched in discourses which are explicitly moral, and frequently moralizing, in orientation. The stereotypes in question may be unambiguously derogatory (such as the violent Native American or the sexually rapacious African American) or may exhibit attributes that might be construed as 'positive' by certain cultures and 'negative' by others (such as the obedient, faithful, patient African servant); but, either way, they imply an assessment of the moral character of the racial or ethnic group the indi-vidual represents. Such evaluations often work retrospectively to justify a history of racism and colonialist persecution. The constitutive role played by racial and ethnic stereotypes, particularly sexualized ones, in the propagation of moral ideology is famously exemplified by *The Birth of a Nation* (D. W. Griffith, 1915), where the characterization of the African American Gus (played in blackface by Walter Long) as a murderer and would-be rapist of white women serves to shore up the myth of white moral supremacy. In terms of this book's poststructuralist ethical framework, the inherent violence of the stereotypical construct consists in its reduction of the other to a fixed, one-dimensional image underpinned by an essentialist conception of identity.

In the 1980s, film theorists influenced by developments in feminist film theory and postcolonial studies began to challenge the premises on which corrective stereotype analysis and concomitant discussions of 'positive images' are based. In their article 'Colonialism, Racism and Representation' (1983), Stam and Spence note that these approaches rest on a reductive under-standing of film as a more or less transparent reflection of political reality, and, in cataloguing a limited set of stereotypes, fall prey to a version of the essentialism they attack.[1] These co-authors argue for attention to 'the *mediations* which intervene between "reality" and representation', that is, to 'narrative structure, genre conventions and cinematic style rather than ... perfect correctness of representation'.[2] While Stam and Spence frame their objectives in explicitly political terms, I would suggest that their argument is also enabling for ethical criticism. Although they do not refer directly to ethics, other terms reveal that their conception of politics is rooted in ethical principles. For instance, relations between viewers and film protagonists are conceived in terms of 'respect', 'sympathy', 'understanding' and other concepts familiar from moral and ethical philosophies concerned with interactions between individuals or communities.[3] As we shall see, analysis of cinematic codes and spectatorial positioning along the lines proposed by Stam and Spence can expose hidden contradictions in the ethical logic of individual films.

The unarticulated ethical implications of the political project outlined by Stam and Spence raise the larger and vexed question of how politics relates to ethics in postcolonialism. Although continental ethical philosophy, and, in particular, the work of Levinas, has been one of the major influences on postcolonial thought (along with Marxist politics), much research in this field leaves its underlying ethical premises unspoken.[4] That said, a number of key theorists have engaged explicitly with ethical discourses in discussions of the impact of colonial and neocolonial violence on self-other relations. Derrida's work on hospitality and reconciliation, Gayatri Spivak's discussions of responsibility and the singularity of the subaltern and Kwame Anthony Appiah's analyses of cosmopolitanism and identity exemplify the diversity of postcolonial thought at the intersection between ethics and politics.[5] One of the quandaries facing theorists of the postcolonial is how to formulate a coherent ethics without recourse to universal principles rooted in essentialist conceptions of human nature. Is it possible to envisage an ethical system which avoids ethnocentrism and respects the value systems of different cultures while establishing legitimate grounds for engagement, intervention and resistance?[6]

From the perspective of a postcolonial ethics the concepts of 'positive' and 'negative' images are inherently problematic, since they rest on the ethnocentric assumption that all cultures judge the good and the bad by the same universal criteria. As noted above, a characteristic or practice deemed 'positive' by one group may be perceived as 'negative' by another. Used without reference to specific cultural or ideological contexts, these designations obscure the distinctions between different sets of values and systems of morality. Moreover, the quest for affirmative images of historically oppressed racial, ethnic or cultural groups may disavow or distract from this history of oppression and the role that cinema has played in it. What are needed, then, are representations which critically interrogate this legacy and forms of criticism which take account of cultural context and point of view without imposing Western value judgements. In order to explore this notion of ethical work as *interrogation* rather than straightforward *exposition*, the following sections turn to two films which respond in different ways to the pernicious misrepresentations of Africa found in Hollywood and European

cinema. Made by directors from Brazil and Mauritania, these films tackle a specific set of ethical issues pertaining to the responsibility of Western institutions towards African countries in the era of globalization and neoliberal
capitalism. My analysis considers how the films position themselves in relation
to the tropes and codes of dominant Western cinemas in order to establish
why the cinematic strategies of one are more conducive than those of the
other to non-ethnocentric ethical thinking about justice and responsibility.

Through white eyes: *The Constant Gardener*

The first of these films has been viewed as part of a sub-genre dubbed the
'white conscience film' by Dave Calhoun in a discussion of the recent trend
in international cinema of recounting stories about Africa to non-African
audiences. Although this moniker implies a moral commitment to expiating
historical guilt and righting past wrongs, Calhoun criticizes the genre for its
superficial engagement with African history and politics.[7] The genre's ethical
and political shortfalls are brought into focus when it is considered in the
context of the history of Western films set in the continent. In European and
North American newsreels, documentaries and fiction films made during the
colonial era, African countries were frequently stripped of their geographical
and cultural specificity, while their citizens were commonly deprived of
agency, speech and points of view or simply rendered invisible.[8] Colonial
myths and stereotypes have been reformulated in the aftermath of direct
colonial rule. Melissa Thackway notes that today Africa is most often represented as 'the site of famine, poverty, disease and war, or, in other words, as
"Other" to the "economically developed", safe, West'.[9] Most of the recent
films mentioned by Calhoun, including *Hotel Rwanda* (Terry George, 2004),
Shooting Dogs (Michael Caton-Jones, 2005), *Blood Diamond* (Edward Zwick,
2006), *Catch a Fire* (Phillip Noyce, 2006) and *The Last King of Scotland*
(Kevin Macdonald, 2006), distance themselves critically from some of these
suspect conventions whilst consciously or unconsciously perpetuating others.
A film such as *Blood Diamond*, for example, troubles the image of Africa as a
single uniform domain by addressing the specifics of the civil war ravaging
Sierra Leone in the 1990s, including the plight of slaves, child soldiers and
others displaced by the conflict, yet persists in using the continent as a war-
torn backdrop for white adventures. Although one of the two main protagonists, Solomon Vandy (Djimon Hounsou), is a Sierra Leonean villager, and
although he survives the death of the white South African anti-hero Danny
Archer (Leonardo DiCaprio), the film divides its attention unequally between
them. The final scene is striking for the efficiency with which it silences
Vandy while dissimulating this move. Called as a witness at a South African
conference on the conflict diamond trade, he is announced as the 'voice of the
Third World' by the chairman, who urges us to start listening to such
voices. The white audience applauds enthusiastically, but before Vandy has a

chance to tell his story, the closing credits appear. The denouement of *Blood Diamond* hypocritically gags the Sierra Leonean witness while alleviating white guilt through a moral sermon valorizing his (unheard) testimony, thereby undermining the amends-making logic it superficially appears to embrace.

One of the films discussed by Calhoun stands out from the rest by dint of the nationalities of its director and cinematographer. The 2005 cinematic adaptation of British novelist John le Carré's *The Constant Gardener* (2001) brings Brazilian director Fernando Meirelles and Uruguayan cinematographer César Charlone together with a British screenwriter and a British producer. Le Carré has remarked that Meirelles brought a 'Third World eye' to the film, inferring that the director's origins lent the project legitimacy and authenticity, although the hierarchical relationship to the 'First' and 'Second' Worlds implied by the often criticized phrase 'Third World' arguably undermines this inference.[10] The connection between Latin America and Africa established via Meirelles's and Charlone's collaboration on the film might more profitably be considered in relation to debates around 'Third Cinema'. This term was coined by Argentinean filmmakers Fernando Solanas and Octavio Getino in the late 1960s to designate a corpus of film theory and practice devoted to the transformation of social conditions and the conventions of dominant commercial and art cinemas.[11] How does *The Constant Gardener* negotiate these conventions and what are the ethical implications of this?

At the level of plot, the film attempts to rectify past and present cinematic distortions of African history by exposing colonialism's legacy and capacity to reinvent itself. It examines the morally ambiguous activities of transnational pharmaceutical corporations in the continent and the blurry distinctions between humanitarian aid and capitalist profiteering. The fictitious company KDH is testing a new tuberculosis drug on sick, impoverished and unwitting Kenyans, with harmful or fatal consequences. A fleetingly seen poster bearing the German slogan 'Bhopal mahnt' (remember Bhopal) situates KDH's actions within a history of pharmaceutical and military tests in developing countries. However, while the film presents itself as a critique of the West's irresponsible exploitation of these countries, the way in which the story is narrated undermines this ethical agenda and does little to refashion established Western filmic conventions. The murder of an indeterminate number of Kenyans is reduced to a catalyst for a narrative whose primary focus is the killing of British citizen, Tessa Quayle (Rachel Weisz), who had been investigating the drug tests. The story unfolds from the perspective of her husband Justin (Ralph Fiennes), a British diplomat who embarks on a search for her killer. The film declares its figurative point of view through narrative structure – information is generally disclosed to the viewer as Justin discovers it – and the shards of memory depicting intimate moments shared with Tessa which puncture the present. The association between the camera and Justin assumes a corporeal dimension when amongst his wife's computer files he discovers a video of himself waking from sleep; the subsequent shot not only displays his reaction but also mimics it by defocusing, as if the lens, like his eyes, is welling up with tears.

What are the ethical ramifications of the privileging of Justin's point of view? In mediating African experiences through his perception, this code reasserts the sovereignty of the European self and reduces the other to a series of fleeting, shadowy, de-historicized projections. Many scenes are shot on location in Kenya and Sudan and the film has won praise for its portrayal of living conditions in the vast Kibera slum in Nairobi. However, while local people frequently appear in the shots as extras, they rarely speak or interact directly with the European protagonists, in line with the conventions of colonial-era films. A handful of scenes disturb these norms and hint at a desire to escape the confines of a white perspective – we see snatches of a Kibera resident's bicycle ride to work and glimpse locals working in the kitchen of a Nairobi restaurant – but these are brief, fragmentary and barely developed or integrated into the narrative.[12] The most fully fleshed out black character, a Belgian-Congolese doctor named Arnold Bluhm (Hubert Koundé), is spoken *about* more often than he is given the chance to speak for himself. The suspicions aroused in Justin by Arnold's friendship with Tessa and the singularly violent end and sexual torture reserved for Arnold also allude to white sexual stereotypes of black males, although the narrative is careful to debunk these.[13] The film's seductive visual style colludes in our estrangement from African experiences. Reminiscent of the techniques used in Meirelles's and Charlone's 2002 film *Cidade de Deus* (*City of God*), which focuses on the lives of inhabitants of a Rio de Janeiro *favela*, the combination of highly mobile handheld camerawork, frequent close-ups and rapid editing fosters a sense of immediacy and authenticity, yet here it prevents us from delving beneath surface impressions. As it follows Tessa and Arnold around Kibera, the camera picks out a mass of visual details: a wide-eyed baby in a shawl on its mother's back; an open sewer; a chicken pecking at an oil slick. But the incessant motion and breathless cuts prohibit us from deciphering traces that might yield glimpses of the bigger historical and socio-political picture (to take an example at random, we wonder about the story behind the shoes we briefly see lined up in one of the alleys).

One scene initially seems to buck these trends. Our first glimpse of Kibera is an excerpt from *Huruma*, a play appealing for tolerance towards people who are HIV-positive, performed to the local community by Kenyan actors working with the real charity SAFE. The play is rooted in Kenyan theatrical traditions; lines are delivered in a choral style and each character is played by three actors, who move, speak and emote in synchrony. A reading of the film in the 'positive images' tradition might praise this scene as a corrective to Western cinema's repeated erasures of culturally specific identities and practices in Africa. Yet such a reading would overlook the ethical implications of editing and point of view. The film preserves only a few short fragments of the play and the camera cuts repeatedly back to Tessa in the audience, whose effusive receipt of a gift from a local child distracts us from the performance.[14] Here, as throughout most of the film, African culture and history are reduced to easily digestible chunks and mediated through white eyes.

The Constant Gardener shies away from creating any serious ethical trouble with respect to the conventions of the Western thriller and romance genres to which it belongs. In spite of its attention to the specificities of locale, which suggests awareness of the altericidal convention of treating Africa as a homogeneous backdrop, Kenya and Sudan ultimately function as eye-catching settings for a transnational corporate intrigue entwined with a British love story, aligning the film with the tradition of adventure films such as *The African Queen* (John Huston, 1951). The film's conformity to the codes of these various genres conflicts with its apparent critique of Western mythologies. Despite the non-linear narrative, the plot unfolds according to the conventional thriller pattern, as Justin follows clues and gathers evidence, culminating in his exposure of KDH's crimes, an act which costs him his life. While, on the surface, justice is done (Tessa's death is avenged), white transgressions are exposed and punished, and moral order is re-established, the public downfall of the Foreign Office politician Sir Bernard Pellegrin (Bill Nighy) neatly occludes more complex and nebulous transnational configurations of power. Moreover, the fact that the agent of justice is British reiterates the myth of European superiority. The film never envisages the possibility of individual or collective action by the Kenyans directly affected by the drug, depriving them of the opportunity for self-determination. *The Constant Gardener* raises consciousness about the human cost of global capitalism in the non-Western world, but its regressive narrative logic seduces us back into the colonialist supposition that only the white man can 'save' Africa. Although the prioritization of a European point of view does not lead to overtly racist representations of Kenyan and Sudanese communities, it nevertheless rearticulates a Eurocentric moral discourse. The film's adherence to the perspectival and generic conventions of dominant Western cinemas thus reveals its ostensible ethical commitment to dispensing justice and restoring equality to be merely white conscience salving.

Reverse shot: *Bamako*

The ethical contradictions inherent in *The Constant Gardener* are brought into sharper focus when it is compared with a film such as *Bamako* (2006). Although it was directed by Mauritanian-born Abderrahmane Sissako, who grew up in Mali, *Bamako* is another African story destined for a predominantly non-African audience (for the time being, at least). As Sissako explains, film distribution and exhibition in Mali has been disrupted by measures imposed on the state by external financial institutions.[15] *Bamako's* ethico-political agenda intersects with *The Constant Gardener's* critique of global capitalism. Set in the Malian capital, the film stages a mock trial in which African society (the plaintiff) accuses international financial institutions (the defendant) of maintaining Africa in a state of underdevelopment through predatory policies such as Structural Adjustment Programmes. Both films thus constitute attempts to establish responsibility for crimes against Africans. But whereas in *The Constant Gardener* the crimes are brought to light by European activists, in *Bamako* African citizens undertake the investigation themselves. The lawyers and witnesses are non-professional actors who play themselves and were given freedom by Sissako to compose their own speeches. What distinguishes the films from an ethical perspective is less their subject-matter than the points of view they adopt in relation to Africa and the West, and Western media in particular. In a 1995 interview, Sissako draws a parallel between colonialism and the West's imposition of its images on Africa, commenting of the latter 'we are being invaded once again. It's another form of acculturation.'[16] For Sissako, African cinema is capable of reversing and deconstructing what is often called the 'colonial gaze': 'white people have had the privilege of seeing others without being seen for three thousand years. Today, Africans are making films, they can project their gaze elsewhere, outside their continent.'[17] More concertedly than *The Constant Gardener*, *Bamako* interrogates and challenges the reductive images of Africa circulating in Western films and the moral myths and ideologies which lie behind them.

The film alludes to but simultaneously dismantles the linear narrative structures and plot conventions followed by dominant forms of Western cinema. Structurally influenced by African oral traditions, Sissako's narrative is fragmented and multi-layered.[18] A series of subsidiary narratives unfold in parallel with the trial; the most fully developed charts the progressive estrangement of a nightclub singer, Melé (Aïssa Maïga), from her unemployed husband, Chaka (Tiécoura Traoré). Ostensibly, the couple's story is linked to the trial only by physical proximity (they happen to live next to the courtyard where it is taking place). The film avoids weaving its disparate narrative threads together through contrived intersections (of the kind cultivated in other films exploring global relations, such as *Babel* (Alejandro González Iñárritu, 2006)). Sissako's refusal to forge explicit links between the parallel plot lines leaves viewers to make their own connections. Breaking with the classical cinematic convention according to which apparently distinct events are eventually revealed to be causally connected, a norm respected by *The Constant Gardener*, *Bamako* creates correspondences that do not obey any straightforward logic of cause-and-effect. The subplots and other inserted sequences function variously to corroborate testimony heard in the trial (a role served by the reconstruction of scenes from Madou Keita's perilous attempt to reach Europe, which reveal the human cost of Western anti-immigration policies), to call it into question (as when French lawyer Roland Rappaport, who represents the international financial institutions, is butted by a goat) or to depict other dimensions of the economic realities which are the trial's main focus (Melé and Chaka's story reveals the cruel toll international financial policies are taking on interpersonal relations).[19] The inserted sequences enable Sissako to experiment with contrasting modes of narration; indeed, they resemble fragments from the alternative films he might have made instead of *Bamako*. They produce disorienting, elliptical shifts in space, time and point of view which violate the codes of Western narrative and solicit new modes of sense making.

The film's non-linear, disunified form also facilitates the disruption of generic conventions. *Bamako* is not, like *The Constant Gardener*, a 'genre film', but it parodically cites several North American generic traditions as well as paying homage to politicized Latin American genre-bending experiments. One evening, a group of Malian adults and children assemble in front of a television to watch a Western. Entitled *Death in Timbuktu*, this five-minute film within the film embraces the superficial audio-visual trappings of the genre but subverts its iconography and ideology through setting, casting and plot. The territory to be colonized is not the Wild West but Africa and the cowboys are played by an international cast, including African American actor (and executive producer of *Bamako*) Danny Glover, Palestinian director Elia Suleiman, Congolese director Zeka Laplaine, French director Jean-Henri Roger and Sissako himself. Their indiscriminate shooting of African villagers elicits giggles from the Malian audience glued to the screen, an implicit critique of the adverse effects of what Sissako calls new forms of media 'acculturation' on African perceptions. Michael Sicinski points out that *Death in Timbuktu* 'recalls the Brazilian Westerns of Glauber Rocha, which used the framework of genre as an armature for radical content'.[20] It constitutes a nod to 'Third Cinema' traditions in which genre is undermined from within, but one which simultaneously marks *Bamako*'s distance from such projects in terms of style and narrative structure. These discrepancies are highlighted in a later scene when Chaka shoots himself and the menacing musical theme of *Death in Timbuktu* returns, the generic reference politicizing his personal tragedy. Given that justice is one of the traditional preoccupations of the Western, a theme sent up by the senseless violence of Sissako's parody, the genre provides an apt medium in which to reflect obliquely on the progress of the trial. Disrupting generic colour codes, the casting of black actors as cowboys complicates the racial binary opposition between white and non-white indigenous communities around which Westerns are traditionally constructed. *Death in Timbuktu* thereby makes a comment about ethical accountability which contextualizes the indictments of Western economic policies heard in the makeshift courtroom, inferring that responsibility for Africa's future does not lie exclusively with outsiders.

The trial scenes themselves have a superficial generic affinity with the courtroom drama, yet once again, the relevant codes are skewed. The formal setting of the courtroom is eschewed in favour of the courtyard of Sissako's childhood home. Here everyday life and work continue uninterrupted around the hearing: a toddler ambles around in squeaky shoes; women dye fabric and men converse with half an ear to the proceedings; an audience-member breast-feeds her child. Through Sissako's creative use of space and depth of field, the boundaries between the trial and quotidian reality are literally blurred, demystifying, domesticating and democratizing the legal process. Whereas the courtroom drama frequently presents the action from the lawyer's point of view, in *Bamako* no single perspective is privileged and the witnesses are accorded as much screen time as the legal teams. The film's leisurely pace and observational style and the preponderance of shots of people simply listening or waiting disturb the perspectival and identificatory conventions of the genre and dispel the dramatic tension it typically cultivates. Rather than building suspensefully towards a climactic resolution when a lawyer reveals all, *Bamako* validates the process of testimony itself and the truths disclosed by the witnesses. In this respect, it might be read as a corrective to the disingenuous suppression of Vandy's voice at the end of *Blood Diamond*. Sissako's take on the courtroom drama upsets its power hierarchies by insisting on the equality of all participants and reclaiming the law as an instrument of the people, while placing Western juridical codes in question.

The hearing itself challenges prevalent contemporary stereotypes whilst thoroughly problematizing the concept of 'positive representation'. Just as the Western image repertoire of Africa as a site of otherness, danger and abjection is shown to be partial and reductive by the very existence of the trial, so Western perceptions of Africans as passive, mute, uncomprehending victims and of African identities as homogeneous and immutable are contradicted by the participants' performances. Significantly, African and French lawyers work together on the legal teams and men and women play equal roles in the proceedings. The witnesses represent a cross-section of Malian society (and, by the film's implication, of sub-Saharan Africa); they include a farmer (Zegué Bamba), a writer (Aminata Dramane Traoré), a failed refugee (Madou Keita), a professor (Georges Keita) and a former teacher (Samba Diakité). Their depositions are distinctive in terms of form and content. For example, while Traoré delivers an eloquent, erudite polemic against George W. Bush, the G8 and the decivilizing, dehumanizing effects of globalization, Diakité chooses to do no more than confirm his name, place and date of birth and profession and let the audience interpret his silence. The most arresting testimony is a song improvized in Senoufo by Bamba, which also demands deciphering since, unlike the speeches in Bambara and French, it is not translated. Importantly, the witnesses' complaints against the World Bank, the International Monetary Fund, the World Trade Organization and the G8 are punctuated with allusions to African co-responsibility, echoing the logic of *Death in Timbuktu*. Georges Keita, for instance, condemns endemic corruption in the Malian administration, while recognizing that he is implicated in this by his profession. The obstacles posed by African apathy and despair are also acknowledged in a scene where Chaka refuses to repeat his comments about the socially destructive impact of Structural Adjustment Programmes on the grounds that 'no-one will listen'.

At every turn, the highly individualized testimonies presented in *Bamako* and their nuanced allocation of responsibility unsettle the reified binary opposition between active, omniscient, onnipotent Western self and passive, duped and impotent African other. If the film displaces the mute images of supplication that dominate Western media discourse about Africa, it simultaneously shows up the ethical fallacy of 'positive' imaging. Both *Bamako* and film within it suggest that an exclusively affirmative portrait of African communities would gloss over cultural particularities and differences, past and present subjugation and ongoing responsibilities. Moreover, the unpredictable unfolding of the trial heightens awareness of the ethnocentric criteria by which 'positive' and 'negative' attributes and practices are judged; Diakité's silence and Bamba's song, for instance, confound Western preconceptions about what constitutes a 'good' testimony. Both performances confront us with the limits of Western juridical frameworks and ideals of justice. Unapologetic in its utopianism, though realistic in its assessment of the actual prospects for challenge, *Bamako* has been seen as didactic, a charge anticipated in the film by the judge who asks the defence lawyer whether he considers the trial to be partisan.[21] I have attempted to demonstrate, however, that it is indirectly through its deconstructive engagement with Western cinematic conventions, as much as directly through the speeches of the witnesses and lawyers, that the film constructs its ethical vision. Sissako's decision to leave Bamba's song unsubtitled is emblematic of this, in its transformation of one of the implicitly racist habits of colonial-era films, which often neglected to provide translations of African languages, into a mechanism for disrupting Eurocentric readings. For those in the audience who do not understand Senoufo (which includes most of the listeners on screen), the song thwarts the desire to know, affording instead an experience of pure form and a radically disconcerting encounter with alterity, which relocates us from the realm of epistemology into the spheres of ethics and aesthetics.

Some concluding remarks

This chapter has endeavoured to show how two films addressing superficially compatible questions about postcolonial culpability and global capitalism in fact open up irreconcilable perspectives on the ethical encounter disrupted by colonialism. The implication of my comparative analysis of *The Constant Gardener* and *Bamako* is not that African films provide points of view on local particularities and global realities that are inherently 'more ethical' – in this context, less totalizing with regard to alterity – than films emanating from elsewhere in the world; this would imply both an essentialist conception of cultural identity and production and a codified model of ethics. Instead, I have argued that the position adopted by these films in relation to dominant forms of cinema is ethically fraught, for the implication of perspectival and other cinematic codes in colonialism's altericidal vision needs to be exposed and thoroughly problematized. The attempt to interrogate and denaturalize such codes must be seen as an important part of a postcolonial ethical project on the screen. A film such as *Bamako* engages in a dialogue with Western cinema and its colonialist inheritance which challenges Western conceptions not only of the good and the just, but also of their relationship to the beautiful, by asking us to reconsider what constitutes ethical testimony and art. Such a film is thus concerned not only with the ethics of globalization, but also with the globalization of ethics, that is, with how analysis of the power relations between communities and cultures might alter our understanding of what ethics is or ought to be.

Notes

1 Stam and Spence, 'Colonialism, Racism and Representation', 884.
2 Stam and Spence, 'Colonialism, Racism and Representation', 884. For a more extensive examination of the problems with stereotype analysis, see Stam and Shohat, 'Stereotype, Realism and the Struggle over Representation'.
3 Stam and Spence, 'Colonialism, Racism and Representation', 889.
4 See Hiddleston, *Understanding Postcolonialism* for discussion of the impact of Levinasian ethics on postcolonial philosophy and the fragility of distinctions between ethics and politics that are often taken for granted in this context.
5 See, for example, Derrida, *Of Hospitality* and *On Cosmopolitanism and Forgiveness*; Spivak, critical introduction to Devi, *Imaginary Maps*; Appiah, *The Ethics of Identity* and *Cosmopolitanism: Ethics in a World of Strangers*.
6 For a discussion of postcolonial ethical agency, see, for example, De, 'Decolonizing Universality'.
7 Calhoun, 'White Guides, Black Pain', 32.
8 For an overview of the conventions of documentaries and newsreels produced by the colonial authorities, see Thackway, *Africa Shoots Back*, 31–2.
9 Thackway, *Africa Shoots Back*, 36. Thackway cites Raymond Depardon's documentary *Afriques, comment ça va avec la douleur?* (1996) as an example of this representational trend.
10 'John le Carré: From Page to the Screen', interview included as an extra on the Universal Pictures DVD of *The Constant Gardener* (2006). For a critique of the term 'Third World' and discussion of alternative terminology, see Young, *Postcolonialism*, 4–5.
11 For an in-depth discussion of Third Cinema, see Wayne, *Political Film*.
12 Significantly, an extended version of the bike ride appears amongst the deleted scenes included in the extras on the Universal Pictures DVD of the film. Only selected fragments of this make it into the final cut.
13 Todd McGowan argues that the film 'plays on the white fear of black sexual potency ... only in order to reveal the groundlessness of the fear and to show that the real danger lies in capitalist power and the British state, both of which are shown as thoroughly white' ('The Temporality of the Real', 58).
14 The play appears in its entirety as an extra on the Universal Pictures DVD of the film.
15 Sissako explains: 'In 1990 the big financial institutions forbade the government to subsidise culture and forced the state to sell the theatres. Previously there were 40 cinemas in Mali but today there are only three' ('Finding Our Own Voices', 31).
16 Sissako, 'Interview: Abderrahmane Sissako', 199.
17 Sissako, 'Interview: Abderrahmane Sissako', 200.
18 For a discussion of the structural, stylistic and thematic influences of orature on Francophone African cinema, see Thackway, *Africa Shoots Back*, 59–92.
19 Sissako suggests that these cut-aways also serve as temporary reprieves from the intensity of the trial, allowing the viewer to escape the physical confines of the courtyard, and perform a relativizing function by portraying a spectrum of reactions to the event on the street ('La Conscience que l'Afrique n'est pas dupe', 20).
20 Sicinski, 'A Fragmented Epistemology', 17.
21 See, for example, Ukadike, 'Calling to Account', 39.

Chapter 4

Ethics, spectatorship and the spectacle of suffering

Libby Saxton

In Ingmar Bergman's 1966 film *Persona*, an actress, Elisabet Vogler (Liv Ullmann), attempts to escape her existential anguish by withdrawing from the world, but finds it persistently intruding on her. Suffering from an unidentified illness, which leaves her unable or unwilling to speak, she convalesces in a psychiatric hospital and a house on the coast, with only her nurse, Alma (Bibi Andersson), for company. One of the ways in which other people's lives impinge on Elisabet's privacy is through historical images. In an early scene, the actress is pacing her hospital room when her attention is caught by a television report. As the cinematic and televisual frames momentarily

Figure 4 Persona

coincide, we watch with her documentary footage of the Buddhist monk Thich Quang Doc burning himself to death in Saigon in 1963 in protest against the war in Vietnam. The film cuts between these hard to view images and progressively closer shots of Elisabet, illuminated by the televisual flicker, as she backs away from the screen in horror, her mouth covered by her hand. *Persona* is one of the earliest films to explore what Susan Sontag calls the 'quintessential modern experience' of watching catastrophes unfolding in distant corners of the globe.[1] As Sontag reminds us, the conflict in Vietnam was the first to be broadcast on global television in daily instalments, thus introducing 'the home front to new tele-intimacy with death and destruction'.[2] The invasion of *Persona*'s screen by images which do not belong to its fiction disturbs and disorients the viewers in and of the film. How does Elisabet's imagined predicament in Sweden relate to actual events which took place in Saigon? No clue is provided by the television commentary on the soundtrack, which avoids direct reference to the actions of the monk. The scene encourages reflection not only on the connections between Western viewers and those caught up in the faraway conflicts played out on the television screen, but also on the manner in which cinema frames and mediates pain and works to implicate its audience in this process. Presciently, *Persona* invites us to contemplate our ethico-political relations to the multifarious images of bodily and psychological trauma which are so readily available in our culture.

One of the perennial ethical problems which has preoccupied commentators on the visual arts and culture is what it means to view images of other people's pain. 'No other spectacle can raise the ethical question of what to do so compellingly as suffering', claims Lilie Chouliaraki.[3] The question 'what to do?' pertains as much to the positions we adopt in watching such spectacles as to how we act on the knowledge of what we have seen. Pictures of real and ongoing anguish, such as the documentary footage in *Persona*, pose questions about the viewer's obligation towards those on the screen: what are acceptable ways of looking and legitimate responses? Suffering staged for the viewer, such as the psychological torment experienced by Elisabet and Alma in Bergman's film, provokes consideration of the ambiguous allures of the iconography of pain, its ethical risks and possible justifications.

Over the past few decades, the concurrent proliferation of image technologies and mediatized atrocities has given rise to an interdisciplinary body of writing on the spectatorship of suffering taking place elsewhere. Recent debates have centred on photographs and television images of war and other calamities and the responses they elicit in Western viewers far removed from danger but not necessarily from responsibility. Less attention has been paid in this context, however, to the spectacles of suffering, both real and staged, we encounter in cinema, and the ethical dynamics of our interactions with them. As highlighted by the juxtaposition of photographic, televisual and filmic images of torment in *Persona*, cinema, like photography and television, allows us to witness others' actual or simulated pain from a distance in space and time. As technological advances have increased our exposure to images of catastrophe, the relationship between cinema and distant suffering has become a discernable concern in certain forms of modern and postmodern filmmaking.

The capacity of representations of painful experiences to stimulate ethical debate is reflected in the filmic examples discussed in previous chapters of this book (such as the potentially intrusive images of distressed children in *Être et avoir* and the traumatic events articulated by the witnesses in *Bamako*). Whereas these case studies focused on the interactions between characters or social actors and directors, and between filmic content and form, my contention in this chapter is that scenes of suffering can bring into focus the ethically fraught interconnections between film protagonists and spectators. More specifically, the chapter explores how films negotiate the asymmetrical power relations between those watching and those suffering, and the political hierarchies consolidated by mainstream Western news discourse. It looks firstly at the models of viewing which emerge in recent writings on photography, television, war and pain, asking what they can contribute to our understanding of film spectatorship, the nature of its association with other people's torment, and the capacity of cinematic images to attract, distract or hold us to account. It goes on to consider whether certain filmmaking practices can open up different perspectives on atrocity images generated by competing technologies by repositioning them in new contexts where they put cinema's fictions into question.

Distant pain and tele-intimacy

The moral position of the subject witnessing another person's distress has long been a classic topic of philosophical debate. According to Jean-Jacques Rousseau, fundamental to the human being's natural goodness is the universal sentiment of 'pity', an 'innate repugnance to see his fellow suffer' which is experienced prior to rational reflection, and makes us reluctant to cause other people harm.[4] For Kant, on the other hand, natural inclinations towards compassion are without moral value; it is our rational sense of moral duty which ought to motivate us to act compassionately.[5] The obligation to act to alleviate others' suffering is common to many systems of religious and moral thought, whether it is grounded in appeals to nature, reason or faith. In discussions of this duty, there is frequently an emphasis on unmediated vision as a catalyst for compassion and on-scene moral action. The biblical parable of the Good Samaritan is a paradigmatic example of this valorization of the ethically transformative potential of face-to-face encounters.

As Chouliaraki points out in *The Spectatorship of Suffering* (2006), however, these dominant ethical norms, which nominate the Good Samaritan as the 'ideal moral citizen', are 'out of pace with our contemporary experience of suffering'.[6] Modern technologies of visual representation expose us to others' pain from a spatial and (unless the images are live) temporal distance. They surround us with scenes of misery in which we cannot immediately or directly intervene, disrupting the chain reaction linking contemplation, compassion and action. Consequently, such spectatorship is sometimes regarded as inherently morally suspect. In *Regarding the Pain of Others* (2003), an essay on photographs and other pictures of war and atrocities, Sontag alludes (with scepticism) to misgivings of this kind:

> Images have been reproached for being a way of watching suffering at a distance, as if there were some other way of watching. ... It is felt that there is something morally wrong with the abstract of reality offered by photography; that one has no right to experience the suffering of others at a distance, denuded of its raw power.[7]

Critiques of the mediation of pain along such lines tend to posit an opposition between eyewitnesses, whose look is legitimized by their presence at the injurious event and exposure to potential danger, and mediate witnesses, whose look is unlicensed because they remain at a safe remove, reliant on visual technologies. So whereas camera-operators embedded with military forces, for example, establish their right to look by putting their bodies on the line, those who watch footage of victims of war from their sofas do so without moral justification. Moral qualms about such distanced spectatorship are exacerbated by the propensity of certain kinds of atrocity images to abstract or sanitize their subject-matter or turn it into an object of voyeuristic fascination.

Nevertheless, the notion that there is something intrinsically pernicious about the mediate witnessing of suffering has been challenged by critics who propose more nuanced accounts of the interactions between the viewer and the viewed. These interventions emphasize the ethico-political agency and responsibility of the spectator over the purportedly immoral 'effects' of such images. In *Distant Suffering: Morality, Media and Politics* (1993), Luc Boltanski remarks:

> Take the case of a spectator contemplating a suffering unfortunate from afar, someone unknown to him and who is nothing to him, neither relative nor friend nor enemy even. Such a spectacle is clearly problematic. It may even be that this is the only spectacle capable of posing a specifically *moral* dilemma to someone exposed to it.[8]

For Boltanski, watching suffering from a distance can act as a spur to ethical thought and action. The 'moral dilemma' posed by such a spectacle consists in deciding how to respond; in Boltanski's account images imparting knowledge of suffering confer on us an obligation to do something about it. Drawing on Hannah Arendt's *On Revolution* (1963), Boltanski analyzes the distinction between compassion, which he associates with face-to-face encounters and local acts, and pity, which 'generalizes and integrates the dimension of distance', as he assesses the value of humanitarian orientations towards the particular and the universal.[9]

Other commentators argue for the ethical and political value of engaged reflection over that of socially constructed sentiment or affect. Chouliaraki's analysis of the ethical values embedded in news discourse is critical of the 'regimes of pity' produced by television. She notes that the division between those who watch and those who suffer reinforces contemporary economic and political divisions, consolidating an asymmetry of power which is a throwback to colonial relations.[10] Instead of healing these divisions, she argues, the 'dispositions of pity' cultivated by Western television news generate care only for those 'like "us"'.[11] Chouliaraki concludes that the production of emotion should be combined with an emphasis on 'detached reflection – on the question of *why* this suffering is important and what we can do about it'.[12] Sontag too advocates reflective rather than sentimental responses. She warns that the illusion of closeness fostered by televisual media – what she oxymoronically dubs 'tele-intimacy' – works to conceal political hierarchies:[13]

> The imaginary proximity to the suffering inflicted on others that is granted by images suggests a link between the faraway sufferers – seen close-up on the television screen – and the privileged viewer that is simply untrue, that is yet one more mystification of our real relations to power. So far as we feel sympathy, we feel we are not accomplices to what caused the suffering. Our sympathy proclaims our innocence as well as our impotence. To that extent, it can be (for all our good intentions) an impertinent – if not an inappropriate – response.[14]

For Sontag, the manufacturing and experiencing of sympathy can thus be strategies of disavowal, ways of denying our agency and responsibility. In other words, our empathic reflexes are liable to distract us from the causal relations between our privileges and others' misfortunes. For this reason, Sontag urges us to stand back from such images and consider how we are implicated in the plights of those portrayed. Regarding the pain of others can be an occasion 'to reflect, to learn, to examine the rationalizations for mass suffering offered by established powers'.[15] Thus conceptualized, ethical viewing might involve reading images of suffering against their moral grain while scrutinizing the integrity of the emotional pay-offs commonly associated with liberal guilt and affect.

Cinema, altericide and ethical implication

According to critics such as Boltanski, Sontag and Chouliaraki, then, the act of contemplating others' suffering is not innately problematic, but rather those modes of representing and responding which instrumentalize this spectacle to shore up or naturalize the socio-political status quo. The rhetoric of mainstream news coverage works to dissimulate and discourage reflection on the unequal relation between protected Western viewer and vulnerable non-Western other, for instance by fostering a narcissistic pity which masquerades as altruism. Dominant modes of reportage shirk the ethical work of investigating how the viewer's privileges are connected to, or, in certain cases, predicated upon, the suffering of the person seen. These critics view spectatorship as charged with responsibility by suffering, while offering different accounts of what an ethical response would entail.

What, then, of the position of *Persona*'s viewers, who are confronted alternately with 'real' atrocities and suffering invented for their edification or gratification? Boltanski's contention that *only* the spectacle of actual suffering inflicted upon an unknown other poses 'a specifically *moral* dilemma' to the spectator overlooks the ethical charge attached to the other spectacles of pain that circulate in our culture, including those we encounter in films. While cinema lies outside the scope of Boltanski's study, his claim that images of suffering can prompt ethical self-scrutiny is applicable, I want to argue, to film spectatorship, and to re-enacted as well as 'real' events. This is not to suggest that a viewer watching pain simulated by consenting actors is a film is accountable in the same sense as, for example, a spectator witnessing atrocities on the television news, or looking at a photograph of a war victim, but that these different situations may illuminate each other's ethical stakes.

One critic who has explicitly investigated the relationship between these experiences of viewing is Aaron, whose discussion of ethical response and responsibility in cinema is influenced by Sontag's and Judith Butler's analyses of photographs of atrocities and torture.[16] Film spectatorship, Aaron contends, is inherently 'hooked on the "real" or imagined suffering of others':

> What I mean by this is that spectatorship depends upon our inter-subjective alignment with the prospective suffering of others. ... The other's pain is both a commonplace of cinema but also something we are always implicated in, not only as consumers but as consensual parties in the generation of characters' suffering for our entertainment.[17]

While the dynamic outlined by Aaron does not apply to every film or experience of viewing, it suggests that spectators and film protagonists are yoked together in ways that might properly be called 'ethical', a possibility left uninterrogated by most major theories of film spectatorship. For Aaron, whose model of the ethical encounter is shaped by Levinas's thought, film viewing is always 'ethically loaded' because 'it represents a negotiation of personal pleasures and others' interests'.[18] In this account, the subject–object relations underpinning what is often called 'gaze theory' are reconfigured in terms of an encounter between self and other, and exposure to alterity is understood to be political through and through.

The imbrication of suffering and spectatorial desire discussed by Aaron poses ethical questions which are by no means specific to the medium of film. As Boltanski points out,

> we know that one of the main motivations of fiction is the staging of suffering ... For over 2,000 years and with astonishing persistence, the question of viewing suffering has been raised in relation to fiction, and more precisely to the theatre, as a moral problem.[19]

How, then, does this problem relate to the 'dilemma' (to use Boltanski's term) posed by pictures of 'real' pain? Do Aaron's film spectator, 'hooked on' a blend of historical and fantasized suffering, and the viewers of photographic and televisual atrocity images discussed by Boltanski, Chouliaraki and Sontag share any common ethical ground? While acknowledging the importance of distinguishing between representations of staged and unstaged violence, Aaron argues that there are connections between the ways in which they implicate viewers:

> I am not in any way trying to level the experience of seeing blood spurting from severed limbs in a war film and seeing the limbless corpses of the aftermath of a suicide bomber in a CNN report – it matters very much that some acts really happened – but to recognise the importance of placing them, albeit at either ends, of some kind of continuum of spectatorship.[20]

Aaron's assertion that these two viewing experiences belong on the same ethical continuum is corroborated by consideration of the constructed nature of photographs and news discourse. As Sontag notes, many of the best-known war photographs taken prior to the Vietnam conflict turn out to be staged; besides, photographs, like all images, are selective: 'to photograph is to frame, and to frame is to exclude'.[21] Moreover, there has been widespread debate about the propensity of contemporary modes of image-production and diffusion to obscure the distinctions between real and fabricated violence, between reportage and spectacle.[22] This too is acknowledged by Sontag, who observes that since Vietnam, 'battles and massacres filmed as they unfold have been a routine ingredient of the ceaseless flow of domestic, small-screen entertainment'.[23] In the light of the increasingly blurred boundaries between entertainment and information, it may be helpful to conceive of 'real' and unreal suffering as providing critical perspectives on each other, without conflating the dilemma presented by the former with the questions posed by the consensual pleasures afforded by cinematic stagings of pain.

While Aaron's aim is to demonstrate that film spectatorship, in its alignment with others' pain, is always ethically implicated, and to delineate the strategies through which films have traditionally sought to disavow this implication, my own concern here is more specifically with the ways in which films negotiate the surfeit of images of suffering that circulate in competing visual media and interrogate our responses to them. A number of writers have examined the potential of cinematic and videographic practices to resist the Western mass media's tendency to suppress alterity (by averting attention from non-Western casualties) and derealize suffering. In his analysis of television coverage of the 1991 Gulf War in *Devant la recrudescence des vols de sacs à main* (*Owing to an Increase in Handbag Thefts*, 1991), Serge Daney compares and contrasts the electronic spectacles he calls 'le visuel' (the visual) with the cinematic image. Whereas 'le visuel' adopts a uniform perspective – '[*the*] *point of view of power*, in other words, of a shot without a counter-shot (of a shot which annihilates its counter-shot)' – cinema can register heterogeneous perspectives and 'bear witness to a certain *alterity*'.[24] Geoffrey Hartman pursues an intersecting agenda in an essay on the mediation of violence and suffering in the 'dot com era', where he compares the 'redemption' of reality performed, in Kracauer's account, by film with the 'ghosting of reality' found in contemporary mainstream movies and television.[25] Drawing on psychoanalytic theories of trauma, Hartman argues that this 'unreality-effect' functions as a psychic defence against the 'hyperarousal' caused by violence in films and on the news.[26] According to Hartman, co-founder and project director of the Fortunoff Video Archive for Holocaust Testimonies at Yale, survivor videography can 'counteract the glossy or ghostly unreality' characteristic of the televisual through its 'minimal visuality'; the restriction of the visual field to an individual embodied voice maximizes the 'mental space' opened up by the image and creates a new 'affective community'.[27]

Taking its cue from Daney's and Hartman's contentions that cinema and videography can constitute sites of resistance to the altericidal practices and numbing 'unreality-effect' of mainstream media, the rest of this chapter turns to selected scenes from three films which dramatize this possibility by casting their protagonists as witnesses to mediated violence and pain. At crucial moments in each film, the narrative is interrupted as the screen is invaded by documentary images depicting suffering or death. My readings ask to what extent the interpolation of these factual images calls our relationship to the fiction into question, by arousing our interest in the often disavowed connections between viewing self and imaged other.

Witnessing atrocity in *Persona*, *The Passenger* and *Caché*

Elisabet's glimpse of Quang Doc's suicide in the televized images that infiltrate *Persona* is not her only encounter with the pain of others distanced from her in time and space. Later in the film, as she lies on her bed leafing through a tattered book, she comes across another historical image. Turning up the lamp, she places the image on her bedside table, rests her head on her hands and scrutinizes it. A reverse close-up shot reveals it to be a now iconic photograph of women and children being arrested by Nazi soldiers in Warsaw. The film cuts back to Elisabet's face, also framed in close-up, its stillness mirroring the stasis of the snapshot. Only her eyes move, roaming intently around the photograph. The camera follows her lead. As the music crescendos, a series of extreme close-ups picks out individual figures and details: a young boy standing in the foreground, peering at the camera, with his arms raised; the butt of the gun trained on him; the faces of soldiers posing for the picture; the face of a civilian woman glancing across at them. Both the film and the photograph capture their subjects in the act of looking, making an object of the gaze itself. Yet the camerawork simultaneously questions the relationship between vision and comprehension. The closer we are brought to the photograph, the harder it becomes to make sense of it. The close-ups fragment the arrest scene, obscuring the subjects' eye lines and reorganizing spatial relations, while drawing attention to the photograph's materiality by revealing its graininess and signs of decay. Our perplexity at the image is compounded by the difficulty of reading Elisabet's face. In contrast to her expressive reaction to the television footage, here she remains impassive, her response indecipherable despite the camera's proximity.

Citing a series of divergent critical readings of this scene, and noting in particular their contradictory perceptions of Elisabet's reaction to the photograph, Peter Ohlin describes it as 'an icon of the instability of interpretation'.[28] For Ohlin, the photograph triggers reflection on the relationship between biological and mechanical reproduction, while other commentators link it in different ways to the thematic preoccupations of the film. What is pertinent in the current context is the interpretative conundrum it generates and the manner in which this illuminates the film's broader concern with the ethical charge of the look. The scrupulous attention accorded to the photograph by Elisabet and the camera, as it imitates the exploratory motion of her eyes, perplexes and tantalizes the viewer. We are not shown whom the book belongs to or how the snapshot came to be tucked inside it. Nor is its presence justified by any straightforward connection to the narrative. Like the documentary footage from Vietnam, the photograph intrudes unbidden, without preamble or contextualization. The relationship between the Holocaust, the war in Vietnam and Vogler's fictional predicament remains indeterminate. This ambivalence is exacerbated by the interpretative difficulties posed by the snapshot itself (as analyzed in detail by Richard Raskin in a book devoted to the photograph, *A Child at Gunpoint* (2004)), and particularly uncertainty about the degree to which the scene was staged. 'Real' and unreal suffering thus bleed into each other within the photograph just as they do within the film, complicating the viewer's response. Whereas Elisabet appears transfixed in horror by the monk's self-immolation, the manner in which the film interpolates the historical images invites alternative reactions. While the Holocaust photograph and the footage of Vietnam may solicit involuntary emotion, the film's refusal to integrate them securely into the narrative promotes reflective responses by enlisting us in acts of decoding and sense making. In spite of Elisabet's attempt to isolate herself from reality, then, and in spite of the abstract spaces, seemingly severed from history, in which its narrative unfolds, *Persona* thus counters the denial of ethical and political agency which Chouliaraki and Sontag identify in mainstream media discourse, and the altericidal rhetoric which Daney condemns in television coverage of the First Gulf War. It does so by compelling reflection on the interconnections between Elisabet and those she witnesses in images, and the disturbing possibility of her implication in their suffering.

The ethico-political relations between Western viewers and violence in what they perceive as faraway lands are more explicitly interrogated in Michelangelo Antonioni's *The Passenger* (originally entitled *Professione Reporter*; 1975). A series of straightforward thematic parallels can be drawn between *The Passenger* and *Persona*: both depict protagonists undergoing forms of existential crisis; both explore these crises through the motif of the *Doppelgänger*; both are preoccupied with the instability of identity and, in particular, with the ways in which identity is shaped through encounters with pain and death both close at hand and far away. However, whereas *Persona* focuses on the ambiguous position of the mediate witness to such events, in *The Passenger* mediated visions are juxtaposed with face-to-face confrontations. In contrast to Elisabet, whose physical distance from the violence she glimpses in images positions her as an on-screen surrogate for the film spectator, David Locke (Jack Nicholson), Antonioni's central protagonist, a journalist by profession, is an eyewitness to foreign conflicts. Moreover, whereas in *Persona* external images materialize and exacerbate the protagonist's interior anguish, in *The Passenger* the existential drama is played out in and through the images themselves. When we first encounter Locke, he is gathering material for a television documentary on 'postcolonial Africa' and seeking access to guerrilla forces in Chad. After he stages his own death by swapping identities with another man, a colleague in London, Martin Knight (Ian Hendry), sorts through his footage, explaining to Locke's wife Rachel (Jenny Runacre) that he is compiling a filmic portrait of the 'late' reporter. In the course of *The Passenger* we see three sequences from Locke's films of Africa, as Knight and Rachel view them on a moviola. While Rachel may superficially appear to be a minor and insubstantial character, it is profitable in the current context to consider the role she plays as an observer, witness and interrogator of images in the editing room scenes in particular.

Two of the excerpts from Locke's footage are staged for the film. The first appears on a small monitor in the centre of the shot, to which the camera draws closer as the scene progresses. This extract is in black and white and shows the ruler of an (unidentified) African country being interviewed by an off-screen Locke, and steadfastly denying the existence of opposition forces. The film cuts to Rachel and Knight, who discuss Knight's project, and then, in a colour flashback, to the original scene of the interview, as Rachel, who was present, remembers in voice-over how she accused her husband of 'accepting too much', failing to challenge his interlocutor's responses, and thus implicitly colluding in his distortion of history. In the third excerpt from Locke's films, which intrudes on the diegesis in full-frame and colour, its status indicated initially only by the whirring of the moviola, we encounter a character identified in the credits simply as the 'witch doctor'. Once again, the integrity of the Western media's gaze is called into question, but this time by the actions of Locke's interviewee, who observes that Locke's questions reveal more about himself than his subjects, before taking the camera and revolving it to face his questioner. A cut to the moviola followed by a counter-shot reveals Rachel watching intently as the witch doctor turns the tables on Locke, breaking what the reporter elsewhere refers to elliptically as 'the rules'. The physical gesture of appropriating and redirecting the camera, which fascinates Rachel, effects a reversal of the 'colonial gaze' and invites critical reflection on the Eurocentric conventions of Western interviews.

The first and third fragments of Locke's footage form a hermeneutic frame which conditions our responses to the second, the only sequence in *The Passenger* which was not shot by Antonioni's cinematographer Luciano Tovoli. Here too, the frames of the moviola and the film coincide as alien images infiltrate the screen without temporal or spatial contextualization. The shots in this sequence are conspicuous in their alterity: some are unsteady or out of focus; the angles, long shots and use of zoom indicate that particular constraints were placed on the camera-operator; their muted colours suggest poor quality film; the temporal ellipses between images resemble the narrative conventions of newsreels. Extracted from documentary footage of undisclosed provenance, this sequence depicts the execution of a rebel leader by a military firing squad on a beach somewhere in Africa.[29] A cut away to the editing room captures Rachel's appalled reaction. While her horror recalls Elisabet's response to the monk's suicide in *Persona*, Antonioni does not, like Bergman, exploit the expressive potential of close-ups of his protagonist's face; instead, we hear Rachel suppressing a gasp and see her hand gesticulating at the very edge of the frame, before she stands and removes herself from the camera's field of vision. Rachel's on- and off-screen presence as a witness not only validates the reality of the documentary footage, but also, in conjuction with her comments, creates space for a reappraisal of Western viewers' relationships to scenes of distant violence ostensibly unconnected to their privileges. Here as elsewhere in the film, her analytical and emotional responses to Locke's footage constitute the 'counter-shots' that Daney finds suppressed by the altericidal discourses of the televisual, insofar as they expose the 'colonial gaze' as a source of ignorance rather than information. In this reading, Rachel's contestatory ethical vision is validated, rather than undermined, by her assertion, when she sees her husband's dead body in *The Passenger*'s extraordinary final scene, that she does not know him.

My final test case is a single scene from Haneke's recent film *Caché*. Haneke's films are explicitly critical of the ethnocentric modes of looking fostered by the image-systems Daney calls 'le visuel', which repeatedly encroach on their narratives through the television and provide acerbic commentaries on the diegetic action. Inattentive consumers of mediated suffering populate Haneke's so-called 'Vergletscherungs-Trilogie' ('glaciation trilogy') *Der siebente Kontinent* (*The Seventh Continent*, 1989), *Benny's Video* (1992) and *71 Fragmente einer Chronologie des Zufalls* (*71 Fragments of a Chronology of Chance*, 1994)), a motif recapitulated in *Caché*. Like Locke, the anti-hero of *Caché* inhabits the media sphere, hosting a literary talk show on the television. But, in contrast to Antonioni's protagonist, Georges Laurent (Daniel Auteuil) refuses to acknowledge his bad faith when he finds himself under scrutiny from the eye of his conscience.

In the scene in question, which unfolds in a single shot, Georges and his wife Anne (Juliette Binoche) discover that their teenage son has gone missing. However, other events, whose connections to the main narrative need to be deciphered, simultaneously compete for our attention. The scene is prefaced by half a minute of full-screen television footage, which reappears on a plasma screen in the Laurents' book-lined living room. In its size and position, the screen bears a visual resemblance to a window, and although it offers no transparent view of the world, it is through this screen that mediated reality intrudes on the family's bourgeois lives, providing the catalyst for the plot. While in previous scenes Georges and Anne have watched threatening anonymous videotapes on the screen, on this occasion the television is tuned to the EuroNews channel. In the course of the scene, it shows coverage of the coalition forces' actions in Iraq, the investigation into the torture of Iraqis at the hands of the American military in the Abu Graib prison, and images of dead and wounded Palestinians in the Occupied Territories. Although this montage calls into question Daney's designation of 'le visuel' as 'shot without a counter-shot', its cinematic framing turns atrocity into wallpaper. Georges is positioned to the left in the foreground of the shot, his attention focused on Anne on the right, who glances briefly at the television on entering the room before turning her back on it. Apparently unrelated to their personal predicament, the news is reduced by their dialogue in the foreground to background noise. Yet the television screen is centred in the shot, resisting this reduction and preventing us from tuning its images out.

The disorientating network of intersecting frames and image-technologies constructed in *Caché* not only encourages reflection on the distancing, derealizing effects of mediated violence which concern Hartman, but also establishes links between distinct outbreaks of postcolonial violence. Via the televized images in the background of this scene, the film posits a connection between contemporary events in Iraq and the Occupied Palestinian Territories and the (unimaged) atrocity which haunts the film and may be

indirectly related to the disappearance of Anne's and George's son: the massacre of hundreds of pro-FLN demonstrators at the hands of French police in
Paris on 17 October 1961. The point of these juxtapositions is not to
establish equivalence between separate instances of brutality but to force us
to rethink the ways in which images conceal and reveal the workings of
power. In *Persona* and *The Passenger*, our gaze is held by the attentive
looking of an on screen witness, an act we are invited to emulate. In *Caché*,
in contrast, it is the protagonists' indifference to reports of horror which
exposes our co-implication. Rather than simply celebrating exemplary reactions to suffering or punishing immoral ones, agendas which would reinforce
the dominant but outdated ethical norms identified by Chouliaraki, these
three films are concerned to demystify our relations to pain endured by
others.

Some concluding remarks

This chapter has explored how selected theoretical texts and film scenes
model or figure the ethical relations between spectators and images of
simulated and actual suffering. It has attempted to demonstrate the pertinence of debates which have thus far focused predominantly on photographic
and televized images of pain to film spectatorship, through discussion of
films which reframe such images, interrogate the ideological biases embedded within them and promote analytical responses over disingenuous forms
of sentiment. By incorporating pictures of actual violence into their fictions,
Persona, *The Passenger* and *Caché* pose questions about the relationship
between spectatorial responsibility and desire, highlighting what Aaron
describes as 'the complex and alluring tension between witnessing violence
and in some way being entertained by it'.[30] Just as the films expose the
instability of the documentary evidence, so this interpolated material puts
the framing fictions in turn to the test, by disrupting their coherency and
challenging their significance. We are held to account not only as witnesses
to 'real' brutality but also as consenting viewers of pain staged for our
entertainment. They remind us too that the problems posed by images of
mediated suffering are inextricably entangled with questions of race and
gender. With the exception of the Holocaust, the conflicts witnessed, alluded
to or allegorized in *Persona*, *The Passenger* and *Caché* – in Vietnam, Chad,
Algeria, Iraq and the Occupied Palestinian Territories – are legacies of
Western colonialism and imperialism, while the privileged position accorded
to women as witnesses in *Persona* and *The Passenger* further specifies the
implication of the viewer. These films insist that what and how we view has
consequences, that spectators are not isolated from the spheres of ethical
action and accountability, but that our privileges – including the privilege of
looking – are linked to others' suffering in ways we need to actively
interrogate.

Notes

1 Sontag, *Regarding the Pain of Others*, 16.
2 Sontag, *Regarding the Pain of Others*, 18.
3 Chouliaraki, *The Spectatorship of Suffering*, 2.
4 Rousseau, *Discourse on the Origins of Inequality (Second Discourse)*, 36.
5 See Kant, *Groundwork of the Metaphysics of Morals*.
6 Chouliaraki, *The Spectatorship of Suffering*, 2.
7 Sontag, *Regarding the Pain of Others*, 105.
8 Boltanski, *Distant Suffering*, 20.
9 Boltanski, *Distant Suffering*, 6.
10 Chouliaraki, *The Spectatorship of Suffering*, 4–5.
11 Chouliaraki, *The Spectatorship of Suffering*, 13.
12 Chouliaraki, *The Spectatorship of Suffering*, 13.
13 Sontag, *Regarding the Pain of Others*, 18.
14 Sontag, *Regarding the Pain of Others*, 91.
15 Sontag, *Regarding the Pain of Others*, 104.
16 Aaron, *Spectatorship*, 87–123; Sontag, *Regarding the Pain of Others*; Butler, *Precarious Life*.
17 Aaron, *Spectatorship*, 112.
18 Aaron, *Spectatorship*, 88.
19 Boltanski, *Distant Suffering*, 21.
20 Aaron, *Spectatorship*, 122.
21 Sontag, *Regarding the Pain of Others*, 41.
22 See, for example, Žižek, *Welcome to the Desert of the Real!* and King (ed.), *The Spectacle of the Real*.
23 Sontag, *Regarding the Pain of Others*, 18–19.
24 Daney, *Devant la recrudescence des vols de sacs à main*, 185, 193 (my own translation).
25 Hartman, 'Memory.com', 5.
26 Hartman, 'Memory.com', 4, 3.
27 Hartman, 'Memory.com', 11.
28 Ohlin, 'The Holocaust in Ingmar Bergman's *Persona*', 242.
29 In their spoken commentaries on the Sony DVD of *The Passenger* (2006), Nicholson recalls only that Antonioni chose this sequence from a selection of films of executions which had been made available to him, while Mark Peploe, who wrote the story and co-wrote the screenplay, acknowledges that he has forgotten the name of the condemned man.
30 Aaron, *Spectatorship*, 121.

Chapter 5

Pornography and the ethics of censorship

Lisa Downing

Pornography is the enduring target of much ethical and political debate. Objections to hardcore pornography tend to follow one or both of two principal rationales: (1) (heterosexual) porn objectifies women, leading to misogynist attitudes; (2) pornography desensitizes the viewer and leads to copycat behaviour ('standard' porn leads to rape; sexually violent (BDSM) porn leads to murder). These are, then, respectively, an assertion about the ways in which the form and content of porn structure spectatorial attitudes (a debate that might take place within academic film studies, as well as sociology or political activism); and an assertion about the (causal) relationship between viewing a representation and acting in the world. They are often harnessed together in the service of feminist anti-pornography rhetoric, such as that produced by Andrea Dworkin and Catherine McKinnon in the 1980s. In works such as *Pornography: Men Possessing Women* (1981) and *Intercourse* (1987), Dworkin offered readings of written and visual

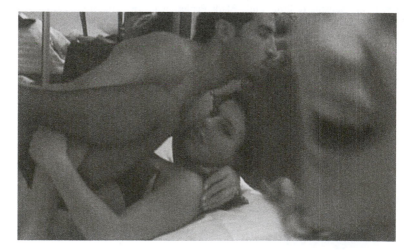

Figure 5 Baise-moi

pornography that sought to demonstrate the dehumanizing and objectifying qualities of male-produced heterosexual pornographic representations of women:

> the female is the instrument; the male is the center of sensibility and power ... The object's purpose is to be the means by which the lover, the male, experiences himself: his desire. ... the object, the woman goes out into the world formed as men have formed her to be used as men wish to use her.[1]

Lawyer Catherine McKinnon then used such rationales to attempt to effect legal measures against the production and distribution of pornography, arguing that the practice of gender inequality Dworkin described as the dynamic of porn translated directly into cultural and institutional misogyny:

> Pornography institutionalizes the sexuality of male supremacy, which fuses the erotization of dominance and submission with the social construction of male and female. Gender is sexual. Pornography constitutes the meaning of that sexuality. Men treat women as who they see women as being. Pornography constructs who that is.[2]

Critics engaging with the ethics and politics of porn differ considerably in their attitude towards explicit spectacle, and the Dworkin/MacKinnon line is by no means the only position adopted. Other critiques of porn have come from the perspective of philosophy. For Mary Caputi in *Voluptuous Yearnings: A Feminist Theory of the Obscene* (1994), after Bataille, 'obscenity' is a cultural necessity, as it is the realm of taboo and transgression, the experience of transcendence of our limits. It is a concept that is both sacred and profane. However, a society such as ours, that fails to recognize the necessity of the obscene, produces instead pornography. Pornography, seen in this light, is a mode of representation that rehearses an archaic belief in the essential nature of male and female. It is a distillation of 'the archeplot of power relations';[3] a sclerotic mode endlessly repeating an Aristotelian belief in the 'resonance between nature and culture'[4] that reifies the distinction between male subjectivity and female objectification. A surprisingly similar argument can be found in Baudrillard's *De la séduction* (1979). Here the French postmodern philosopher argues that the commercial production of pornography is located in, and is the result of, a masculinist and heteropatriarchal axis of power that restates, by continued repetition, the legitimacy, inevitability and 'hyperreality' of phallic sexuality in commodified form. This is a book that has been accused of making problematic assumptions about femininity.[5] However, despite its detractors' objections, Baudrillard's intervention on the pornography debate is important for having taken a discourse previously located in Anglo-American academia into the sphere of continental thought.

Critics arguing in favour of pornography often do so from the point of view of an ethical and political engagement with anti-censorship. Gillian Rodgerson and Elizabeth Wilson's *Pornography and Feminism: The Case Against Censorship* (1992) argues that

> as feminists, we have a responsibility to be critical of those images we find sexist, racist or exploitative and to counter them in the most effective way there is, not by seeking to get them banned, but by initiating a much more wide-ranging debate about sex.[6]

They also argue strongly against the (inconclusive) assertions that, according to a slogan coined by Robin Morgan, 'pornography is the theory, rape is the practice'. Rodgerson and Wilson conclude that 'Andrea Dworkin is wrong. It is not pornography itself that lies at the heart of women's oppression or indeed anyone's oppression. ... Pornography may mirror the sexism of society but did not create it.'[7]

Linda Williams's nuanced argument regarding the workings of power in specifically filmic pornography, *Hardcore: Power, Pleasure and the Frenzy of the Visible* (1989), concurs that the sexual problems of patriarchy cannot be solved by censoring hardcore. The commonly evoked distinction between 'good', feminine, softcore erotica and 'bad', masculine, hardcore pornography is an unhelpful one, according to Williams. She takes issue with those feminist critiques that locate the offensiveness of hardcore pornography in the centrality it accords to the image of the penis and phallic sexuality (exemplified by the 'money shot'), which Baudrillard terms 'hyper-real'. 'Satisfied simply to deride the organ of presumed male power itself, rather than the system of oppositions by which the meaning of the penis is constructed, the critique does not even approach the discursive root of the problem of pornography and sexual representations for feminism', writes Williams.[8] This highlights the problem central to much psychoanalytically informed criticism (for which Freud himself is partially responsible, with his rather literal concept of 'penis envy'): the idea that phallic power derives directly from the possession of a penis *itself*, not from the privileged meanings that a patriarchal society ascribes to being male. Williams reminds us that, in a Lacanian reading at least, 'the phallus is fundamentally not real and not possessed by anyone'.[9]

It would be an error to assume that the survey of attitudes summarized above represents a set of debates that belong entirely in the past – in the hey day of Dworkin's campaigning. On 26 January 2009, a law that criminalizes the possession of 'extreme images' came into force in the UK. The law makes it illegal to possess a pornographic image (where pornography is defined as 'of such a nature that it must reasonably be assumed to have been produced solely or principally for the purpose of sexual arousal'), if it depicts a (consensual) act which results, or is likely to result, in serious injury to a person's anus, breasts or genitals, or an act which threatens or *appears to* threaten a person's life. The law does not differentiate between simulated acts and actual acts, and makes criminal the perusal of images of practices that it is not criminal to carry out. The logic subtending this legal decision suggests that the act of viewing is more powerful and dangerous that the fact of doing. The law was passed, after considerable opposition from human rights and BDSM community activists, as the direct result of the campaign of the mother of a murdered girl, Jane Longhurst. Longhurst's murderer, Graham Coutts, was found to be in possession of violent pornographic imagery, which, it was argued, spurred him to strangle Longhurst to death.[10] This case demonstrates effectively that the assumption that viewing dangerous images can lead to criminal acts is current in the cultural imaginary, as well as in legal and political discourse, at the time of this book going to press. It also demonstrates the special status that continues to be accorded to pornography, even if pornography here represents not the erect penis of Linda Williams's case studies in *Hardcore*, but acts that would only be erotic to a 'minority taste', and that many otherwise pro-pornography liberals might be tempted to decry *precisely* on the grounds of 'taste'; because the acts depicted represent to them the 'obscene' (in Caputi's sense). If an image of one of the 'extreme acts' named in this bill has been produced for a purpose *other* than to sexually arouse – e.g. as in the case of a horror film, to entertain – then it would not be illegal to possess and view it. 'Pornography' retains a status all of its own, perhaps because of the moral unease that the idea of pleasure creates. This might also explain the odd fact of this law criminalizing the one who looks – the possessor not the producer – of the image. Pleasure is dangerous, perhaps, insofar as it is unpredictable; it is impossible for any faction or political agenda to co-opt or direct it. Feminists such as Dworkin might object to the pleasure some men (and women) find in some hardcore heterosexual pornography. The Christian or political right, or certain normative psychiatrists, might object to the pleasure some people find in images of unusual and non-normative sexual practices. Pleasure becomes, in pornography debates, a matter of crucial ethical import as it is the only 'product' that is assumed to be certain to issue from the production of porn, and it is not a product that can be put to good utilitarian or social use. It is perhaps for this reason that pornography is so contentious.

In what follows, I shall touch on some of the assertions made about pornography by both the anti- and pro-pornography camps, in my reading of a French narrative art film that makes use of explicit sex scenes and actors taken from the porn industry, Despentes's and Trinh-Thi's *Baise-moi* (2000). This film blurs the very distinction to which I have just referred – the distinction between pornography and other types of spectacle produced for different purposes, based on the impossible criteria of establishing *intention*. By focusing here on a film that very self-consciously engages with, borrows from, and reflects upon the genre of pornography – rather than on a commercial porn film – I intend to show that the ethical valence of such filmic features as manipulation of generic form, decisions about point of view, and acting style can problematize a straightforward supposition of what heterosexual pornography *is* and *does*. Just as would be the case with any other type of filmic spectacle, pornographic images can elicit reactions from the spectator that might run counter to generic expectations. I do not wish to claim that it would be impossible to demonstrate the workings of such counter-viewings or reading against the grain in the case of a commercial porn film. Such a film might well produce reactions in the spectator that do not fit neatly the stereotypical assumptions of the binary responses of either sexual arousal or disgust. However, I am particularly interested in what happens to heterosexual pornographic conventions when they are juxtaposed with other filmic codes, here codes of violence, and when they appear in a film co-signed by two women.

Baise-moi and the ethics of the gaze

In recent years, a strand of French filmmaking has emerged that attempts to transgress the distinction between mainstream narrative film and pornographic spectacle by putting on display bodies and sexual acts. While some of these films have been directed by the male *enfants terribles* of contemporary French cinema, such as Noé (*Seul contre tous*, 1998; *Irréversible*, 2002), several of the most prominent examples have been authored, perhaps surprisingly, by women, most notably Catherine Breillat, whose *Romance* (1999) portrayed an explicit female odyssey of sexual experimentation including anonymous promiscuous sex and S/M practices. When in 2000, Despentes and Trinh-Thi released *Baise-moi*, an adaptation of Despentes's 1994 novel, it was in the context of this filmic culture of corporeal and sexual (over)exposure. However, in numerous ways this film expands upon and exaggerates the game essayed by directors such as Noé and Breillat, by placing hardcore sex scenes alongside sequences of chillingly insouciant designer violence. The attention that centred on the film came, however, not only from the right-wing lobby in France (the *Front national*) determined to achieve that elusive and subjective trick of classification and prove that this was 'porn not art' in order to deny it a commercial certificate,[11] but also from feminist academic critics. The main questions it has provoked address the status of the proximity of sex and violence, and the gendering of the two. Critics asked: is this female-directed movie in which women are shown being raped, enjoying filmed pornography and engaging in stylized mass murder that explicitly references Tarantino's cinema of postmodern designer violence, an empowering revenge film or sheer exploitation?[12] How should we understand the status of actresses Raffaella Anderson (Manu) and Karen Bach (Nadine), professional porn stars transformed into art-film actresses (without giving up the hardcore)?

While some critics condemned the film out of hand as a confused and wrong-headed attempt to usurp masculine sexual aggression and violence for a feminist agenda, while continuing nonetheless to objectify the female body in the grand tradition of heterosexual pornography,[13] others argued that it offered a challenging and subversive response to the genre of pornography and a critique of mainstream representational models of male violence on women.[14] *Baise-moi* employs several devices to show up, firstly, how sex and gender are culturally constructed and commodified, and secondly how the construction of sex is *made* to signify as natural. By setting the opening of the film in a harsh urban underworld, in which the toughest dominate, and men use force to get their way with women (seen, shockingly, in the unflinchingly brutal rape sequence), the film sets up the understanding that these women cannot be other than the products and constructions of an environment which imagines them. It shows how, in a specific imaginary milieu, sex and violence are inevitably wedded together. Moreover by making Nadine a prostitute and Manu a porn star, the film shows how it is through a commodified version of sex and the instrumentalization of the body that the society in question understands sexuality *per se*. It is not coincidental that Nadine is shown watching scenes from Noé's *Seul contre tous* as she turns a trick. As well as referencing directly the trend for explicit sexual representation in experimental French cinema of which this film itself is a part, the brutal, macho setting of *Baise-moi* becomes recognizable as an actualization of the dystopian worldview offered by the protagonist of *Seul contre tous*, the misogynistic, homophobic and incestuous butcher played by Philippe Nahon. The culture portrayed in *Baise-moi*, then, actualizes in a fictional space the worldview that Andrea Dworkin represents as the social reality of power relations between the sexes in her emotive texts. This said, for the most part, the film avoids the easy victim feminism that would cast the women as the passive foils of a masculinist culture (Nadine is a proud consumer of the porn that Manu makes), and the male violence that is the norm in the brute reality of the society portrayed is transformed on their bodies and through their performance into a slick, existential nihilism. They become the stylized products of a misogynist culture, in which they then take action, an action appropriate to the nightmare of that culture.

The film works hard to undermine discourses that map domination/submission onto male/female bodies by appealing to 'natural' sexed and gendered characteristics. It does this by means of a critical reflection on culture. On escaping this grim urban sphere, the two women drive out to the coast. The longstanding symbolic association of women's sexuality and the sea is played upon here, but not in the predictable and hackneyed way that would reinforce the culture/nature binarism, suggesting a 'pure' female sexuality that one could hark back to if only it were possible to undo culture. (This would imply an originary, natural essence that patriarchy mutilates, rather than the possibility of imagining an alternatively constructed way of 'being' that would be the product of a different sort of culture.) Instead, when Manu is filmed looking out to sea, the sea at first appears as a digital image – a series of flickering white-on-black particles. Then, a moment later, it reappears as a mobile photographic image of turbulent, romantic foam-tipped waves. By de-naturalizing, temporarily, that most natural of all elements, the sea, the directors suggest that female sexuality, by analogy, is also constructed by codes of representation, and that it *appears* natural and inevitable in pornographic filming practices, as in the cultural imaginary, *because of* rather than despite the mediating presence of technological equipment. In this way, the non-pornographic scenes of *Baise-moi* can be seen to undermine rather than shore up what Caputi describes as the 'archeplot of power relations' central to anti-porn critique, and may encourage the spectator to view the sex scenes differently also – via a viewing denuded of a belief in female or feminine 'nature'. This would approximate a queer strategy for understanding gender and sex as constructed categories, such as proposed by Judith Butler's deconstructive feminist theory.

However, for all its self-awareness and its at times effective and satisfying mockery of the discourses, genres and modes it also occupies, there are numerous stumbling blocks to reading *Baise-moi* as a film that is wholly concerned with deconstructing the ideologies it addresses to allow for ethically alternative viewing responses. Indeed, in numerous ways, the film merely repeats the assumptions structuring and underpinning the genres to which it refers. By staging the rape of Manu, for example, as a formative event that propels her shooting of her boyfriend and subsequent murderous spree, the film works within the law of cause and effect of traditional narrative cinema. More damning still for a film that purports to up-end such logical commonplaces, the denouement delivers an exact replica, rather than a refusal or subversion of the dominant ideology. As in a whole range of male-directed films, in which troublesome women are eventually punished by death or incarceration (the erotic thriller in the mould of *Fatal Attraction*, Adrian Lyne, 1987) or forced to take their own lives as the only available exit from patriarchal law (as in the disingenuous ending of *Thelma and Louise*, discussed in Chapter 2 of this book), Manu is ultimately shot dead while Nadine is reincorporated into the social machinery by means of her arrest in the closing frames, after a sentimental scene in which she returns Manu's body to the sea.

This substantiates Linda Ruth Williams's claims that this film is, in numerous ways, 'basically *Thelma and Louise* get laid'.[15] Like *Thelma and Louise*, it is a brave attempt to explore female friendship and rebellion in a context and by cinematic means appropriate to the moment in which it is made (taking advantage, for example, of a climate in which debate existed in France, following the scandal of Breillat's *Romance*, concerning the question of whether the relaxation of censorship rules in that country pertaining to violent or erotic material may be interpreted as a gesture of liberation for women). However, this is a film which ultimately refuses to go 'all the way' in its challenge to the dominant tradition. One might ask, then, what is the point of adding hardcore sex to the *Thelma and Louise* model, when this does not transform the outcome or meaning of female rebellion in the logic of the film as a whole, and when women are still punished?

The question of why the directors choose to film 'real' sex is an important one. I have written elsewhere about the extent to which, by retaining the mode of realism (the desire to film real penetration, real oral sex), films such as *Romance* seem to operate according to a belief that the act of heterosexual genital sex constitutes the ultimate truth of sexuality. The revelation they offer is simply to show us that which we are supposed to desire to see; that which is usually hidden, suggested, or symbolized in mainstream films.[16] This is a similar argument to the one Williams makes in *Hardcore* when writing 'sex, in the sense of a natural, biological and visible "doing what comes naturally", is the supreme fiction of hard-core pornography; and gender, the social construction of the relations between "the sexes", is what helps constitute that fiction'.[17] One of the problems encountered in watching and thinking about *Baise-moi*, then, is that its exposure of *deliberately* 'real' sex – scenes that could be footage cut straight from a commercial porn flick – juxtaposed with the presentation of deliberately 'pretend' violence, risks suggesting the 'truth value' of one set of images, while insisting upon the surface performativity of the other. It risks upholding, at the level of the visual, the myth of the 'natural' or 'inevitable' status of sex, which the film has worked hard at the discursive level to undercut, by means of the various strategies of self-aware parody, denaturalization and intertextuality I have discussed. *Baise-moi* presents a conundrum then: how can we take seriously the critique of normative codes of sex and gender, and the suggestion of alternative ways of apprehending the sexually explicit spectacle, in a film that simultaneously appears to take the 'reality' of sex itself so seriously while very evidently playing at violence? One potential answer might be offered by suggesting that certain spectators would draw much more pleasure from the fictional scenes of female-on-male violence, than from the 'real' scenes of hardcore, undermining the hierarchy of transgression suggested in the real–unreal formula.

However, to return to the problem of how to reconcile the apparent contradictions ascribed to the status of the sexually explicit images in this film, Breillat has stated that the meaning of such an image depends on the way the director films it. She claims that much depends on 'whether it is looked at with a vision that is hideous and obscene or with love'.[18] Her statement suggests that an ethics of filming – a looking 'with love' at previously despised images – may transform and challenge their meaning. Some of the problems and paradoxes *Baise-moi* raises may be reconciled by showing ways in which, by exploiting the very ways of looking *within* (as well as *at*) sex, this film manages to skew the treatment of desire. Mainstream hardcore heterosexual pornography, perhaps more than any other spectacle, functions by exploiting the subject–object relation. Regardless of whether we accept those rather one-dimensional anti-porn feminist arguments that contend that the woman is always positioned as victim–object and the man as sadist–subject in mainstream porn, it is clear that porn functions by appealing to a voyeuristic mechanism that draws pleasure from looking at the body, what it is doing, what is being done to it. I shall argue here that the *primary* challenge posed by *Baise-moi* lies not in its exploitation of female sexuality and violence in the service of generic parody or experimentation, but in a particularly original deployment of the onscreen dynamic of voyeurism that borrows from and enlarges the scope of pornography. It is found in an attempt to capture configurations of scopic desire that at once reference and go beyond the simple mechanism of looker and looked-at and – by extension – the limiting subject–object model of relationality on which traditional theories of pornography and spectatorship rest.

Theories that contend that there is no properly 'feminine gaze', originating with Mulvey's celebrated 1975 article, are well known in cinema studies. According to Mulvey, in classic narrative cinema, the viewer occupies a masculine position; he is aligned with the agency and desire of the onscreen male hero. The position of femininity, on the other hand, is a matter of embodiment rather than subjectivity: the woman on screen connotes what Mulvey terms 'to-be-looked-at-ness'.[19] This theoretical model, designed to describe mainstream narrative cinema has obvious resonances with some of the anti-porn feminist accounts discussed at the beginning of this chapter, which merely exaggerate the pernicious cause and effects of this dynamic of objectification. The idea of a female spectator getting pleasure from the filmed spectacle of the woman's body has been explained either in terms of her occupying a 'masculinized', 'transvestite' role in her identification with the masculine agent,[20] or a masochistic one, in her identification with the objectified female body.[21] Though queer theory has gone some way towards challenging the meanings of this rigid binaristic division, privileging the instability of gender identifications and the subversive power of mobile fantasy, such gender–binary theoretical models grounded in 1970s ideology still hold considerable weight in the field of academic film studies. I would like to argue, however, that the presentation of the female pairing of *Baise-moi* allows new light to be cast upon this long-standing problem. In an article that discusses desire and identification in films portraying female pairs (*All About Eve*, Joseph L Manckiewicz, 1955 and *Desperately Seeking Susan*, Susan Seidelman, 1985), Jackie Stacey has argued that 'the rigid distinction between *either* desire *or* identification, so characteristic of psychoanalytic film theory, fails to address the construction of desires which involve a specific interplay of both'.[22] While the films Stacey discusses achieve this 'specific interplay' by a relation of simultaneous wishful identification and difference between their characters, *Baise-moi* achieves a similar aim by its particular

depiction of visual desire across the subjectivities and bodies of the Nadine/
Manu pair. It is my contention that the way in which certain scenes of *Baise-moi*
are filmed offers not only a gaze admitting of both desire and identification,
but also a reciprocal gaze that marginalizes the subject–object one, both at
the level of the diegesis, and in the construction of the cinematic spectacle
for the viewer. This is not a case of the 'transvestite' female gaze, that false-
consciousness-provoked usurping of the masculine position, but rather the
surprising presentation of a pair of reflecting, desiring gazes that confirm and
authenticate the other's desire, creating an inter-subjective, inter-visual
realm. This suggests a desire that operates subversively *alongside* rather than
outside of the (masculine) imaginary, which, within the world of the film,
encodes the gaze as possession of the object. That Manu and Nadine are literally, socially *outside the law* is necessary and appropriate, as it echoes their
condition of looking and desiring from a position that is on the margins of
the laws of spectatorship; but that inevitably references them as all trans-
gressive gestures and discourses reference the limits they seek to exceed.

A key scene of *Baise-moi* which features explicit sexual action may be
profitably analyzed in order to substantiate my propositions, and to explore
some ways in which, while conforming to type, it works to subvert viewer
expectations. The sequence in question is set up conventionally, almost as a
textbook example of the pornographic genre. It opens on a shot of Manu's
buttocks and raised leg, in close-up, in the foreground of the frame. She rips
the gusset of her tights as a titillating spectacle for the man on the bed, as in
a striptease. The type of pulsating music chosen to accompany the scene will
be familiar to watchers of commercial pornography. Next, the camera
meanders over a woman's and a man's body entwined on a bed, in various
poses. The close-ups on body parts central to the grammar of pornographic
filming, are used here to create precisely the effect feminist critics tell us
they have – to depersonalize the filmed being and reduce subjectivity to
corporeality. In the case of this sequence, it means that the viewer is at first
unsure whether it is Manu or Nadine being filmed – their individual identities seem subordinate to their status as bodies. The close-ups grow more
and more distorting as physical frenzy increases. Then the camera pulls back
and the frame widens to reveal the two women having sex with two men on
twin beds. We focus on Nadine's face and see that she is looking across at
Manu. Pleasure and desire are visible on her face, but they seem to be
directed through her gaze at the other, and not to emanate from the physical
action she is engaging in with her sexual partner. At the moment when
Nadine takes her eyes off Manu and looks back at what (whom) she is doing,
Manu – habitually the watched rather than watcher – looks over at Nadine,
completing their circuit of the desiring gaze.

It would be possible to argue, I suppose, that this play with the female-
on-female gaze *could* take place in a mainstream pornographic movie. After
all, the idea of a woman sexually desiring another woman is a feature not

only of lesbian practice and politics, but of the appropriating pornographic imaginary, and so-called 'lesbian scenes' feature in much mainstream pornography created for a heterosexual male audience. However, this fantasy is not allowed to come to fruition in *Baise-moi* for the prurient spectator – perhaps because, in the type of world the film evokes, there would be no possibility (for the viewer or the participants) of experiencing it any other way than as an extension of the pornographic subject–object imagination. Tenderness and trust between the women are much in evidence in their protective attitude towards each other (Manu shoots dead a man in the street who makes a lewd pass at Nadine, in a scene reminiscent of the shooting of the rapist in *Thelma and Louise*), whereas sex acts between the two women are conspicuous by being debarred from the onscreen action. By contrast, heterosex and murderous violence are laid out for our examination in the most graphic terms: the film constitutes an unrelenting parade of men being blown and then being blown away.

However, what is going on here is neither the divorce of passion from emotion and sexual attraction from 'pure' friendship, nor a romantic idealization of female love as cerebral and pure, as against the brute physicality of heterosex or male desire. We have seen that their friendship is presented in such a way that we should understand it to have an erotic dimension. We know that Nadine enjoys watching Manu's professional appearances in pornographic films, from a conversation they have in the car early on in the film. And we witness, in the sequence I have just described, her scopic pleasure in watching her friend have sex with a man on the other bed. Yet her enjoyment of watching Manu's body does not lead her to a depersonalizing objectification of the other, but to respect and friendship and, moreover, to an answering desirous gaze in which watched becomes watcher, rendering the difference between those positions fluid and interchangeable rather than fixed and fixing. An ethics that admits of the desiring gaze is hinted at in however fragile and skeletal a form in the filmed interaction between the two women. Why, though, is any sex act between the women – an event that is, in many ways, the logical unspoken outcome of the narrative – debarred in this way?

Revisionist readers of *Thelma and Louise* have argued that the intensity of the emotional relationship portrayed between Susan Sarandon's and Geena Davis's characters signals a subtle subtext of lesbian desire that is never shown explicitly, except in the suggestive but chaste kiss that precedes their leap into the abyssal Grand Canyon. For one critic, 'the discrepancy between ... the women's passion for each other and its lack of sexual expression ... is the gap I have to fill'.[23] In *Baise-moi*, I would suggest, the discrepancy between the emotional closeness and visually fuelled desire of the female characters for each other on the one hand, and their physical engagement in uniquely heterosexual sex, filmed according to the rules of mainstream pornography (the close-up, the split-crotch shot, etc.) on the other, opens up a gap through which we might espy an alternative narrative of desire.

If, as I argued earlier, what pornography does is to deliver up to us that which we *are supposed to want to see*, and thereby confirm our appetite for the (apparent) thing itself, it embodies the principle of the self-fulfilling prophecy. Pornography viewed in this light would fuel desire according to a mechanism reminiscent of a Deleuzian and Guattarian model of desire, in which the boundless, machine-like process of desire produces and proliferates ever more objects for its own satisfaction.[24] I am persuaded that *Baise-moi*, by offering us a disposable, stylized, commodified version of heterosex and designer violence on a plate, as it were, while only *hinting* at the possibility of the desire between the two women, draws attention to a different level of the *real* which it deliberately forecloses. I would suggest that this refusal to show same-sex sexual acts is not born of prudery, but is designed to show us that, in the exaggerated, dystopian, heterosexist culture of the diegesis, in which consumerism and pornography are the only forms of erotic relationality portrayed, when so much is on display, that which is not shown regains subversive power.

These points are thematized in the film when the young man with whom Nadine has been having sex, in the sequence analyzed above, says he would like to watch the two girls perform sixty-nine on each other, and they instantly tell him to leave. Then, the remaining man, who was previously Manu's bed partner, goes over to Nadine and kisses her, while Manu settles down to become the *voyeuse*. He becomes in this moment, then, a shared toy, a sexual proxy between them, in a suggested gendered inversion of the model of homosociality proposed by Eve Kosofsky Sedgwick, in which women are the sanctioned shared objects passed between men as a guarantee against the threat of socially despised homosexuality.[25] Here, however, it is not because of their homophobia that Nadine and Manu refuse to engage in sexual activity with each other, but because the film is constantly aware of the cliché of voyeuristic fascination offered by scenes of girls together for heterosexual men, not only the character who is made to leave here, but the 'imagined' male viewer too. The film, then, exploits heterosexual pornographic codes but only so far as to allow commodified heterosex to be the repetitive, visible 'given' that constructed the possibility of Manu and Nadine – porn star and prostitute – *in the first place*. Their silenced, invisible – but constantly suggested – resistant desire signals the embryonic possibility of transgressing the codes determining their construction from within.

Some concluding remarks

My discussion of *Baise-moi* in the context of the ethics of pornography has sought to show that the meanings attributed to looking at female bodies or acts of heterosexual sex are not so black and white or one-directional as accounts such as Dworkin's (or even Mulvey's) suggest, since meanings reside in the manipulation of subject–object relationality (both on and offscreen); in the ways we are directed to look by the framing of the image; in the gazes that we witness on screen as they pass between characters or actors – as well as in the nature of the *object* being filmed. While it is fairly easy to show (as my reading of a generically troubled explicit French art film has attempted to do) that the 'fact' of gendered objectification can be skewed, undermined and critiqued *within* the creation of sexually explicit representation, as well as in critical discourse about it, it is harder to make conclusive ethical arguments either way for the effects of pornographic material on the viewing public.

This book on film and ethics is committed to thoughtful consideration of the range of ways in which the image engages energies that impel us to ask questions about self and other; responsibility and desire. To claim that film and ethics matters is to claim that the stakes of viewing are high. Yet to take an ethical position on pornography does not necessarily entail either championing it or condemning it. It does not even necessarily involve *believing in* the category of pornography as a special, unique and uniquely dangerous form of representation.

The question of what is, or is not, 'real' seems key to some debates in porn, yet not to others. A film's certificate may well be determined by whether a penis is shown going into a vagina, or whether two bodies are simply rubbing together, simulating intercourse. Moral panic about the contested existence of the snuff movie is entirely concerned with whether or not someone really dies on screen.[26] Whereas the UK's 'extreme images' law does not care if the picture or clip I have on my computer screen depicts – for example – a woman strangling a man, or a woman *pretending to* strangle a man. If the photograph or video was made to arouse my (kinky, non-normative, paraphiliac) desire, then – in this context, and following this logic – it is pornography, it is dangerous, and I am, as a result, a criminal. We may begin to see, then, that according too much attention to the category of 'reality' in relation to pornography can be an ethical and hermeneutic red herring. Representation is never straightforwardly 'real', whether the acts represented are simulated or are actually taking place. Representation is a matter of shades of meaning, achieved via a complex and multivalent apparatus, and – like intention – its ontological status is not directly or singularly identifiable. While sexism, non-consensual violence and other forms of socio-economic, ethnic and sexual power imbalances are definitely 'real' at the level of social life, it is easier to attack representations than the complex and multivalent sources of social injustice. It is also very easy to scapegoat pornography, particularly non-normative or minority taste pornography, in the spurious and often disingenuous name of 'protecting the vulnerable' – a strategy beloved of the tabloid press, whose sensationalist coverage of the Jane Longhurst murder and championing of Liz Longhurst's campaign for criminalization of 'extreme images', contributed to the passing of the controversial law in 2009. We might do well to ask today, as Rodgerson and

Wilson provocatively asked in 1992: 'Could it be that, like so many others, the anti-pornography campaigners have fallen for the view that, because we live in a "media society", the media is the only reality?'[27]

Notes

1 Dworkin, *Pornography*, 110–11.
2 Mackinnon, *Feminism Unmodified*, 148.
3 Caputi, *Voluptuous Yearnings*, 2.
4 Caputi, *Voluptuous Yearnings*, 2.
5 For a brief summary of the ways in which this work has been accused of problematic sexual politics, see: Bristow, *Sexuality*, 141–7.
6 Rodgerson and Wilson, *Pornography and Feminism*, 15.
7 Rodgerson and Wilson, *Pornography and Feminism*, 67.
8 Linda Williams, *Hardcore*, 266.
9 Linda Williams, *Hardcore*, 266.
10 More information about this law and political/academic responses to it can be found on the website of the activist group 'Backlash':
http://www.backlash-uk.org.uk/ (accessed 29/01/09).
11 Linda Ruth Williams, 'Sick Sisters', 28.
12 I refer to the allusion in *Baise-moi* to an episode from *Pulp Fiction* (1994). The scene in which a man, who is about to be killed by Nadine and Manu in a bar, is forced to crouch on all fours and squeal like a pig, cites Tarantino's own citing of a scene from Boorman's *Deliverance* (1972), creating several layers of intertextuality.
13 Linda Ruth Williams, 'Sick Sisters', 28–9.
14 Vincendeau, '*Baise-moi*', 38.
15 Linda Ruth Williams, 'Sick Sisters', 28.
16 Downing, 'Between men and women', 30.
17 Linda Williams, *Hardcore*, 267.
18 Sklar, 'A Woman's Vision of Shame and Desire', 26.
19 Mulvey, 'Visual Pleasure and Narrative Cinema'.
20 See: Mulvey, 'Afterthoughts on "Visual Pleasure and Narrative Cinema" inspired by King Vidor's *Duel in the Sun*'.
21 See, for example: Doane, 'Film and the Masquerade: Theorizing the Female Spectator'.
22 Stacey, 'Desperately Seeking Difference', 378.
23 Kabir, *Daughters of Desire*, 211.
24 Deleuze's and Guattari's model of desire as productive of its objects is a reaction against the model of desire as lack-driven, propounded by psychoanalytic discourse, particularly that of Jacques Lacan, which holds that desire lies in the unbridgeable gaps between the subject, the symbolization of the subject's desire, and the desired thing.
25 Sedgwick, *Between Men*.
26 See Avedon, 'Snuff: Believing the Worst', 126–30.
27 Rodgerson and Wilson, *Pornography and Feminism*, 40.

Section 2

Introduction to Section 2

Theory, ethics, film

In recent years, theoretical film studies has been invigorated by the approach of reading/viewing cinema alongside and through philosophical texts (both analytic and continental). The study of film and ethics is evidently an important part of this rapprochement of visual culture and thought, but – as we have stated before – the relevance of ethical philosophy to film has not previously been accorded the import it merits. Section 2 of this book contributes to the emergent field of 'film philosophy' by discussing in detail, and placing in dialogue, a wider range of currents in continental ethical philosophy than have previously been addressed in relation to film studies.

The chapters in Section 1 proposed a series of ethical insights about form, content and spectatorship, without grounding these fully in continental philosophical debates. This section aims to demonstrate the gains of reading film and philosophy in conjunction with each other. For example, at the end of Section 1, we began, using films as case studies, to discuss the ethical implications of the fixed model of viewing elaborated by gaze theorists and to suggest that this model was conceptually insufficient. We posed a range of ethically informed and urgent questions about the meanings of images and our relationships to them: can we envisage a viewing relationship that does not work in a straightforwardly objectifying way? Does ethics as an optics disrupt the neat subject–object relationship of the gaze?

In Section 2, we attempt to explore these questions more fully by engaging with poststructuralist, psychoanalytic, and postmodern philosophical models that unsettle the mechanism of objectification underpinning gaze theory and figure the interactions between viewers and films in more complex ways. The philosophical frameworks in question are often in conflict with each other regarding the nature and status of the ethical encounter. It is by taking on board a series of differing perspectives that we acknowledge the complexity and multivalency of the ethical energies at play within the experience of cinema.

Any study that considers what it means to 'experience' an art form suggests some engagement with the idea of phenomenology. The notion that the ethical might be the experiential, relational, cognitive or spiritual modality *through which we view the world*, is a suggestive one for any theory of the function of modes of cultural production that appeal to vision. The cinematic apparatus presents to the viewer something other than him or herself, in the light shone by the projection equipment onto the screen. In this, it is a perfect metaphor for phenomenology. Rather than taking phenomenology as our philosophical framework, however, we take instead this broad idea of 'the phenomenology of cinema' as our object. The thinkers with whom we engage, such as Levinas, Derrida, Foucault and Lacan, are ones who are influenced by, but largely reacting against, classical phenomenological theory such as that by Edmund Husserl and Maurice Merleau-Ponty. In Levinas's account, for example, the phenomenological model is insufficiently ethical. It presupposes that the Other is the object of the one within a dyadic structure. Levinas calls this 'totality' and suggests that an ethical model of otherness would follow on from an openness to 'infinity', in which the Other is irreducible to 'my' perception. For Levinas, the alterity of the Other comes 'without mediation' and 'signifies by himself'. It is the appearance of the other that calls the subject to a consciousness founded in ethical responsibility. This contention is pertinent to the cinema, since the subject–object relation of looking and being looked at are the active–passive mechanisms assumed by almost all theoretical models (especially those of Metz and Mulvey) to underlie spectatorship. We might posit, then, that viewing is always potentially an ethically charged encounter, but one that is inevitably *manipulated* in cinema, rather than unmediated, as in Levinas's account of the ethical epiphany. It is this specifically cinematic manipulation of the ethical relation that is of principal concern to us here. Chapter 6, which focuses on Levinas, argues that one of the ways in which the altericide of the subject–object relation (the Other's reduction to an object of my perception) may be avoided is through a disruption of the visual relationship between viewer and filmic subject-matter. The chapter draws parallels between Levinas's reservations about the visual and Lanzman's refusal to represent the Holocaust in *Shoah*.

One of Foucault's reservations about phenomenology lies in its privileging of the category of the individual and its location of truth within experience. Foucault sees the ethical as residing in the spaces between socially imposed moral codes and the individual's (historically located) response to them. To assume that an ethics can be created from perception alone is socially naïve according to Foucault, as the subject exists within power relations and may be at once the subject and object of any interaction. A way in which this can be helpful for our consideration of film lies in the links that can be made between perception and surveillance. Voyeurism as a mechanism of cinematic pleasure is endemic to the psychoanalytic model of subject–object relations. Foucault's suspicion of phenomenology is matched by his suspicion of psychoanalytic structures. In the force field of Foucaldian power, the subject is watched from multiple and infinite vantage points such that he or she eventually internalizes this process of watching/being watched and self-surveys. The idea that watching does not take place in a linear way, and that we are all implicated in our own scrutiny, offers a corrective alternative to the uni-directional model of both phenomenology and gaze theory. One of the aims of Chapter 8 is to advance a reading along these lines.

These are two examples of the ways in which the thinkers addressed in this section simultaneously question phenomenological traditions, while offering alternative theories of perception that restore to the phenomenology of cinema its full complexity.

In the Introduction, we briefly discussed the opposition between a Levinasian privileging of the other and an ethics built on fidelity to the self. In the chapters of this section, we look in more detail at these two currents of thought and assess their applicability to an ethically informed theory of the cinema. We have already suggested that ethicizing the cinematic experience means conceptualizing it in terms of responsibility and desire (where these are not straightforward opposites), rather than simply in political or moral terms. In the chapters of Section 1, as already noted, the imperative of responsibility and the ethical right to pleasure were often counterpointed uneasily with each other. Section 2 explores more explicitly the applications of an ethics of alterity and an ethics of the self, by means of detailed considerations of what these currents (exemplified, respectively by Levinas and Derrida on the one hand, and Foucault, Lacanian thinkers and Badiou on the other) might offer for cinema studies.

Levinas's, and to a lesser extent Derrida's, resistance to figurality on ethical grounds makes them challenging thinkers with which to rethink cinematic representation. They encourage us to ask whether it is possible to witness self–other relations on screen, and to find ways of looking at cinematic subjects, that do not commit violence to the Other. Derrida in particular engages with the difficulty – or even impossibility – of being a consummately responsible social agent (and spectator), since responsibility to any one other being (or to any one interpretation of a filmic image) comes at the price of another. Saxton's discussion of Derrida in Chapter 7 explores a theoretical framework for taking further her enquiry into responsibility and spectatorship begun in Chapter 4. Lacan and Žižek, conversely, offer models of ethics that sit uncomfortably alongside the privileging of otherness advocated by Levinas and Derrida. Their model of ethics as destitution of the ego in pursuit of the Real of desire, however, is similarly concerned with abandoning easy notions of a centred moral self and interrogating the limits of being. Reading psychoanalytically informed queer theory by Lee Edelman alongside Lacan and Žižek allows for an interrogation of value judgements that appear so obviously ethical that they risk going unquestioned. The ideals of family, solidarity, community and futurity are unflinchingly explored as ideologies of potential oppression in Edelman's provocative, 'anti-social' readings of Hitchcock's cinema, which are analyzed in Chapter 9.

Postmodern theory to some extent further complexifies, and to some extent resolves, the productive tensions highlighted above. In its refusal to reify hierarchies or privilege a given position as 'true' or 'right' (making it the opposite both of fundamental religious discourses *and* poststructuralist continental thought-experiments such as Badiou's anti-ethical ethical absolutism), postmodernism can serve in various ways to highlight the impossibilities of forcing compatibility on a range of competing viewpoints, that may each offer valid reading, thinking and viewing strategies with regard to different films and different ethico-political contexts. We end our book with Downing's consideration of postmodern ethics in Chapter 10 because postmodernism's work of relativization (which is distinct from moral *relativism*) is particularly valuable. It helps us to unpick some of the grand narratives of modernity that structure the ways in which we might think didactically about film and ethics, and offers us instead a series of strategic counter-readings and counterintuitive philosophies. Via explorations of ethical encounters with the non-human, for example, it expands our horizon of thinking about ethics, and forces a break with the enduringly anthropo-centric terms in which ethics is habitually conceived – even in those forms that resist a traditional humanism. This second section of our book, then, theorizes the moving image's unique potential to intensify and make acute at times, while skewing and deforming at others, the specifically ethical dimension of looking at the cinema screen or, particularly in the context of postmodern practices, of viewing new digital media.

Chapter 6

Blinding visions

Levinas, ethics, faciality

Libby Saxton

In recent discussions of the ethical dimensions of film, the name Emmanuel Levinas has cropped up more frequently than that of any other philosopher. Yet on the surface Levinas's writings may not seem the most promising starting point for research in this field. References to cinema are extremely rare in his work and serve a purely illustrative function. Moreover, while he does not explicitly criticize film, his philosophy manifests an abiding suspicion of the aesthetic and the visual, which he associates with forms of domination and violence. In the preface to *Totality and Infinity: An Essay on Exteriority*, Levinas describes ethics as an 'optics', a formulation which appears conducive to reflection on a medium which has historically appealed first and foremost to our sense of sight. But he immediately qualifies this description by dissociating the ethical relation

Figure 6 Shoah

from the field of the visible: 'it is a "vision" without image, bereft of the synoptic and totalizing objectifying virtues of vision, a relation or intentionality of a wholly different type – which this work seeks to describe'.[1]

Nevertheless, it is my contention in this chapter that, precisely because of his hostility towards vision and images, Levinas's thought offers a crucial resource for re-viewing film in ethical terms. If Levinas had little to say about cinema, the appearance of explicit references to his texts in recent films, such as Godard's *Notre musique* (*Our Music*, 2004), and acknowledgements by other contemporary directors, including Jean-Pierre and Luc Dardenne and Josh Appignanesi, that his work has influenced theirs, suggest that cinema, at least, has something to say about Levinas.[2] Over the past decade, Levinas's writings have inspired readings of documentary, of specific genres (such as the action film), of the work of individual directors (including Quentin Tarantino, Patrice Leconte, Michelangelo Antonioni, the Dardenne brothers and Andrei Tarkovsky) and of film spectatorship.[3] Commentators have begun to announce a 'Levinasian turn in film scholarship'.[4] While scholars of film have engaged with Levinas's insights into aesthetics and politics, it is his discussions of ethics that have been the central focus of attention. This reflects the privileged place occupied by ethics, as 'first philosophy', in Levinas's thought and is in line with the wider reception of his work in the humanities.[5] Much of the writing on Levinas and film to date acknowledges Levinas's critiques of art and vision before proceeding to look beyond them to aspects of his thought that appear less inimical to analysis of visual culture. In this chapter, I want to linger longer with Levinas's misgivings about images and explore their connections with what has been described as an anti-ocular or iconoclastic current in film practice itself.

In order to give these connections a historical grounding, it is necessary briefly to outline two intersecting cultural contexts in which Levinas's work may be read. Locating Levinas within a broader tradition of scepticism towards the visual in twentieth-century French thought, Martin Jay credits him with an important role in the revival of intellectual interest in France in the 1970s and 1980s in Judaism and particularly in the biblical interdiction on creating graven images or idols. As Jay points out, 'Levinas explicitly tied ethics to the Hebraic taboo on visual representation and contrasted it again and again to the Hellenic fetish of sight, intelligible form and luminosity'.[6] Levinas repeatedly returns to the Second Commandment not only in his texts on religion but also in his writings on aesthetics and ethics, where it accrues meanings that exceed a purely theological interpretation. In postwar French thought, this interdiction has filtered through from sacred into secular discourse and has acquired special resonance in ongoing debates about the difficulty of adequately representing the Holocaust or Shoah. The persistent claim that the Nazis' attempt to annihilate the European Jews and other communities remains unsusceptible to representation, and more specifically the assertion that it cannot or should not be recuperated within images, often derive from a particular understanding of the *Bilderverbot*. While Levinas remained reluctant to speak directly about this event, the epigraph to *Otherwise than Being or Beyond Essence*, which dedicates the book to the memory of those murdered by the Nazis, hints at the degree to which it haunts his philosophical project.[7] More specifically, Levinas scholars have speculated about the extent to which his concerns about art may be seen as a reaction to the Holocaust. Thus if Judaism is one of the contexts explicitly informing Levinas's approach to images, another, intimately connected yet this time implicit, may be the legacy of the extermination camps. Moreover, Levinas's discussions of art intimate that the atrocities perpetrated by the Nazis may have a bearing on his view of the kinds of image to which the interdiction applies. Tracing shifts in Levinas's attitude towards art over the course of his career, Jill Robbins observes that on those exceptional occasions 'when Levinas *does* speak positively about art, ... that art always has a relation to the Holocaust'.[8]

This chapter explores the relationship between some of Levinas's texts and one of the most influential films to have emerged out of the cultural contexts described above, *Shoah* (Claude Lanzmann, 1985). Lanzmann's film has provoked debates about the ethics of representation in its own right. While Levinas has rarely been mentioned in this connection, and Lanzmann makes no explicit reference to his work in his published interviews and essays, the filmmaker's concerns intersect on several fundamental levels with the philosopher's. Indeed, I want to argue here that Lanzmann's images are hospitable to certain key aspects of Levinasian ethics at once in spite and because of Levinas's mistrust of the hegemony of the eye. Lanzmann trained as a philosopher and his films can be viewed as a form of philosophical inquiry informed, like Levinas's writings, by the traumatic events of the Holocaust. Moreover, Lanzmann, like Levinas, questions the legitimacy of representation and, in particular, of the visual image. *Shoah* tends to be seen as the paradigmatic example of a strand of anti-visual, even iconophobic filmmaking which responds to the challenges to representation posed by the camps. Lanzmann, like Levinas, is explicitly preoccupied with the interdiction on images and its exigencies in postwar thought and culture. Both adopt positions which have been labelled iconoclastic. However, reading Levinas and viewing Lanzmann's film alongside each other serves to call this designation into question.

The chapter falls into two sections. In the first, I engage with Levinas's writings on ethics, aesthetics and the 'visage', or 'face', of the Other, focusing in particular on an essay on the prohibition against representation, and consider what light they throw on our relationship to film images. I am interested here, more specifically, in how Levinas's critique of representation as liable to 'thematize' and thereby reduce the 'visage' to a projection of the Same, may be brought to bear on filmic sounds and images and the ways in which they address, compel and command us as spectators. The second section takes the form of a case study, reading Lanzmann's film both with and against Levinas's insights into the propensity of images to blind and deafen us to the Other. It is not my contention that *Shoah* constitutes a straight-forward filmic illustration of Levinas's philosophy, let alone an exemplary model of Levinasian ethics in action. On the contrary, it will become clear that key aspects of Lanzmann's approach as a filmmaker are directly at odds with the modes of relating envisaged by Levinas. What I am suggesting instead is that Levinas and Lanzmann pose questions to each other which can alter our understanding of the work of each. The chapter concludes with some remarks on the broader implications of Levinas's thought for film and spectatorship, and vice versa, focusing on the ethical potentialities of the image as interface between self and other.

Levinas: *Bilderverbot* and *visage*

In his controversial early essay 'Reality and its Shadow' (1948), where he takes issue with the view of literature as 'committed' advanced by Jean-Paul Sartre, Levinas makes a passing but significant reference to the Second Commandment: 'The proscription of images is truly the supreme commandment of monotheism, a doctrine that overcomes fate, that creation and revelation in reverse'.[9] Levinas returns to this proscription over three decades later in 'The Prohibition against Representation and "The Rights of Man"' (1984), an essay which has so far received less attention from his commentators. Here he engages with the prohibition in a more sustained way and in terms that reveal the extent to which it informs his broader project, in tandem with the Sixth Commandment ('you shall not murder'). This essay originally appeared in a volume which attests to the renascent interest in the interdiction noted by Jay: *The Prohibition against Representation* (1984), selected proceedings of a conference held in Montpellier in 1981, organized by Adélie and Jean-Jacques Rassial, during which philosophers, psychoanalysts, writers, painters and filmmakers debated the implications of the prohibition for current developments in their fields. Levinas's contribution takes the commandment as a point of departure for a discussion of our relation and responsibility to the other. He begins by warning that the commandment only applies to certain images and should not be taken out of its Biblical and Talmudic contexts, but nevertheless questions whether it may only be understood 'in the limited sense of a religious rule, and a purely repressive one at that'.[10] This paves the way for a rehabilitation of the interdiction in line with his broader ethical project, which is more often descriptive than prescriptive. For Levinas, the suspicion of images of beings at the heart of Judaism may also be interpreted as a denunciation of a certain reductive or acquisitive mode of thought, of 'an *intelligibility* that one would like to reduce to knowledge'.[11] Representation is reconfigured in the course of his argument variously as 'thought thinking the thing', 'the adequation of thought with its other', 'an intentionality', 'a thematisation ... of what lets itself be designated – ultimately or immediately – by a demonstrative, and in a word concretely, with the index finger'.[12] As a corrective to such a form of thinking and the 'deep-seated immanence or atheism', even 'temptation to idolatry', he discerns in this context in sight and knowledge, Levinas endeavours to imagine a 'thought freed of all representation' which infers 'a *meaningfulness* prior to representation'.[13] What is particularly compelling in this context about the prohibition against representation is that it acknowledges the transcendence which is proper to the relation to the Other but which is overlooked in perception:

> This transcendence is alive in the relation to the other man, i.e. in the proximity of one's fellow man, whose *uniqueness* and consequently whose irreducible *alterity* would be – still or already – unrecognised in the perception that stares at [*dé-visage*] the other.[14]

The word-play in the final phrase of this sentence is revealing (the hyphenated 'dé-visage' might be translated as 'stares' or 'defaces'), for in Levinas's account, that which cannot 'give itself' in representation is 'the uniqueness of the unique that is expressed in the face [*visage*]'.[15] In *Totality and Infinity* Levinas describes 'visage' as 'the way in which the Other presents himself, exceeding *the idea of the Other in me*'.[16] But he explains that the term does not refer exclusively to a human face.[17] Nor does it allude simply or primarily to something that we can see. Despite his use of vocabulary associated with vision, Levinas strips the face of its habitual meanings as a phenomenon that appears in the visible world, an object of perception: 'one can say that the face is not "seen". It is what cannot become a content, which your thought would embrace; it is uncontainable, it leads you beyond'.[18] Levinas clarifies that rather than *appearing* to me, the face *expresses*, *signifies* and *speaks*, addressing and commanding me from a position beyond the perceptual field. As such, it reveals itself 'without the intermediary of any image'; indeed, it incessantly 'destroys and overflows the plastic image it leaves me, the idea existing to my own measure'.[19] Levinas pursues these insights further in 'Interdit de la représentation et "Droits de l'homme"', where he asserts that the epiphany of the face is 'refractory to the image': 'Beneath the plasticity of the face [*figure*] that *appears*, the face [*visage*] is already missed. It is frozen in art itself'.[20] The face cannot be captured in representation, which would reduce it to immobility, re-appropriate its alterity and silence its address. Françoise Armengaud, glossing Levinas, explains that the face is not only unique but also 'essentially non-duplicable; it has no double, no shadow, no copy, no portrait'.[21] In other words, it is the face of the Other that forms the proper foundation and object of the prohibition against representation; it is in its epiphany that 'an "unheard of command" or "the word of God" is heard'.[22]

Put simply, then, Levinas explicitly grounds his conception of ethical relations in the *Bilderverbot*: 'the ancient, biblical call and command …

awakens the subject to a responsibility for the other'.[23] However, his commentary on the prohibition appears to further problematize the task in hand: the attempt to forge connections between his thought and filmic representation. Levinas's account of a face which is 'refractory to the image', poses a series of questions to film viewers.[24] If the face of the Other eludes representation and cannot be encountered in images, if it expresses the Second Commandment as well as the Sixth, how could a visual medium reveal alterity or call us to responsibility in the manner described by Levinas? Is it possible to conceive of ways in which cinema might expose us to this face without 'defacing' or 'effacing' it – without reducing it to an object of perception? Is the prohibition against representation signified by the face not always already violated as images of the other are captured on celluloid or translated into digital data? Or might certain films challenge Levinas's understanding of the prohibition? In a related vein, how does the cinematic apparatus disrupt and reconfigure a Levinasian model of relatedness? Film is unable to emulate the immediacy and spontaneity of the 'face-à-face', or face-to-face, envisaged by Levinas insofar as the camera mediates otherness and manipulates our look. Furthermore, as mentioned elsewhere in this book, influential psychoanalytic accounts of the apparatus have habitually placed the viewer in a position of dominance and transcendence over the object viewed. This paradigm inverts the asymmetrical structure of the Levinasian encounter, where it is the Other who calls the self into question. As Cooper observes, 'a Levinasian-inspired theory of viewing would necessarily posit a space beyond subject/object relations, which is crucial for an opening to otherness'.[25] What kinds of viewing relations might preserve the proximity and separation proper to what Levinas calls 'a relation irreducible to the subject–object relation: the *revelation* of the other'?[26]

Lanzmann: the speaking face and the missing body

In order to address some of these questions in a concrete context, I turn now to *Shoah*, Lanzmann's nine-and-a-half-hour film about the production line of death which ended in the gas vans or the chambers in the Nazi extermination camps. *Shoah* is dominated by images of faces – those of survivors, perpetrators and bystanders – and places – the murder sites, revisited for the film. It breaks with the conventions established by previous films about the camps by evoking the past without reconstructing it using actors and sets or archive footage. Historical images are rejected by Lanzmann because few of those which survive relate directly to the mass extermination, while reconstructions he views, contentiously, as inherently fictionalizing and domesticating in the aftermath of an event of such magnitude. Lanzmann summarizes his key misgivings about representation in his provocative critique of *Schindler's List* (Steven Spielberg, 1993):

The Holocaust is unique first of all in that it erects around itself, in a circle of flames, a limit which cannot be breached because a certain absolute of horror is intransmissible: to claim to do so is to make oneself guilty of the most serious sort of transgression. Fiction is a transgression; I profoundly think that there is a prohibition on representation.[27]

While Lanzmann asserts elsewhere that it is not his intention to impose taboos, perpetuate interdictions or 'sacralize' the event,[28] many of his commentators hear echoes of the Second Commandment in remarks of the kind cited above and see a secular form of religiosity visualized in his film.[29] Whether or not we accept this reading of *Shoah*, which remains at odds with the director's own and is informed by his extra-filmic commentaries as much as by his images, Lanzmann's qualms about representation and its capacity to reduce and violate its object provide a pertinent Levinasian point of entry into his film. However, in one obvious but important respect at least, Lanzmann's response to the *Bilderverbot* diverges sharply from Levinas's: while the director rejects images of the past, he invents and multiplies images of the present, embracing visual representation in order to reflect on its perceived limitations from within.

Before examining some of the ways in which *Shoah* alludes to these limitations and the ethical meaning with which they become charged, it is important to distinguish between two kinds of relations established by the film: those between Lanzmann and his filmic subjects, which remain difficult to reconcile with Levinasian principles; and those between the film and its viewers, which seem to me to be more compatible with the philosopher's preoccupations. Structured around Lanzmann's personal obsessions, *Shoah* is arguably a film about its director as much as about anything else, for the testimonies he elicits tend to be channelled through and shaped by his own vision and agenda, which are often conspicuously prioritized over those of his interviewees. Critical debate about the film has dwelt with suspicion on the ethical implications of Lanzmann's apparently manipulative or coercive handling of some of his interviewees, for example by continuing to film even when this is clearly against their wishes or resorting to deception.[30] Whether or not his ends justify his means, a Levinasian critique of these strategies would charge Lanzmann with re-appropriating the alterity of his witnesses and their depositions to the extent that he refuses to allow them to put his own place at risk.

If a Levinasian reading of *Shoah* must contend with Lanzmann's self-positioning as filmmaker, interviewer and, in certain cases, as camera-operator, the pertinent question in the current context is whether this reduces his subjects to objects of perception and knowledge, or whether and how they resist this. Lanzmann accords us visual access to his witnesses primarily through medium and close-up shots of their faces. For better or worse, the face has long been cinema's privileged subject, where it has been transformed through the close-up into a spectacle, an incarnation of unspoken or unspeakable truths, an originary signifier whose meanings can never be stabilized or exhausted.[31] Under Lanzmann's lens, the faces of the German and Polish perpetrators and bystanders become the site of a multitude of micromovements, which offer a silent but involuntarily illuminating commentary on the witnesses' testimony. During these interviews, the facial close-up sometimes functions as a lie detector, exposing the inconsistencies, half-truths or barefaced untruths which punctuate the witness's account. The images of the faces of the survivor-witnesses, however, signify differently, breaking with the cinematic tradition mentioned above by progressively dismantling the myth of the face as the veracious expression of an interiority, the locus of a privileged relationship to the real. While any generalization about the witnesses' faces in *Shoah* risks denying the irreducible singularity of each, what is particularly disconcerting about a number of the survivors' expressions, notably those of Simon Srebnik, Rudolf Vrba, Filip Müller and Abraham Bomba, is their habitually impregnable impassivity. The camera repeatedly lingers on these faces, inviting us to scan them for insights into the past and the present, yet even when the witnesses are remembering the most excruciating suffering, their faces often remain inexpressive, deadpan, at once unreadable and available to a multiplicity of readings. A number of deportees have reflected upon the violence that was inflicted – at once literally and metaphorically – upon the human face in the Nazi camps.[32] Drawing on such testimonies, Nancy ventures that 'the question of the representation of the camps is none other than that of the representation of a face which has itself been deprived of a representation and a gaze'.[33] While he does not explicitly refer to Levinas here, Nancy's argument at this juncture recalls the Levinasian notion of a 'visage' which calls representation into question. If, on one level, the survivors' faces in *Shoah* bear witness to the enduring effects of violation and privation, on another level, they attest to the limits of representation both in their resistance to a definitive reading and in their refusal, at pivotal moments, to reveal anything at all. These images ultimately offer us no purchase either on the witnesses or on the traumatic experiences they recount. In the absence of direct images of the past, the survivor's face becomes the site where trauma is visually registered and where the interdiction on direct representation is affirmed. In this way, the visible face also signifies something beyond the visible, something that eludes our vision and escapes our grasp. To clarify: this is not to suggest that the real, human faces of the survivor-witnesses in *Shoah* can be read as representations of the Levinasian 'visage', which exceeds and undoes any image we attempt to form of it; what concerns me here instead are the ways in which these faces resist reduction to visible phenomena, sources of knowledge or objects of aesthetic contemplation and the possibility that this preserves an opening onto alterity.

Crucial to this opening is language. One of the key means by which Lanzmann reactivates the prohibition against representation is by consistently privileging the word over the image. While Lanzmann, like Levinas,[34] is interested in the ethical significance of non-verbal forms of expression (as demonstrated, for example, by the numerous occasions on which the camera continues to linger on the witness's face after he or she has fallen silent), language and its relationship with alterity simultaneously emerge as pivotal preoccupations for both. In *Totality and Infinity*, speech is identified as a central component and expression of the ethical relation with the Other: 'The face speaks. The manifestation of the face is already discourse'.[35] In the relation of language, moreover, 'the essential is the interpellation, the vocative', which maintains the other 'in his heterogeneity'.[36] In line with Levinas's concerns, *Shoah* addresses its audience and evokes the alterity of the traumatic past primarily through discourse. The film interpellates us not only as spectators but also, and perhaps most significantly, as listeners. The witnesses appear first and foremost as sources of language, and it is as speaking faces, talking heads, that they resist reduction to objects of our perception. The priority which Lanzmann grants to audition over vision – to oral over visual modes of access to the past – is thus in keeping with Levinas's reflections on the ways in which the 'visage' reveals itself and on the prohibition against representation which it expresses. The *Bilderverbot* is reiterated in *Shoah* in the disjunctive relationship between voice and image, between the atrocities described by the witnesses and the empty, derelict and deceptively tranquil murder sites to which they return in the present. Furthermore, it is through oral testimony that *Shoah* makes manifest the absence of those faces Lanzmann cannot or chooses not to show yet whose experiences remain the central subject of the film: the missing faces of the dead. If *Shoah* invites us to read the survivor's face as a screen in the double sense of the term (as a blank surface onto which the action is projected and as a partition which conceals the action from view), as the survivor speaks, the film screen opens onto a face in the Levinasian sense, insofar as it directs attention beyond itself towards an otherness which cannot be recuperated in images.

Some concluding remarks

Paradoxically, then, *Shoah* transposes some of Levinas's concerns about the potential for treachery and violence inherent in images into a visual register. But in so doing it also qualifies them. On the one hand, the film echoes Levinas's warning that visual representation is liable to freeze or destroy otherness and suggests that the events of the Holocaust are particularly susceptible to such violation. Whereas Levinas and Lanzmann both pronounce explicit interdictions on images in their writings, however, the film is less didactic; rather than articulating proscriptions, it communicates its mistrust of images of atrocity through its omissions and refusals. On the other hand, this visual critique of the visual simultaneously challenges Levinas's dismissal of images and qualms about art. *Shoah* presents us with one set of strategies by which film, in Levinasian terms, might expose us to alterity without domesticating or simply effacing it. In this sense, it anticipates Levinas's suggestion that the Second Commandment may not be a purely repressive stricture, but may sanction attempts to signify otherwise, prior to or beyond vision, intelligibility and knowledge.

While it is possible to identify parallels between Levinas's and Lanzmann's projects deriving from their shared concerns about the perils of certain forms of figuration, it is equally important to acknowledge the discrepancies between them. Lanzmann's treatment of some of his interviewees raises questions about consent and the rights of filmed subjects of the kind that have been widely debated in discussions of ethics in documentary (as mentioned in the introduction and Chapter 1), yet which are only tangentially related to 'ethics' in the sense which Levinas gives to the term. Unlike Levinas's writings, *Shoah* does not accord ethics precedence over epistemology; nor does it grant the other priority over the self. The boundless responsibility towards alterity conceptualized by Levinas is subordinated in the film to a quest for historical knowledge which is informed by a political agenda. *Shoah*'s much-discussed blind spots – the institutional complicity of the French in the deportations and the experiences of women in the camps, to take two examples – may be explained as a consequence of its exclusive focus on the machinery of extermination. Nevertheless, in a way that recalls Levinas's equivocation over whether the Palestinian can occupy the position of 'the other', the film's elisions limit the sphere of responsibility, which Levinas insists elsewhere must be understood as infinite.[37] In the terms of Levinas's argument at least, Lanzmann's prioritization of political agency leads, in these particular contexts, to an evasion of ethical responsibility.

Moreover, while I have maintained that *Shoah* exposes its viewers to alterity, this is not to suggest that it – or any film – stages an ethical encounter between viewers and images of the kind envisaged by Levinas, which cannot be understood as an empirical event. As Renov points out, 'given the conditions of capture and reproducibility that govern nonfiction media, we can assume that no documentary practice can meet the ethical standards of the [Levinasian] encounter, simulating a mode of thought better than knowledge'.[38] The delay between filming and viewing, the absence of the imaged subject and the duplicability of the image all render cinema incapable of recreating the unpredictable, unmediated, unique and daunting confrontation with the Other from which Levinasian ethics derives. What I have tried to demonstrate here instead is that *Shoah* renegotiates the relationship between viewing self and imaged other in ways that resonate more deeply with Levinas's thought than competing strands of philosophical inquiry. I noted above that a Levinasian model of viewing relations would contrast sharply with those posited in psychoanalytic accounts of the film apparatus. *Shoah*'s reluctance to grant us visual access to the past and prioritization of oral witnessing disrupts the mechanisms of objectification outlined in the canonical interventions of Baudry, Metz and Mulvey (which are based primarily on analysis of classic narrative cinema). Lanzmann's film disturbs the illusory positions of sovereignty and transcendence afforded to viewers in such accounts. Like Levinas's writings, it attempts to imagine instead 'a relation irreducible to the subject–object relation'.[39] Precisely by impeding our vision and frustrating our desire to see, *Shoah* implicates our gaze and charges it with responsibility. Crucially, a Levinasian reading of the film enables us to articulate the ethical dynamics of this process.

So why take Levinas to the cinema? This chapter has highlighted convergences between his thought and a film which is unusually reticent about representation, and shown how the former brings the ethical dimensions of the latter into focus. But, as mentioned at the outset, Levinas's insights have more often been applied to films that are significantly less ambivalent about the visual and emerge from different historical, intellectual and cultural contexts. More straightforwardly and directly than *Shoah*, such films call into question Levinas's critique of what he calls 'the eternally present order of vision' as inherently totalizing.[40] Viewing films *with* Levinas always involves a degree of viewing *against* the iconoclastic thrust of his writings. This negotiation is essential if we are to avoid downplaying the specificity of the medium in the service of an autonomous and in some ways conflicting theoretical agenda. Levinas's denigration of vision, so intimately bound up with his conception of the ethical, provokes us to look differently at the images on the screen, to seek out those fissures in their being through which alterity intrudes. In turn, films can alter our reading of Levinas by rehabilitating vision without instrumentalizing the image, by visualizing others without reducing them to projections of the self, and by envisaging an ethical 'optics' which illuminates the visible as much as the invisible.

Notes

1 Levinas, *Totality and Infinity*, 23.
2 In the scene in question in *Notre musique*, an Israeli journalist flicks through a copy of Levinas's *Entre nous* (1991) while contemplating in Levinasian terms the significance of the reconstruction of the Mostar bridge in Bosnia-Herzegovina, which will reconnect the Catholic Croats and Muslim Bosnians who live on opposite sides on the River Neretva. See also Dardenne, *Au dos de nos images* and Appignanesi and Baum, '*Ex Memoria*: Filming the Face'.
3 See, for example, Renov, *The Subject of Documentary*, 148–67; Cooper, *Selfless Cinema?*; Botting and Wilson, *The Tarantinian Ethics*; Downing, *Patrice Leconte*; 106–30; Aaron, *Spectatorship*, 111–113; and the essays in the 2007 special issue of *Film-Philosophy*, 'The Occluded Relation: Levinas and Cinema', ed. Cooper.
4 Cooper, 'Introduction: The Occluded Relation: Levinas and Cinema', iii.
5 Levinas, *Totality and Infinity*, 304.
6 Jay, *Downcast Eyes*, 546, 548, 555.

7 Robert Eaglestone argues that 'Levinas's thought is saturated with the thought of the Holocaust' to an extent that is often overlooked by his readers ('Inexhaustible Meaning, Inextinguishable Voices', 249–250).
8 Robbins, *Altered Reading*, 133.
9 Levinas, 'Reality and its Shadow', 141.
10 Levinas, 'Interdit de la représentation et "Droits de l'homme"', 107.
11 Levinas, 'Interdit de la représentation et "Droits de l'homme"', 109.
12 Levinas, 'Interdit de la représentation et "Droits de l'homme"', 108–110.
13 Levinas, 'Interdit de la représentation et "Droits de l'homme"', 108, 113.
14 Levinas, 'Interdit de la représentation et "Droits de l'homme"', 110.
15 Levinas, 'Interdit de la représentation et "Droits de l'homme"', 108.
16 Levinas, *Totality and Infinity*, 50.
17 Levinas, 'Peace and Proximity', 167.
18 Levinas, *Ethics and Infinity*, 86–7.
19 Levinas, *Totality and Infinity*, 200, 51.
20 Levinas, 'Interdit de la représentation et "Droits de l'homme"', 112, 110.
21 Armengaud, 'Faire ou ne pas faire d'images. Emmanuel Levinas et l'art d'oblitération'.
22 Levinas, 'Interdit de la représentation et "Droits de l'homme"', 112.
23 Levinas, 'Interdit de la représentation et "Droits de l'homme"', 113.
24 For a more general discussion of the implications of Levinas's writings for art and visual and sensible experience, see Crignon, 'Figuration: Emmanuel Levinas and the Image'.
25 Cooper, *Selfless Cinema?*, 19.
26 Levinas, *Totality and Infinity*, 73.
27 Lanzmann, 'Holocauste, la représentation impossible', vii.
28 See, for instance, Lanzmann, 'Parler pour les morts', 14.
29 See, for example, Lacapra, *History and Memory after Auschwitz*, 100.
30 See, for instance, Todorov, *Facing the Extreme*, 275–276.
31 For analysis of the privileged position and evolving meanings of the face on screen, see Aumont, *Du visage au cinéma*.
32 See, for instance, Antelme, *The Human Race*, 52–53 and Levi, *If This Is a Man*, 103.
33 Nancy, 'La Représentation interdite', 92.
34 For an account of the privileged place which Levinas reserves for non-verbal communication, see Critchley, *The Ethics of Deconstruction*, 177–180.
35 Levinas, *Totality and Infinity*, 66.
36 Levinas, *Totality and Infinity*, 69.
37 Levinas, 'Ethics and Politics', 294.
38 Renov, *The Subject of Documentary*, 157.
39 Levinas, *Totality and Infinity*, 73.
40 Levinas, 'The Servant and her Master', 157.

Chapter 7

Deconstructive ethics

Derrida, Dreyer, responsibility

Libby Saxton

In Carl Theodor Dreyer's celebrated film *Ordet* (*The Word*, 1955), a seminarian who has been driven mad by reading Kierkegaard believes that he is Christ. Johannes's claims meet with disbelief and exasperation from his family until, in the culminating sequence, he appears to perform a miracle, raising his sister-in-law from the dead. On a first viewing, it is difficult to know what to make of this denouement. It is at odds with the film's hitherto realist style, rationalist perspective and sceptical portrayal of religious mysticism. The 'miracle' seems to trouble the coherency of the narrative rather than offering closure through religious redemption. Furthermore, until the final scene, Johannes's perceived duty to God appears to contradict his obligations to his family, recalling the 'teleological suspension of the ethical'

Figure 7 Ordet

which Kierkegaard finds in the biblical story of Abraham and Isaac.[1] In *The Gift of Death* (1999) Derrida, drawing on Kierkegaard, attempts to show how absolute, unlimited responsibility (epitomized by the test of faith faced by Abraham) conflicts with responsibility in general: our ethical obligations towards other human beings. In Derrida's secular account, 'what can be said about Abraham's relation to God can be said about my relation without relation to *every other (one) as every (bit) other* [*tout autre comme tout autre*]'.[2] But if every responsible act involves neglecting other responsibilities, and thus, in Derridean terms, a form of violence, how should we decide what to do? In what follows, I explore how Dreyer's films and Derrida's text grapple with this question.

The broader aim of this chapter is to suggest some ways in which Derrida's writings might contribute to our understanding of film and ethics. Given the far-reaching influence of his work in Europe and the United States over the past fifty years, it is perhaps surprising that Derrida has not had a more decisive impact on film studies. As poststructuralism became a dominant theoretical paradigm in Western humanities faculties, film theory absorbed some of Derrida's critical insights, appropriating deconstructive accounts of textuality and subjectivity in part circuitously via feminist, queer and postcolonial theory. Yet, unlike their counterparts in literary studies, relatively few scholars of film have engaged directly with Derrida's texts. His work has been described as a 'structuring absence' in film theory and his impact on film criticism has remained fragmented and localized.[3] One of the likely reasons for this is that his early writings at least appeared to prioritize language over vision and perception. Levinas's suspicions of the visual are echoed in places by Derrida, who shows how the 'metaphysics of presence' grounding totalizing modes of thought over-invests in metaphors of light and sight. It is in order to deconstruct such totalities that Derrida recurrently returns to motifs of blindness, disrupting the logic of sameness by demonstrating that vision is always threatened by the possibility of its negation.[4] As a consequence, to many theorists, Derridean deconstruction may have seemed less hospitable to film than Lacanian psychoanalysis, with its frequent recourse to visual scenarios.[5]

Derrida's to date limited and largely indirect influence on film studies may give rise to two misleading impressions: firstly, that film lies outside of the scope of his concerns; secondly, that his writings on other topics have little relevance to debates in this field. However, in spite of his hostility towards totalizing forms of vision, Derrida has frequently analyzed visual representations and sometimes incorporated them into his texts. Moreover, in the last decade of his life he co-wrote a book and published a series of extensive interviews devoted in whole or part to cinema.[6] He also appeared in several films, including *Ghost Dance* (Ken McMullen, 1983), *Derrida* (Kirby Dick and Amy Ziering Hoffman, 2002) and perhaps most notably *D'ailleurs Derrida* (Safaa Fathy, 2000). Derrida's reflections on the cinematic image resuscitate themes familiar from his other works, including mourning, the trace, testimony, belief, blindness and, most frequently, the spectre or phantom: 'In order to understand cinema, we must think together the phantom and capital, the latter being itself a spectral phenomenon.'[7] The connections he posits between cinema and spectrality hint suggestively at the medium's political and ethical dimensions (in the sense which Derrida gives to these terms): its capacity to disturb historical time and alert us to an open, unforeseeable future, to summon up the absolutely other and unsettle the opposition between presence and absence.[8] However, while Derrida's discussions of film serve in this chapter as a point of orientation, my primary focus is his rethinking of traditional ethical concepts. The texts discussed here make few references to the moving image, but the chapter indicates ways in which they might enrich our viewing by forging links with thinking encountered in the films of Dreyer.

Derrida and ethics

One of the charges that has been repeatedly levelled against deconstruction is that it is ethically irresponsible, or at least evasive and obscurantist when confronted with the urgent moral problems of our age. Derrida's critics have objected that his concepts of 'différance' and 'undecidability' undermine the grounds of ethical action and lead to moral relativism. During much of his career, Derrida's engagement with ethical themes was intermittent and oblique. But in the last two decades of his life, notably in the wake of the Paul de Man controversy, he began to turn more frequently to explicitly ethical as well as political concerns and endeavoured to demonstrate how these were integral to the deconstructive project. As mentioned in the introduction to this book, in Levinas's writings Derrida identifies a sense of the ethical which is in one sense bound to and yet in another severed from the suspect Western metaphysical tradition. However, Derrida's deconstructive readings attempt to show how the ethical relation described by Levinas contains within itself the possibility of its own betrayal. In *Totality and Infinity* and *Otherwise than Being or Beyond Essence* Levinas alludes to the figure of 'le tiers', the third party who 'looks at me in the face of the Other' and points beyond the two-way asymmetrical relation to questions of justice, equality and humanity, albeit contentiously conceived in terms of fraternity.[9] In 'A Word of Welcome' (1997) Derrida stresses the paradoxical implications of the third: 'it is as if the unicity of the face were, in its absolute and irreducible singularity, plural *a priori*'.[10] According to Derrida, the third affords protection against ethical violence, but, in so doing, it threatens the purity of the relation to the unique. In this way it alerts us to a 'double-bind':

> if the face to face with the unique engages the infinite ethics of my responsibility for the other in a sort of *oath before the letter*, an unconditional respect or fidelity, then the ineluctable emergence of the third, and with it, of justice, would signal an initial perjury [*parjure*].[11]

Since the third appears in or with the face, this perjury is originary. In Derrida's account, then, ethics is haunted from the outset by that which opposes, violates or negates it, and therefore any attempt to erect it into a master-discourse or totality should be viewed with suspicion. Just as justice is shown to be founded on a primordial perjury, so too other ethical concepts are revealed to be contaminated by the non-ethical. In Derrida's texts from the late 1980s onwards, questions of decision-making and justice, virtues such as responsibility, hospitality and forgiveness, and notions of giving, promising and testifying are analyzed in the light of this ethical double-bind.

While the ethical topics with which Derrida engages are firmly rooted in the Judaeo-Christian tradition, his aim is to imagine what ethics would look like without transcendental guarantees. In *The Gift of Death* he considers the relationship between religious faith and ethical responsibility. Developing lines of enquiry initiated elsewhere in his work, he argues, counter-intuitively, that responsibility should 'exceed mastery and knowledge'; while it might seem that we can only make a responsible decision on the basis of what we know, such knowledge would make the decision programmatic and therefore, by Derrida's criteria, irresponsible.[12] In this sense, a responsible decision always involves a leap of faith, or, from another perspective, momentary madness. Moreover, for Derrida, who engages here with essays by Jan Patočka, Christianity is central to the genealogy of responsibility since it provides us with the motif of an 'abyssal dissymmetry in the exposure to the gaze of the other' and with 'a new significance for death, a new apprehension of death, a new way in which to give oneself death or put oneself to death [*se donner la mort*]'.[13] Following Levinas, Derrida asserts that responsibility 'demands irreplaceable singularity', and that only the anticipation of death, whether our own or another's, can enable us to experience this irreplaceability.[14] In order to explain the implications of responsibility as singularity, Derrida turns to Kierkegaard's discussion in *Fear and Trembling* (1843) of Abraham's willingness to sacrifice his only son in response to God's command. A scandalous decision by any conventional ethical standards, its moral for Kierkegaard, who is arguing here against Kant and Hegel, is that acting in accordance with universal ethical codes may lead us to neglect our 'higher' or 'absolute' duty to God.[15] In Derrida's commentary on Kierkegaard, Abraham's predicament reveals 'ethics as "irresponsibilization": as an insoluble and therefore paradoxical contradiction between responsibility *in general* and *absolute* responsibility'.[16] For Derrida, the extreme biblical example offers an insight into our everyday experience of responsibility: 'I cannot respond to the call, the request, the obligation, or even the love of another without sacrificing the other other, the other others.'[17] Derrida surmises that 'the concepts of responsibility, of decision, or duty, are condemned *a priori* to paradox, scandal, and aporia', since responsibility, in its singularity, always betrays or sacrifices ethics, the realm of substitution and universalization.[18] To be responsible I must make a decision, but my decision will never be responsible enough.

Characteristically, there is some equivocation in Derrida's conclusions. For instance, Abraham is described as 'at the same time the most moral and the most immoral, the most responsible and the most irresponsible of men' – does this mean we should follow his example or not?[19] Ethics, we are told, 'must be sacrificed in the name of duty', while this sacrifice must simultaneously recognize, confirm and reaffirm ethics; but Derrida does not explain how this might be achieved in practical terms.[20] Commentators have also pointed out internal inconsistencies in his argument. Dominic Moran argues that Derrida not only remains reliant on conventional distinctions between 'good' and 'evil' which he sets out to deconstruct; he also contradicts himself by insisting on the singularity of every decision only to present Abraham's implicitly as a paradigm. Moran asks: 'By providing a case-study of absolute responsibility, by exemplifying the unexemplifiable, does not Derrida prevent or inhibit one from acceding to it? Does this not make his entire project of rethinking responsibility *irresponsible*?'[21] At the same time, Moran and other critics have objected to Derrida's reluctance to demonstrate how deconstructive ethics might be applied in concrete situations. Questions about exemplification and application arise throughout this book, and particularly in this second section, as we consider the intersections between film and theoretical discourses of ethics. While cinema supplies us with examples of ethical and unethical attitudes and practices, we have emphasized that using films merely to illustrate philosophical positions is fraught with risk, as this tends to imply a hierarchy in which cinema is subordinated to philosophy and to lead to selective, impoverished accounts of individual films. In my chapters on Levinas and Derrida such an approach would simply be nonsensical, since an ethics of singularity cannot be exemplified (in contrast, for instance, to Kant's universal ethics or Žižek's Lacanian ethics, which he explains by using examples from Hitchcock's films). Moreover, the inherent reproducibility of the filmic image disallows experience of the singular. Just as, for Walter Benjamin, mechanical reproducibility strips the artwork of its 'aura', so the technology of film robs the ethical encounter of its uniqueness and irreplaceability. Dreyer's films are interesting from this perspective since they explore the tension between irreducibly singular religious experience and the intrinsically pluralizing function of cinematic technology.[22]

With fear and trembling: *The Passion of Joan of Arc*

It might initially seem counter-intuitive to place the films of Dreyer, a humanist working in a Protestant environment who was drawn to Christian subjects, in dialogue with Derrida's anti-humanist, secular account of ethics. However, many of the obsessions of these films reappear in *The Gift of Death*: religion, faith, sacrifice, responsibility and the relationship between life and death; and in their treatments of these topics both Derrida and Dreyer are influenced by the existentialist thought of Kierkegaard. Moreover, the narratives and visual textures of Dreyer's films display gaps and excesses which undermine totalizing humanist or religious interpretations. David Bordwell notes that critical writing on Dreyer's work has adopted three broad approaches – religious, humanist and aesthetic – and goes on to lament critics' tendency to 'domesticate' the films by ignoring those elements which do not fit with their preferred interpretation.[23] The following analysis suggests that *The Passion of Joan of Arc* (1928) and *Ordet* disturb these fixed categories by questioning both Christian and humanist understandings of ethical agency. Both films depict the subjection of women within patriarchal Christian cultures, a recurrent theme in Dreyer's work, and point critically to cinema's complicity with this ideology while continuing to operate within it. Both perpetuate a series of stereotypes of gender and sexual orientation. In Mark Nash's analysis of *Gertrud* (1964) the '"trouble" haunting the Dreyer-text' is the repressed problem of bisexuality.[24] Taking my cue from Derrida, I want to focus here instead on the 'trouble' caused by the competing conceptions of responsibility, singular and general, religious and ethical, brought into play in the two earlier films, and their problematic relationship to patriarchal violence.

The Passion of Joan of Arc has been described as an 'intensely and ambiguously religious' film.[25] Drawing on the historical transcripts of the trial, this silent film reconstructs the final hours of the life of Joan (Renée Falconetti), during which she is interrogated by pro-English clergy, convicted of heresy and finally burnt at the stake. It dramatizes Joan's encounter with the numinous, the solitary, agonizing process of reflection through which she arrives at the decision to sacrifice her life, and her vigilant approach to death. While the outcome of Joan's decision is known to the viewer from the outset, the film stresses that it remains unknown to her by depicting her vacillations and paroxysms of confusion, foreshadowing Derrida's conception of the decision as a (secular) act of faith, made in fear and trembling rather than knowledge. At the heart of the film lies what Derrida calls 'the *mysterium tremendum* of Christian responsibility', the asymmetrical gaze of the transcendent other and the sacrificial gift experienced as a terrifying mystery.[26] Joan's human capacity for terror and suffering is emphasized throughout the film; in this, she differs from the otherworldly, divine heroine of Robert Bresson's *Le Procès de Jeanne d'Arc* (*The Trial of Joan of Arc*, 1962). Dreyer's Joan is charged not only with a spiritual mission but also with an earthly one, a political and ethical obligation to her King and fellow French citizens, and, as we shall see, the film evokes her struggle to reconcile these two callings. In its dual focus on her spirituality and her humanity, her duties to the transcendent and immanent worlds, *The Passion of Joan of Arc* anticipates Derrida's reflections on the aporetic logic of responsibility, while repositioning a woman at the centre of this aporia.

The story of Joan's decision is told through static close-up images of her face, which is often decentred within the frame but forms the moral and spiritual centre of the film. Mary Anne Doane sees *The Passion of Joan of Arc* as the epitome of a filmic genre which uses facial close-ups to exploit the 'cultural and epistemological susceptibility' to 'the opposition between surface and depth, exteriority and interiority'.[27] Its expressivity intensified by the blank backgrounds against which it is usally framed, Falconetti's face threatens to negate this opposition by exteriorizing her interior struggle. In its seeming transparency, it works to guarantee the truth of her suffering and transcendental vision. Joan thus initially appears to be the perfect embodiment of the autonomous, unified humanist subject. As Sean Desilets points out, critics have tended to view her as a semantically stable counterpoint to the chaos which surrounds her, evoked through the film's deconstruction of diegetic space via close-ups, disruptive editing and avoidance of establishing shots.[28] Unlike Abraham's act of faith, Joan's 'gift of death' does not pit her directly against the universal ethical order by requiring her to violate the bonds that bind her to other human beings. The threat to this order is posed instead by the cruelty and hypocrisy of the Church. The camerawork and editing highlight Joan's ethical purity by framing her separately from her judges and troubling matching eye-lines, insisting on her refusal to collaborate in the economy of violence. At first glance, then, it appears that Joan's earthly and spiritual missions, or (in Derridean terms) her responsibility to the other and all the others, 'the ethical or political generality', are mutually reinforcing.[29]

However, a fissure begins to open up between these two orders in the final third of the film, when Joan's private spiritual drama is precipitated into a public social milieu. Joan is carried outside on a stretcher to face further haranguing in a cemetery, where a crowd has gathered to watch. In a series of brief medium shots, we glimpse the townspeople predominantly as an anonymous mass, decentred in the often canted frame and flanked by English soldiers. When the clergyman Erard (Jean d'Yd) attempts to convince her to sign a recantation, Joan protests 'I have done no-one any harm', insisting on the compatibility of her religious and ethical principles. Another member of the clergy, Loyseleur (Maurice Schutz) tries a different tactic of persuasion: 'You must not die now. Your king still needs your help'. Contradicting Joan's claim, Loyseleur's remark prises apart and opposes her duty to God to her ethico-political responsibility to her country and fellow citizens, and shortly afterwards she signs. The film then crosscuts between Joan's prison cell, where her hair is shorn, and a fairground, juxtaposing her humiliation with the townspeople's celebrations. Having retracted her recantation, Joan is led outside for execution, where the crowd mills around the stake. Images of Joan clutching a cross to her body are intercut with close-ups of a baby feeding at its mother's breast. As the fire takes hold, the film continues to cut between Joan and the crowd, and the camera pans in close-up across faces expressing pity and compassion. The editing thus establishes a connection between Joan's agony and the suffering of the citizens, who are now individualized by the camerawork. Yet, in this sequence, as throughout the entire film, Joan never interacts with the townspeople, or even appears in the same shot as them (with the exception of an elderly woman who gives her water). During her public exchange with Erard, she is shown in close-up against a plain white backdrop, just as in the interior scenes, and in her final moments she is framed alone against the stake, her separation from the surrounding crowd reinforced by the non-coincidence of their eye-lines.

So, while the cuts locate Joan's drama within a social context, the *mise-en-scène* and framing of the individual shots seem to tell a different story, removing her spiritual mission from the ethical realm of human interaction and social and kinship bonds. The superficial logic of the narrative reconciles her responsibilities to God and to the French citizens; Joan's 'gift of death' inspires the townspeople to revolt against their occupiers. In this reading, her act of faith casts her as an exemplary ethical heroine for the onlooking citizens, who act here as on screen surrogates for the film viewers. Yet the manner in which Joan is filmed disrupts this interpretation by decontextualizing her experience and emphasizing her alienation from what Derrida, following Kierkegaard, calls the 'ethical generality'.[30] In the last few minutes of the film, this generality moves into the foreground and occupies the entirety of the frame as members of the rioting crowd are beaten and slaughtered by the guards. The spiral of violence unleashed by Joan's sacrifice points to the incompatibility of her earthly and spiritual duties, ironically echoing the pernicious logic of her persecutor Loyseleur. The drawn-out depiction of the killings throws the singular, unique and irreplaceable (the responsible) out of alignment with the general, substitutable and universal (the ethical). The focus of the narrative has shifted from the gift to its human cost. By the end of the film, the illusion of the transcendental unified subject has been replaced by a 'fantasy of the body in pieces': all that remains of Joan is a blazing corpse surrounded by the shattered bodies of her people.[31]

The threat of violence to the female body which haunts *The Passion of Joan of Arc* casts its drama of responsibility in a different light. In their fragmentation of Joan's form, the close-ups and the rapid cuts used in certain scenes mimic the torture inflicted upon her by her onscreen tormentors. James Schamus notes that in a discussion of the film Dreyer attributes a sadistic function to the close-up as an effect of torture.[32] Viewed in the light of this analogy between direction and pain-infliction, the celebrated images of Joan's face point to a controlling authorial presence and suggest a stereotypical combination of male sadism and female masochism. The form of the film draws attention to the collusion of the cinematic apparatus in the acts of gendered violence perpetrated in the name of religion at the narrative level. For Nash, 'the main interest of the Dreyer-text is that, although caught up in the traditional theological view of cinema with its "god-like" author, mysteriously present "everywhere", that is nowhere, it nevertheless presents this ideology as a highly problematic one.'[33] The asymmetrical gaze which Derrida attributes to the Christian God, the infinite other who 'sees without being seen', is ambiguously conflated in this film with the gendered gaze of the filmmaker.[34] If the film's religious discourse can be interpreted as an allegory of the relationship between author and text, then Joan's treatment at the hands of a male director can be viewed as a critique of the patriarchal ideology of Christianity. *The Passion of Joan of Arc* suggests that the exorbitant responsibility, the responsibility beyond ethics, described by Derrida is implicated in a contagion of patriarchal violence which exposes the female subject to the threat of annihilation.

Suspending (dis)belief: *Ordet*

The relationship between faith and ethics is thematized more explicitly in *Ordet*. The protagonists of this film openly debate conflicting conceptions of religious and moral responsibility; at this level, the narrative intersects once again with the concerns of *The Gift of Death*. Set in a rural Danish community, *Ordet* revolves around a local dispute between two Protestant sects, the Christians of Grundtvigism and the Inner Mission, which espouse different views of the purpose of faith and the nature of a righteous life. According to Morten Borgen (Henrik Malberg), the patriarch of the Christians of Grundtvigism, whereas as his sect believes that its duty is to rejoice in a life enriched by faith, the puritanical Inner Mission advocates self-torment and embraces death. Although the former group constitutes the film's primary focus, Dreyer's continually tracking camera, lengthy takes, and avoidance of close-ups, which contrast with the techniques used in *The Passion of Joan of Arc*, suggest an attentive, sceptical observer who is reluctant to pronounce a definitive judgement on any belief-system prematurely. Within Morten's family, a series of more nuanced positions emerge. Morten admits that he is racked by doubts and no longer believes in miracles. Although this conviction will be tested in the course of the film, Dreyer's non-judgemental portrayal of Morten's uncertainty echoes Kierkegaard's defence of rational doubt as an essential component of faith. However, when Morten's son, Mikkel (Emil Hass Christensen), admits to his wife Inger (Brigitte Federspiel) that he has no faith, she reassures him with a different argument: 'But you have something more important: a heart, and goodness.' While Inger herself believes that 'many tiny miracles occur all around us', her contention that moral virtue and love for other human beings are ultimately more significant is directly at odds with the conclusions Kierkegaard draws from the story of Abraham and Isaac. Inger's humanist ethics also conflicts with Derrida's reading of Kierkegaard, for it does not tolerate aporiae.

Inger's remark about goodness might be understood as an implicit reference to another of Morten's sons, Johannes (Preben Lerdorff Rye), who seems in contrast to embody the contradictions discussed by Kierkegaard and Derrida. We are introduced to this mysterious character in one of the opening shots of the film, where, standing on a hillock with his arms outstretched, he berates the 'hypocrites' for their faithlessness and proclaims himself God's prophet. Johannes clings doggedly to his belief in his divinity and is regarded alternately with pity and frustration by the Borgen family; only Maren (Ann Elisabeth Rud), Mikkel and Inger's young daughter, have faith in his claims. While the adults attempt to rationalize Johannes's behaviour, the film withholds any satisfactory psychological explanation for it. In Kaj Munk's play *Ordet* (1932), on which Dreyer based his screenplay, Johannes's madness is attributed in a Freudian fashion to the death of his fiancée. The film omits this detail; we are told only that his delusions took hold while he was studying theology (Kierkegaard is mentioned here) and became tormented by doubt, prefiguring his father's spiritual quandary. Mikkel's flippant reference to Johannes's deleterious reading habits may hold a clue to his predicament. Kierkegaard's remark that 'the instant of the decision is madness' is cited by Derrida to support his contention that every responsible decision requires a leap beyond rational calculation.[35] Is Johannes's 'madness' the condition of possibility of the 'hyperethical' decision (a term Derrida uses to describe Abraham's sacrifice), or has he been driven mad by undecidability?[36] The *mise-en-scène* and particularly the manner in which Johannes is framed and lit, further unsettle the boundaries between responsibility, mysticism and insanity. The low angle shots of Johannes preaching on the hilltop, wearing a long, billowing cloak, and, shortly afterwards, a medium shot of him holding a candle which resembles William Holman Hunt's painting of Christ, 'The Light of the World' (1853–54), collude in his self-beatifying fantasy. Like Joan's, Johannes's movements and sight lines are independent from those of his interlocutors, and when he speaks it is more frequently to quote from the Bible than to engage in dialogue. In their religiosity, the images of Johannes dignify his actions without corroborating or refuting his claims, whilst emphasizing his estrangement from the ethical realm. Johannes might be Kierkegaard's 'knight of faith', or he might just be mad, or both.

The final scene of the film exacerbates this ambivalence. Inger's return to life at Johannes's bidding after she has died in childbirth is both unexpected and unlikely. The most obvious explanation is unsatisfactory: having recovered his sanity, Johannes is empowered by Maren's faith to perform a miracle, an act which superficially resolves the contradictions between his duty to God and to his family. Other factors hint that the denouement is not merely a simplistic affirmation of the redemptive power of Christian faith or the self-coherence of responsibility. The scene ties off a submerged narrative thread concerning reproduction and male filiation. Earlier in the film, a pregnant Inger promises Morten a grandson in exchange for his consent to the marriage of his youngest son Anders (Cay Kristiansen). Inger breaks her promise for the baby dies at birth, at which point it seems she must also die, unable to sustain the male family line. Up to this point, the sub-narrative follows an all too familiar pattern of male authority and female self-sacrifice in order to overcome a male death. Yet Inger's 'resurrection' interrupts this reactionary pattern. The final shot of the film shows her in close-up, just after she has learnt of the death of her child, her cheek pressed against her husband's. While this image constitutes an unequivocal affirmation of heterosexual coupledom, it breaks with the classic narrative film convention according to which the primary purpose of the formation of the couple is a reproductive future (discourses of 'reproductive futurity' are discussed in detail in Chapter 9). The fantasy of the fragmented body evoked by *The Passion of Joan of Arc* returns in *Ordet*, but here the broken body belongs to the male infant (Mikkel informs us that the child is literally 'in four pieces'), while the woman's body remains intact and desiring. Rather than constituting an unequivocal validation of religious faith, then, the closing shot issues a challenge to patriarchal Christian ideology in its decoupling of heterosexual intimacy from the production of sons and its refusal to predetermine the future.

Closure is further postponed by the sheer implausibility of the 'miracle', which reminds us of the illusory nature of cinematic images and solicits an act of faith from the viewer as well as from the protagonists. In an interview in *Cahiers du cinéma*, Derrida defines the film medium's specificity in terms of its 'regime of belief': 'At the cinema there exists an absolutely singular modality of *believing*: a century ago we invented an unprecedented experience of belief. ... At the cinema, we believe without believing, but this belief without belief remains a belief.'[37] The final scene of *Ordet* both exploits and exposes this mode of 'belief without belief' (which is sometimes described in terms of unconscious mechanisms of fetishism: 'je sais bien, mais quand même'). Anticipating the connections suggested by Derrida between cinema, belief and spectrality, Inger's impossible awakening unsettles the binary oppositions between belief and disbelief, absence and presence, the living and the dead. Nash observes that the 'Dreyer-text' 'suspends not only disbelief, the romantic precondition for the aesthetic, but also, in its religious signification, belief'.[38] The 'miracle' in *Ordet* creates an association between our willingness to suspend disbelief in the cinema and religious faith, implicitly referencing yet simultaneously registering suspicion of theological accounts of the medium and the often-cited parallels between the director and God. The film's denouement probes the connections between duty, faith and film spectatorship, while resolutely refusing to resolve either the mystery of Johannes's actions or the aporia of responsibility.

Some concluding remarks

This chapter has argued against a prevalent tendency to dismiss deconstruction as unconcerned or evasive with regard to ethical issues and for its capacity to help us unpick the incoherencies of ethical discourses in film. In *The Gift of Death* Derrida contends that insofar as it is grounded in a liberal consensus, a set of generally agreed principles, ethics itself constitutes an evasion of responsibility. For scholars of film, the value of his account of responsibility as aporetic lies in its potential to alert us to the symbolic violence of overly complacent moralizing discourses in film practice and theory. While it would be misguided to seek examples of the singular responsibility described by Derrida in any cultural text, his argument encourages us to attend to the gaps, uncertainties and contradictions produced by discrepant discourses of responsibility in cinema. The subject-matter of Dreyer's films makes them particularly susceptible to such an analysis. By juxtaposing multiple conceptions of duty, virtue and faith, *The Passion of Joan of Arc* and *Ordet* warn us against taking any of them at face value, undermining straightforward religious or humanist interpretations. However, while these films foreshadow a number of Derrida's concerns, they also pose questions to Derrida about the relationship between responsibility and gender. Noting the marginal role played by women in the story of Abraham, Derrida asks:

> Would the logic of sacrificial responsibility within the implacable universality of the law, of its law, be altered, inflected, attenuated, or displaced, if a woman were to intervene in some consequential manner? Does the system of this sacrificial responsibility and of the double 'gift of death' imply at its very basis an exclusion or sacrifice of woman?[39]

While Derrida prefers to leave these questions 'in suspense', Dreyer's critical investigations of women's treatment at the hands of male authorities suggest that any responsible account of responsibility must take into account the gendered dynamics of its genealogy.[40] *The Passion of Joan of Arc* and *Ordet* reveal a set of disturbing connections between the Christian paradigm of unconditional duty, patriarchal violence, idealized female (self-)sacrifice and the cinematic medium. In so doing, they highlight a need to rethink the gender conventions which underpin the logic of responsibility outlined in *The Gift of Death*.

Neither Derrida's writing nor Dreyer's films offer a set of normative guidelines for making responsible decisions. However, in drawing attention to the paradoxes of responsibility, they warn us against totalizing models of ethics. *Ordet* and *The Passion of Joan of Arc* stage the Derridean drama of decision both within the diegesis and at the level of the interaction between viewer and film. In line with the conundrum posed by the final scene of *Ordet*, they suggest that responsible viewing might have less to do with rational sense-making than with leaps of faith and moments of madness.

Notes

1 Kierkegaard, *Fear and Trembling*, 46.
2 Derrida, *The Gift of Death*, 78.

3 Lapsley and Westlake, *Film Theory*, 65. Derrida's influence on the British journal *Screen* has been compared to that of a presence in 'off-screen space', or 'a fish in water, never openly breaking the surface' (Easthope, 'Derrida and British Film Theory', 189, 187). Important exceptions to this general trend are Brunette and Wills, *Screen/Play* and Smith, 'Deconstruction and Film'.

4 See, for example, Derrida, *Memoirs of the Blind* and 'Lettres sur un aveugle', in Derrida and Fathy, *Tourner les mots*, 71–126. For a discussion of Derrida's ambivalent attitude towards visual themes, see Jay, *Downcast Eyes*, 498–523.

5 See Brunette and Wills, *Screen/Play*, 16–21 for comparison of the impact of Derrida and Lacan on developments in film theory.

6 See, for example, Derrida and Fathy, *Tourner les mots*; Derrida and Stiegler, *Echographies of Television*; Derrida, 'The Spatial Arts'; Derrida, 'Le Cinéma et ses fantômes'.

7 Derrida, 'Le Cinéma et ses fantômes', 79 (my own translation).

8 See *Spectres of Marx* (1993) for Derrida's most extended discussion of spectres, politics and ethics.

9 'Language as the presence of the face does not invite complicity with the preferred being, the self-sufficient "I-Thou" forgetful of the universe ... The third party looks at me in the face of the Other – language is justice. ... The epiphany of the face qua face opens humanity' (Levinas, *Totality and Infinity*, 213).

10 Derrida, *Adieu to Emmanuel Levinas*, 110.

11 Derrida, *Adieu to Emmanuel Levinas*, 33.

12 Derrida, *The Gift of Death*, 8, 25–6.

13 Derrida, *The Gift of Death*, 29, 32.

14 Derrida, *The Gift of Death*, 51.

15 Kierkegaard, *Fear and Trembling*, 61.

16 Derrida, *The Gift of Death*, 62.

17 Derrida, *The Gift of Death*, 69.

18 Derrida, *The Gift of Death*, 69.

19 Derrida, *The Gift of Death*, 73.

20 Derrida, *The Gift of Death*, 67.

21 Moran, 'Decisions, Decisions', 120.

22 Sean Desilets makes a similar point in relation to *The Passion of Joan of Arc*: 'Mysticism is a radically singular experience' ('The Rhetoric of Passion', 78).

23 Bordwell, *The Films of Carl-Theodor Dreyer*, 1–3.

24 Nash, 'Notes on the Dreyer-Text', 87.

25 Heath, 'God, Faith and Film', 94.

26 Derrida, *The Gift of Death*, 9.

27 Doane, 'The Close-Up', 96.

28 Desilets, 'The Rhetoric of Passion', 57.

29 Derrida, *The Gift of Death*, 71.

30 Derrida, *The Gift of Death*, 78–9.

31 Nash, 'Notes on the Dreyer-Text', 105.

32 Schamus, 'Dreyer's Textual Realism', 323.

33 Nash, 'Notes on the Dreyer-Text', 87.

34 Derrida, *The Gift of Death*, 5.

35 Quoted in Derrida, *The Gift of Death*, 66.

36 Derrida, *The Gift of Death*, 71.

37 Derrida, 'Le Cinéma et ses fantômes', 78 (my own translation).

38 Nash, 'Notes on the Dreyer-Text', 92.

39 Derrida, *The Gift of Death*, 76.

40 Derrida, *The Gift of Death*, 76.

Chapter 8

Foucault in focus

Ethics, surveillance, soma

Lisa Downing

Michel Foucault has been relatively little discussed in theoretically informed academic film studies. This may be for several reasons. Firstly, Foucault did not write or speak very much about the cinema, with only one interview, published in *Cinématographie* in 1975, directly addressing the medium. Secondly, Foucault's work is best known for its analysis of discourse; its theorization of the power of words in institutional contexts. As cinema is principally a visual medium, it is perhaps understandable that his work is not, at first glance, the most likely toolkit with which to analyze representations on screen. However, even when writing on power, institutions and discourse, much of Foucault's work uses visual metaphors and models (e. g. the memorable discussion of power and point of view in Velasquez's painting *Las Meninas* [1656] in *The Order of Things*, 1966). Moreover, it focuses – perhaps more than any other body of thought except psycho-analysis, to which it offers a theoretical counterweight – on the mechanisms of watching, particularly in the context of social surveillance (*Discipline and Punish*). Foucault's theory of surveillance makes challenging arguments

Figure 8 Trouble Every Day

about the ubiquity and complexity of forms of observation, scrutiny and control in modern societal institutions. Importing this model to the mechanism of the gaze at and within film might allow for a way of thinking about watching that re-politicizes and re-ethicizes some of the clichés of gaze theory.

Foucault's work also rethinks sexuality and corporeality in ways that question psychoanalytic diagnostic epistemologies. The first volume of his tripartite *History of Sexuality*, *The Will to Knowledge*, published in 1976, a year after *Discipline and Punish*, makes powerful claims for the importance of rethinking bodily pleasure outside of the discursive knowledge categories of modernity. As explored in Chapter 5 of this book, much recent filmmaking and debate in film criticism has focused on the ethics of corporeal display. It may be profitable to think through cinematic experiments in somatic representation alongside Foucault's writing on the challenge of redefining the erotic body. In what follows, then, I shall focus on two concepts in Foucaldian thought – surveillance and theories of the body – to explore the possibility of creating a dialogue between his ethico-politically informed philosophy and the medium of cinema; thereby re-energizing both fields.

Surveillance and *Monsieur Hire*

A film that offers a particularly good test case for the use of Foucault's theory of surveillance for thinking about the ethics of looking is Patrice Leconte's *Monsieur Hire* (1989). If Hitchcock's *Rear Window* (1954) is the best-known and most widely discussed of those films which consciously set out to address voyeurism, to be movies about watching and, by extension, 'movie[s] about watching movies',[1] then Leconte's *Monsieur Hire* is a close contender. The similarities between *Rear Window* and *Monsieur Hire* are numerous. Both films exploit the analogy between the illuminated window and the cinema screen as loci of suspense and desire. Both feature a voyeuristic male protagonist in a state of claustrophobic confinement (physical in the case of Hitchcock's Jeff (James Stewart); emotional in the case of M. Hire (Michel Blanc)). And both, broadly, are parables about the dangers of falling in love.

However, the outcome of the sexual relationships in these two films, and the configurations of gendered power they invite us to behold, work rather differently, with the sexual politics of the Hitchcock film providing a more traditional and recognizable cinematic dynamic. In *Rear Window*, Jeff's girlfriend Lisa is so eager to please her lover and ultimately to persuade him to marry her, that she puts her own life at risk investigating the wife-murderer Thorvald, with whom Jeff is obsessed. In *Monsieur Hire*, Alice's loyalty to her murderous boyfriend Émile leads her to frame M. Hire for the killing of Pierrette Bourgeois, which in turn leads to his death. In both cases, the woman carries out an act of sacrifice for her lover, however in *Monsieur Hire*, the victim of the sacrifice is the betrayed other rather than the self. Although motivated by love for a man, Alice in *Monsieur Hire* is not a traditional feminine filmic stereotype. She is neither just a passive object to be looked at (indeed her actions drive the plot forward and precipitate its conclusion), nor a straightforward victim. She incorporates elements of the traditional femme fatale of *noir* (seductiveness, danger, perfidy), but also deviates from the archetype in a number of ways (she is not 'decoded', she remains alive). Hire, the *voyeur*, is not accorded complete mastery through his gaze, and it is he rather than the femme fatale whose death will provide filmic closure. Thus, in its framing and characterization, the film is ambiguous and inventive, exceeding the 'rules' of the narrative which we would expect.

Noting these departures from the generic norm, Abigail Murray's 1993 article 'Voyeurism in *Monsieur Hire*' proposes that Leconte's film restructures the gendered codes of voyeurism, such that '*Monsieur Hire* … sets up the gaze as male but only to bring into question the existing structures of looking in the cinema which are based on the active/male, passive/female dichotomy'.[2] The gaze is indeed set up as male in the very early stages of the film. The credits, accompanied by a baroque score by Michael Nyman, give way to a spectacle of a dead female body lying in a field. The camera pans upwards to show a detective (André Wilms) watching the corpse intently. He then muses, via a voice-over, on the sad fate of the victim. A few frames later, we see the body lying in the morgue and the policeman taking photographs of the dead girl's face. The male gaze takes possessive mastery of this inert female in the most radical way: it immortalizes her mortality. Following this shot of the dead child, we cut to a live child, playing a game of hide and seek on the doorstep with M. Hire. Shortly after, we are offered shots of Alice (Sandrine Bonnaire), dressing to meet her boyfriend and then undressing again to make love to him, silhouetted against the light in her bedroom window. These images are seen from the point of view of Hire, who watches from the shadowy interior of the flat opposite hers. By placing sequences of the murdered body, Hire's game with the little girl and his fascination with Alice in close proximity, Hire's voyeurism accrues associations of sinister intent. These early scenes, then, include both conventional *noir* elements (murder and the spectacle of the alluring woman) and a traditional configuration of gendered surveillance, which the director will later go on to subvert.

The subversion in question is achieved firstly by divesting the male watcher of 'power' in the sense of societal kudos. The figure of M. Hire is disenfranchised by a number of means, the most obvious of which is that he is set up 'as an enigmatic figure, whose demystification and final punishment … constitutes [sic] the main narrative goal'.[3] This is in contradistinction to the mechanism by which the classic narrative film allegedly operates in psychoanalytic theory. According to Mulvey and others, it is the enigma of female sexuality that keeps the masculine viewer riveted to the spectacle. The internal logic of certain generic conventions echoes this relation, particularly the *film noir* which uses the scintillating figure of the femme fatale as a fascinating foil to the quest of the hard-boiled detective. In *Monsieur Hire*, however, it is Hire rather than Alice who is constructed as a sexual enigma. Alice's 'secret' (that she is her boyfriend's accomplice) is revealed halfway through the film. Hire's enigma, on the other hand, unsolved and prematurely fore-closed in his death, aligns him with a long tradition of cinematic women rather than men. The association of Hire with women occurs within the diegetic world as well: we are told that he has a criminal record for indecent expo-sure, which links him with Alice who admits that she takes pleasure in being looked at ('it's nice to be watched' ['c'est agréable d'être regardée']). More-over, and very significantly, the police surveillance to which Hire is constantly subjected casts him also as the most obvious victim of the dominant gaze.

Jean Duffy takes this discussion further by proposing that 'the application of the term "voyeur" to Hire is … rendered problematical by the presence within the film of so many other voyeurs'.[4] These include the detective (a surveillance 'professional'); Alice herself, who returns M. Hire's gaze, watching him as he watches her make love to her boyfriend (only Émile is the unaware object of the gaze in that scene); and the various women, neighbours and children who suspiciously observe M. Hire's movements. The camera, too, moves between unobtrusive 'naturalistic' shots and self-consciously voyeuristic ones, such as the high camera angle which looks down on Hire's walk to work, tracking him across the courtyard in the manner of a surveillance camera.

What is more, the objects of the gaze are equally numerous. They are: Pierrette's dead body; Alice; Hire; Alice's fiancé Émile, when Hire watches him make love to Alice; as well as numerous inanimate objects of con-templation including dead mice. Several players are both watcher and watched; predator and prey at different moments in the film. The presence of several watchers and several objects of the gaze creates a multi-layered and self-reflexive cinema. Moreover, by pluralizing the dominant–passive object–subject structure of the gaze, Leconte allows the debate to move beyond the limits of the gendered relation described by Mulvey, and into the realm of other ethical debates. Jean Duffy points out that although M. Hire's Jew-ishness (he is actually M. Hirovitch, of Russian-Armenian descent) is accorded less obvious significance in Leconte's version than in Simenon's novel or Duvivier's *Panique*, it nonetheless functions as a silent subtext which allows Leconte to construct a properly allegorical tale of persecution.[5]

It has been argued that Leconte has effectively replaced the signifiers of Jewishness with signifiers of perversion in *Monsieur Hire*, such that the mar-ginality in question is sexual rather than religious or ethnic.[6] I have pointed out above that it is Hire rather than Alice who is the siphon of sexual mys-tery in the film, skewing the convention of the femme fatale. It is certainly true that the nature of Hire's sexuality is put into question several times. One could almost say, indeed, that the 'secret' the spectator searches out with regard to Hire is his *sexual* secret rather than the truth of whether he is Pierrette's murderer (though the two are presumed to be linked, at least by the detective). When the detective goads Hire: 'how long is it since you came inside a woman?' ('ça fait combien de temps que vous n'avez pas joui dans une femme?'), he evokes the post-sexological, post-Freudian stereotype of the sexually repressed male whose frustration is channelled into violence. The detective assumes that Hire is a lust murderer, while in fact the motive for Pierrette's crime has been robbery. Thus, perverse sexuality is assumed to be the primary underlying motivation in the society evoked in *Monsieur Hire*. If we read the film as a study of the ways in which access to the individual's sexual secret makes him or her into an object of knowledge and societal control, it becomes clear why a Foucaldian analysis of the functioning of knowledge and power offers a more persuasive tool for reading the film than psychoanalytic gaze theory. Foucault posits in *The Will to Knowledge* that modernity constructs the sexual secret as the secret per se of identity; the key to our essence. The secret is apparently 'revealed' through techniques designed to elicit confession. However, Foucault argues, these techniques are conversely the means by which the secret is retroactively constructed.[7] The confession Foucault has in mind is the narrative invited by the sexologist or psychoanalyst and crafted by the analysand, but the role of the policeman functions in *Monsieur Hire* in a similar way: to tease out sexual confession in order to classify the subject (as a deviant criminal).

However, just as the film upsets the assumption of a dominant–submissive logic of the gaze with its pan-voyeuristic perspective, so it sets up not only Hire, but every character, as potentially embodying one or more 'types' of sexual perversion. Thus, the very notion of sexual normalcy recedes from the picture and the meaning of the normal/perverse binarism is similarly put into question by the film's logic. Alice is shown to have exhibitionist tendencies – she enjoys being watched by Hire as she undresses, and becomes erotically aroused when he touches her clandestinely in the very public sphere of the boxing match. Hire is a voyeur, an exhibitionist and fetishist. He frequents prostitutes and is prone to violent outbursts of sexual rage in their presence. He is also a sensualist, who fetishizes scents and textures (he buys a bottle of the perfume Alice uses in order to evoke her via her scent). The detective displays voyeuristic and sadistic tendencies in his treatment of Hire and a fixation with the (beautifully lit) dead body of Pierrette that borders on the necrophiliac. Only Émile is the exception to this collection of 'perverts'. Émile is a murderer for financial rather than sexual gain, and is seen as a representative of the order of heterosexual and masculine normalcy. Alice comments early on in the film 'I like the way you kiss me. I find that you kiss me like a real man' ('j'aime ton façon de m'embrasser. Je trouve que tu m'embrasses comme un homme'). The portrayal of 'ideal' masculinity is, however, subtly ironized and under-mined by Leconte: the one 'real man' in the piece is also a brutal murderer and is unwittingly spied upon and cuckolded by the scapegoat M. Hire.

Thus, the three main characters (the detective, Hire and Alice) are con-nected by tacit similarities rather than, as might at first appear likely, radical differences. Any difference in their fates is attributable to the positions they occupy in relation to the social order they find themselves in. Hire is presented as an anti-social misfit. Leconte shows how his status as victim and outsider is constructed according to an arbitrary division between sanctioned and unsanctioned positions and behaviour within the symbolic system of the law. When Alice first catches Hire watching her she tells him that, if she wanted to, she could have him arrested, as there is a law against spying on people. The detective is presented as an equally strange (and much less sympathetic) individual than Hire, but, as agent of the law, his persecution and surveillance of Hire and gratuitous voyeurism (e.g. of the corpse) go unchallenged. Hire is punishable *only* because he does not have the symbolic means to ensure that he is not. Hire's self-deprecating demeanour and presence suggest that the character recognizes his own disenfranchisement and internalizes the persecution of the society.

This subtle critique of the power of the gaze as operating in a more complex and fluid relation than that of an obvious dominant–subordinate couple may remind us of Foucault's discussion of the Panopticon in *Discipline and Punish*. The panopticon is an architectural model designed for surveillence: 'around the periphery, a ring-shaped building; in the centre, a tower. The tower has large windows that open out onto the inner facing wall of the ring'.[8] The guard in the middle of the tower can thereby, at any time, watch each of the prisoners in the cells around the inside of the walled building. The effect of this spatial arrangement is to induce in the inmate an awareness of his permanent visibility, which ensures the automatic functioning of power.[9] Oppression, then, works by suggestion and by the operation of a (mis)recognition of guilt on the subject's part, rather than by the exercise of force. By analogy, Hire is constructed by the law as the subject of the legitimate voyeur's gaze. His culpability and punishment are assured not by the hands of individual agents, but by a social organization that rests upon the self-regulating power of surveillance.

The effect of this pluralization of the possession of gaze and perverse desire across the *dramatis personae* of *Monsieur Hire* is twofold. Firstly, it complicates an understanding of watching and desiring as something done by an active (masculine) subject to a passive (feminine) object; and secondly it draws attention to the ethical groundlessness of the persecution of Hire upon which the film's plot rests. *Monsieur Hire* read in this light is more comparable to a Foucaualdian critique of sexual knowledge and surveillance than an account of the gaze and sexuality explicable in Freudian terms. It is my contention, then, that Leconte's film problematizes not only the rules of the gendered gaze, as Murray and Duffy have shown, but also the straightforward conceptual mechanisms we have at our disposal to describe types of desire and relationality that rely on unequal subject–object distribution and the absolute meanings of passivity and activity.

This reading of the film illustrates the dangers of applying wholesale doctrinal feminist film criticism or a model of reading based on the psychoanalytically informed assumption that cinematic representation is always already – and only – about a shared directorial–spectatorial desire. Despite being at first glance an apparently exemplary film with which to test gendered theories of the gaze, as it engages directly with the subject-matter of desirous voyeurism, *Monsieur Hire* is much more simultaneously knowing and challenging of the discourses that name subject positions and desires than has previously been recognized. By addressing and problematizing (thematically and structurally) both the gaze and perverse sexuality, the film forces a meta-filmic and meta-theoretical engagement with the silenced ethical implications underpinning gaze theory. Put more simply, by demonstrating the moral innocence of a 'deviant' voyeur, Leconte's film invites a reflection that does not straightforwardly demonize the gaze *or* fall into easy assumptions about the inevitability of the relation between desire and oppression; sexuality and objectification. It helps us to understand by means of a visual example Foucault's contention about the workings of disciplinary power:

> the exercise of discipline presupposes a mechanism that coerces by means of observation; an apparatus in which the techniques that make it possible to see induce effects of power, and in which, conversely, the means of coercion make those on whom they are applied clearly visible.[10]

Monsieur Hire, read in this light, is a cinematic reflection on cinema's capacity to be either an apparatus that re-inscribes disciplinary mechanisms by forcing us to be complicit with certain normative viewing positions (where viewing means both gazing and holding a fixed view), or a means of revealing and debunking these ways of looking. Monsieur Hire – the character – meanwhile, is at once the specific, disciplined subject of the criminal and sexological powers, and *any* modern subject in the panoptical system Foucault describes.

Body trouble (every day)

In 'Sade, Sergeant of Sex', the *Cinématographie* interview with Gérard Dupont that appeared in 1975, Foucault was asked to comment on the representation of bodies in contemporary films such as Alexandro Jodorowsky's *El Topo* (1970) and *The Death of Maria Malibran* (*Der Tot der Maria Malibran*, Werner Schroeter, 1972). The interviewer asked him if the orgiastic or bloody representation of bodies in these films marked an ethically troubling sort of objectifying sadism. Foucault denies this vehemently. In experimental cinema such as Schroeter's, says Foucault,

> what seems new is ... the discovery-exploration of the body by means of the camera. ... It's an encounter at once calculated and aleatory between the bodies and the camera, discovering something, breaking up an

angle, a volume, a curve, following a trace a line, possibly a ripple ...
and then suddenly the body derails itself.[11]

Foucault opposes this innovative filming of the body and the effects it produces both to any cinematic adaptation of Sade, which, he says, would be a
tiresome repetitive, ritualistic spectacle of perversion (sex according to a
'disciplinary' regime), *and* to the traditional Hollywood method of filming
the woman's body, such as the spectacle of Marilyn Monroe in Billy Wilder's
Some Like it Hot (1959). Foucault thereby makes a similar point to Mulvey's
famous critique – published, coincidentally, in exactly the same year as this
interview. Foucault's assertion that Shroeter's camera breaks up our perception of the body *qua* object, such that that body-object 'derails itself' seems
to suggest that such cinema offers a representational analogy of the way
Foucault would have us *live* the body as the locus of pleasure, via a self-
regulating ethics that moves away from the regime of 'sex-desire' and in the
direction of 'bodies and pleasures'.[12] This accords a particular importance to
cinema as a space in which such experiments might be essayed.

The recent trend in French cinema for extreme corporeal representation,
discussed in Chapter 5 of this book, has been referred to as a revisiting of the
concerns of 1970s filmmakers such as Schroeter, Jodorowsky and, especially,
Nagisa Oshima, whose *Ai No Corrida/ In The Realm of the Senses* (1976) provoked
particular scandal for its portrayal of nudity, genital sex acts, and its final
scenes of fatal erotic asphyxiation. It is productive to bear in mind Foucault's
comments about the filming of the body in innovative ways, and the capacity
this has for breaking the 'carefully programmed regulation'[13] of a Sadeian
conception of sex, when considering the filmmaking of one of these directors of
corporeal excess, Claire Denis. Denis's filmic corpus can be seen as an
extended attempt to confound traditional ways of filming and viewing the
body. In films such as *Beau Travail* (1999), with its unusually lingering focus
on the male body 'in all its density';[14] and more especially in the controversial erotic–horror pastiche *Trouble Every Day* (2001), the human body is
subjected to a radical making-unfamiliar of the kind Foucault describes.

It can be argued that *Trouble Every Day* both offers a critique of the disciplinary model of sexuality described by Foucault and provides a visual
physical alternative to it. Firstly, Denis's film is aesthetically striking for the
deliberately 'clinical' qualities of both the documentary-like camerawork and
the *mise-en-scène*. There are several sequences shot in bright, white laboratories
and hospitals. These underline the film's thematic – and I will argue, ethical – concern with medical science. It is significant that the fatal pair, Coré
(Beatrice Dalle) and Shane (Vincent Gallo), are shown to suffer from homicidal
sexual appetites as a result of undergoing (deliberately vague and unspecified)
scientific experiments on the human libido. Where critic Martine Beugnet
asserts that, the film, 'shows the failure of the scientific response' to the
'ambiguous nature of the addiction suffered by her characters'.[15] I would

argue that this misses the causal relation between science and destructive abnormality hinted at in the film's logic. We know that Coré's and Shane's 'illness' occurs as a direct result of science's intervention; that the monster is *created by* the discipline that seeks to normalize and cure. Coré appears, then, as a monster created by sexual science, in a gesture that literalizes the Foucaldian assertion that science *produces* rather than *describes* or *diagnoses* pre-existing sexual abnormality, and that abnormality in fact appears as truth only by means of the processes of reiteration of authorized sexual knowledge, of which medicine is the primary modern form. Foucault tells us that 'deployments of power are directly connected to the body – to bodies, functions, physiological processes, sensations and pleasures'.[16] Through the deformation of the horror genre, and the central place accorded to the medical, Denis expands horror's scope and offers an unusual cinematic reflection on the ethics of sexual science and the medicalized gaze, in particular its construction and pathologization of the other.

Trouble Every Day plays with certain received discourses of sexual psychopathology using the lexicon of the horror film, deliberately distorted to reveal itself as doing something that is not quite parody or pastiche, but is nonetheless citational. These discourses can be traced back to the very inception of *scientia sexualis* as Foucault conceives of it, the nineteenth century which produced the 'personages' of both the homosexual and the pervert and othered them via the 'medicalization of the sexually peculiar'.[17] As Foucault also shows us, institutional discursivity does not operate singularly or from only one location or discipline. The invention of the 'sexually peculiar' in the nineteenth century pervaded literature, art, and other cultural production, as well as finding expression in the clinic. The urge of Shane and Coré to kill, tear up and eat their sexual partners is reminiscent of Emile Zola's fictional case study of a lust murderer, Jacques Lantier, in *La Bête humaine* of 1890, whose fatal urge is to destroy the female other and 'have her dead like the earth.' ('l'avoir comme la terre, morte!').[18] Significantly, alongside suspense and horror films by Kubrik and De Palma, Denis cites Jean Renoir's 1938 adaptation of Zola's novel as a source of inspiration in making *Trouble Every Day*, placing the history of sexual science at the heart of her concerns.[19] However, the deadly erotic subject-matter of *Trouble Every day* is thematized in a range of ways that could not be more different from Zola's naturalist case-study presentation of Jacques Lantier, which attempts to achieve the aims of science in novel form. This is not to say that the film does not reference the same cultural myths and discourses that *La bête humaine* aped, but to acknowledge that it references them by means of citation, exaggeration and play, rather than reverential imitation.

Trouble Every Day works, then, by literalizing the logic of certain discourses whose ideologies habitually remain tacit, and by juxtaposing them with others, in order to show up their hidden allegiances. The horror genre, from which Denis's film borrows, traditionally features one of two versions of the monster. Firstly, there is the atavistic, primitive, machine-like hunger of the zombie or vampire – most famously embodied in the figure of *Dracula* (Bram Stoker's novel of 1897), a recognizable product of a nineteenth-century cultural imaginary saturated with degeneration theory. Secondly, there is the man-made monster, the creation of science and embodiment of the danger of progress, represented as early as 1818 by Shelley in *Frankenstein*. Coré straddles the two models. She belongs as much to the pages of a nineteenth-century sexological manual such as the influential *Psychopathia sexualis* of Richard von Krafft-Ebing (1886), as the pages of Stoker and Shelley. And, as I have argued, like Frankenstein's monster, she is an aberrant creation of science. However, unlike the sexological treatment of its objects of study, the traditional gothic horror narrative does not foreground explicitly the sexuality of its monsters, which is why, according to theorist of the Gothic, Fred Botting, Freudian psychoanalytic theories of repression and unconscious fantasy have been so widely applied to this genre.[20]

Trouble Every Day undercuts the necessity for such theories as Freudian psychoanalysis, by deconstructing the supposed *underlying* meanings of the generic conventions, which are relocated at the surface of the filmic narrative. The effect of this obsession with surface and the refusal of the camera to look for meaning – even while Shane is shown pursuing a quest for truth through science – is that, to quote Douglas Morrey, 'in this film of surfaces there is no psychology'.[21] It deliberately demetaphorizes and flattens out that which, in traditional gothic, must remain at the level of symbol, constantly evoking and silencing a 'hidden meaning', a terror even worse than what surfaces. The film also foregrounds explicitly the connection between discourses of the supernatural and discourses of science. A commonsense understanding would hold that the objective, rational and positivistic aims of science and the irrational, primitive superstition of supernatural myth would be distinct, indeed opposed. However, this is not the case in the arena of sexual science, and the early texts of sexology consistently borrowed from the lexicon of myth, particularly in the construction of destructive aberrant sexualities. The infamous 'Vampire of Montparnasse', Sergeant Bertrand, a soldier who exhumed and performed acts of sex and destruction on cadavers in 1849, was tried for 'vampirism', as the medico-legal label 'necrophilia', did not at that time exist.[22] The mythical and the scientific have co-existed throughout the history of psychopathology, then, providing us with the very substance of 'sexual knowledge'.

Moreover, as Beugnet has pointed out, the vampirism of *Trouble Every Day* has unmistakably postcolonial implications, in keeping with the concerns of Denis's wider corpus. The research carried out by Léo (Alex Descas), the missing black doctor for whom Gallo's character searches, took place in French Guyana, a territory regulated and othered by colonialism much as other post-enlightenment trends, such as psychiatry, sought to regulate the socially and sexually unruly in Western cultures. And degeneration theory, a discourse contemporaneous with the heyday of colonialism, saw both the

African ethnic population and the sexually deviant European as threats to the continuation of the white European race. It is, says Foucault, 'in this (strictly historical) sense that sex is ... imbued with the death instinct' (*traversé par l'instinct de mort*).[23] As Beugnet writes 'Shane and Coré are contemporary vampires, creatures of a post-colonial era tormented by a curse brought back from a former colony'.[24] *Trouble Every Day*'s mapping of a series of citations of science and reason onto the visual and affective stuff of myth and gothic horror thus articulates a series of culturally silenced dialogues and affects an ethical resurfacing of the work of moralistic and pathologizing othering routinely performed by both health discourses and colonial discourses. It also addresses the violence central to the ideology of mainstream Hollywood cinema, as Denis herself comments:

> American cinema shows a very advanced civilization where the truth belongs to scientists and politicians. Violence in American movies is always due to the bad ones, to the others. Their violence is horrific and pernicious yet depicted as moral because the bad guys always lose in the end. I find this simplistic moral absolutely revolting.[25]

In *Trouble Every Day*, violence is one of the few things that is deliberately not one-dimensional or superficial, but ambiguous. It is not always where we would expect to find it, and is multivalently ethically troubling. Symbolic violence is seen in the results of experimental medical science, and in eroticized physical destruction. The two types of violence act upon and complexify each other. Disgust at the medical and colonial use of bodies is demetaphorized and located on and in the body.

Let us move on now to the ways in which, having critiqued forms of sexual knowledge using generic references and deformations, in ways that closely resemble Foucaldian analyses, *Trouble Every Day* films sex and the body in ways that exceed the knowable and familiar. Denis's film is constructed around a series of visual plays with texture, both organic and inorganic. Surfaces are filmed slowly and ponderously throughout, deliberately refusing the acceleration and pacing that would create suspense in a 'straight' horror film. In filming the body, the camera focuses on expanses of flesh, on genitalia, on cloth covering the body, on blood-soaked skin and shrouds made reflective and liquid, that fill the screen allowing little framing or contextualization. Morrey has written:

> the camera travels at length over the expanse of [a boy's] torso, suddenly become strange and immense: his hairs twitch and flutter like the grasses on the wasteland earlier; mysterious ridges are discovered on his body like the surface of the moon; dark moles appear like planets within this uncharted solar system, gravitating around the shocking black hole of his navel.[26]

The qualities Morey ascribes to *Trouble Every Day* demonstrate how the erotic is mobilized as an encounter with the absolute other in the film. The body here becomes an unrecognizable landscape, rather than the predictable objectification of the sexualized body as thing.

In a particularly striking sequence of *Trouble Every Day*, Coré makes love to a male victim before killing him. Her first gentle caresses to bring him pleasure and the violent, cannibalistic perverse caresses that end in murder are filmed with identical languor. The caresses are also adumbrated in a later scene in which the honeymoon couple, Shane and June (Tricia Vessey), engage in 'vanilla' sex, broken off when Gallo's character runs to the bathroom to masturbate frenziedly. Both sequences are shot with extreme close-ups on the supine bodies, and look similar, refusing the differentiation of sexual taxonomy. The camera's proximity to the bodies throws them into shadow and it is not always clear whose limbs and body parts are whose, or what the interlocked bodies are doing to each other. Only slowly and eventually, in the scene between Coré and her victim, does blood begin to appear on the boy's face, still in extreme close-up; a liquid sexual emission that is unexpected and disorienting. As his face becomes covered and distorted with the blood, the meaning of the sexual scene literally liquefies. Coré licks the blood from the dying face and body and lifts the flaps of skin she has torn open, playing with the wounds as newly made parts of the body; a male body reconfigured as open and accessible. Just as the horror conveyed by the biting and tearing up of the body, consistent with the 'theme' of cannibalism, is undercut by the beauty, indeterminacy and strangeness of the images, so the notion of unitary body-objects ripe for possession and offering automatic interpretability is confounded. The slow destruction of the idea of the body, culminating in a visually stunning scene of Coré spattering the bare white walls with her victim's blood and rubbing herself against them until her own body blends, chameleon-like, into the *mise-en-scène,* suggests the flickering of the image or the momentary disappearance of the body as object.

Rather than violence *qua* violence, there is a melting away of meaning here. The only acceleration allowed for in the sexual murder scene is the intensification of the victim's groans and cries, ambiguously expressing ecstasy or horror; competing with the eerie and insistent extra-diegetic music by the Tindersticks. Sound and image are, then, discordant and stand in contradiction to each other, making the ascription of meaning more difficult, such that it is deferred. Denis refuses to allow us to ascribe meaningful content to the scene *as it is being watched* (though we may retroactively reconstruct it in terms of familiar or conventional epistemology or as a reference to/digression from filmic genre). The caress of the camera becomes a making-strange rather than a movement towards the acquisitive familiarity of possession that can transform even the cannibal's embrace and the vampiric devouring of blood, familiar to us from the codes of horror cinema, into an erotic strangeness. If the film can be read to be providing a Foucaldian meta-critique of depth claims, such as those offered by psychoanalysis and discourses of sexual knowledge, it similarly thwarts habitual mechanisms of sexual knowing at the visceral level, accessed through spectacle. It does not only appeal to a Foucaldian ethics of the body, it enacts it.

Concluding remarks

In this chapter, I have argued that, while Foucault is seldom discussed in the context of cinema, his writings on ethics, the body, sexuality and surveillance make his corpus a key intertext with the works of recent filmmakers and film critics concerned with similar questions, dynamics and problems. The key Foucaldian idea that power – both discursive and visual – operates as a forcefield of relations, a cluster of lines of penetration at the centre of which are bodies and subjectivities, offers an insightful way of re-thinking cinematic concerns with the gendering of the gaze and the dominance of the one possessing it (as a reading of *Monsieur Hire* has shown). Moreover, the Foucaldain exhortation to move from a law-bound system of desire exemplified by pre-structuralist psychoanalytic models of sexuality to an ethical problematization of the meanings of the body as locus of pleasure and power outside of its disciplined and categorized hierarchies of meaning is given expression in recent filmmaking by Claire Denis. The chapter has shown the benefit of taking to the cinema a thinker who, while writing little on film, has produced texts that are insistently reliant on the language of visuality, sight, and space, and whose discussions of these dynamics are always informed with ethico-political energies.

Notes

1 Lemire, 'Voyeurism and the Post-War Crisis of Masculinity in *Rear Window*', 57.
2 Murray, 'Voyeurism in *Monsieur Hire*', 293.
3 Murray, 'Voyeurism in *Monsieur Hire*', 293.
4 Duffy, 'Message versus Mystery and Film Noir Borrowings in Patrice Leconte's *Monsieur Hire*', 218.
5 Duffy, 'Message versus Mystery', 219.
6 Wild, 'L'Histoire resuscitée'.
7 Foucault, *The Will to Knowledge*, 34.
8 Foucault, *Discipline and Punish*, 233.
9 Foucault, *Discipline and Punish*, 234.
10 Foucault, *Discipline and Punish*, 170.
11 Foucault, *Essential Works*, vol. 2, 225.
12 Foucault, *The Will to Knowledge*, 157.
13 Foucault, *Essential Works*, vol. 2, 225.
14 Beugnet, *Claire Denis*, 114.
15 Beugnet, *Claire Denis*, 181-2.
16 Foucault, *The Will to Knowledge*, 152.
17 Foucault, *The Will to Knowledge*, 44.

18 Zola, *La Bête humaine*, 404 (my own translation).
19 Beugnet, *Claire Denis*, 183.
20 Botting, *Gothic*.
21 Morrey, 'Textures of Terror: Claire Denis's *Trouble Every Day*'.
22 See: Vernon Rosario, *The Erotic Imagination*, 60.
23 Foucault, *The Will to Knowledge*, 156.
24 Beugnet, *Claire Denis*, 182.
25 Cited in Beugnet, *Claire Denis*, 182.
26 Morrey, 'Textures of Terror: Claire Denis's *Trouble Every Day*'.

Chapter 9

The cinematic ethics of psychoanalysis
Futurity, death drive, desire

Lisa Downing

In earlier chapters of this book, we have seen how ideas borrowed from psychoanalysis were used in the 1970s and 80s for poststructuralist feminist film theory. Laura Mulvey's canonical essay 'Visual Pleasure and Narrative Cinema' (1975), used concepts of scopophilic desire for the feminized object, and masculine identification with the onscreen protagonist, to explain the gendered and sexuate dynamics of cinematic desiring. Mulvey's work and the responses it provoked drew mainly on Lacan's early concept of the 'mirror stage', introduced in a lecture given in 1949. The mirror stage describes both a developmental stage of imaginary identity formation through which the child must pass, and a scene or stadium in which the adult will continue to play out fantasies of desired wholeness and fearful fragmentation. Early

Figure 9 Shadow of a Doubt

psychoanalytic gaze theory by Metz and Mulvey mapped the spectator's relation to the figure on the screen onto the child's relation to the mirroring parent or other object of wholeness in the figurative mirror. The work of classic cinematic editing sutures over the gaps that haunt the subject, and provides reassuring images of wholeness – masculine subjects with which to identify and shiny feminine body-objects at which to look. I attempted in the last chapter to show how Foucault's critique of power might nuance some of the assumptions of psychoanalytic gaze theory; however, this work of making-more-subtle is also already being undertaken *within* current psychoanalytically informed scholarship. Žižek, for example, has claimed that the gaze is the object, rather than the possession, of a (patriarchal) subject and, therefore, that 'when I am looking at an object, the object is already gazing at me'.[1] Joan Copjec has stated that the viewer is never the master of what he gazes at, but a divided subject of trauma, as well as a subject desiring mastery over that division.[2]

Twenty-first-century Lacanian theorists, then, have been particularly keen to highlight the schismatic and vulnerable nature of the subject as both social agent and as film spectator, and the wobbly, unstable relationship between subject and object positions that psychoanalysis proposes. They have also revisited key psychoanalytic concepts and a range of filmic texts in order to demonstrate that cinema and psychoanalysis are systems that are each capable of shedding light on the workings of the other. The title of Žižek's edited book, *Everything You Always Wanted to Know about Lacan (But Were Afraid to ask Hitchcock)* (1992), encapsulates this strategy beautifully. Žižek's work here, and in *Looking Awry: An Introduction to Jacques Lacan through Popular Culture* (1991), constitutes a politically active employment of psychoanalysis in which the workings of ideology and desire are read as appearing in and through popular culture, thereby elucidating the mechanisms of Lacanian theory and making them accessible to a wide public.

Central to Žižek's analysis is Lacan's notion of the Real as the locus of ethics. Žižek thematizes cinema, and popular culture more broadly, as offering us reflections on, and experiences of, the risk the subject takes with regard to encountering the Real of his or her desire. Films enact the temptations, dangers and lures of the Real, and also demonstrate ways in which subjects meet or fail the ethical challenge of owning up to their desire – which would mean, paradoxically, dis-owning identity, or assuming subjective destitution. Certain literary and filmic popular characters are particularly good at demonstrating the workings of this failure. The figure of the detective is Žižek's principal example of a subject who circumvents the unthinkable encounter with the ethical Real. The detective in the Sherlock Holmes mould offers rational interpretations of odd and uncanny events, Žižek claims, in order to 'break the spell they have upon us, i.e., to spare us the encounter with the Real of our desire that these scenes stage'.[3] Holmes functions as a bulwark against the circulation of libidinal desire that an anonymous murder or other mystery provokes (and one only has to think of

Basil Rathbone's beautifully controlled and carefully asexual performance in the English and US series of Sherlock Holmes films of the 1930s and 40s to gain immediate corroboration of Žižek's point).

The hard-boiled detective, on the other hand, employs a slightly different diversion tactic in classic noir narrative: he resists the femme fatale who embodies a 'promise of surplus enjoyment [that] conceals mortal danger.'[4] Libido is located away from the detective and on to the woman whose role and purpose is to tempt him in this genre. Žižek argues that the femme fatale of noir is the ultimate ethical figure. She is the woman who, having worn numerous conflicting masks of manipulation, despair, pleasure and pain, finally drops all masks when rejected by the detective, and dissolves into abjection. It is in this 'hysterical' breakdown, when her position as an object for men (or 'man's symptom' in the controversial language of the Lacanian gendered system) is finally realized, that her existence *as appearance* is replaced with an authentic *non-existence*. In assuming this 'second death', she becomes 'an object *for herself also*'.[5] The name Žižek gives to this assuming of one's object-status is 'subjectification' (as opposed to 'subjectivity'). A being is 'subjectified' via the realization that one has been an object for the other in a play of Symbolic and Imaginary forces. By leaving behind the masks that constituted oneself as that object, one accedes to an absolutely empty subject-hood. Thus, for Žižek, 'the femme fatale embodies a radical *ethical* attitude, that of "not ceding one's desire", of persisting in it to the very end when its true nature as death drive is revealed'.[6] Žižek concludes that the hard-boiled detective who rejects the femme fatale (e.g. Sam Spade (Bogart) in *The Maltese Falcon* (John Huston, 1941)) persists in a narcissistic Imaginary identity which is wholly unethical, whereas Robert Mitchum's character in *Out of the Past* (Jacques Tourneur, 1947) identifies with the femme fatale's death-driven self-unravelling and embarks on the gesture of (ethical) suicide.

This concern is picked up and developed by fellow Slovenian Alenka Zupančič in her essay on Hitchcock and suicide in Žižek's edited collection and, outside of the realm of film theory, in her philosophical work *Ethics of the Real: Kant, Lacan* (2000). Ethics, in the Lacanian sense, then, is intimately related to death drive and suicide because the challenge of the ethical is to divest oneself of the Symbolic and Imaginary traps of subjectivity (of ego), in order to enter the state of 'subjectification' – 'the gaze by which we confront the utter nullity of our narcissistic pretentions'.[7] It is for this reason that Zupančič can argue that, in the Kantian system, categorical imperatives are compromised moral acts insofar as 'they are not an "in itself" (*an sich*)'.[8] Rather they *describe* an act, they are a prescription; they remain, in short, in the Symbolic. To fulfil the category of the act, an infinite purifying is required. Zupančič claims, after Jacques-Alain Miller, that it is on the basis of the act of (literal and infinitely metaphorical) suicide that Lacan was able to found a version of the act that comes close to the elusive Kantian ideal. As has already been stated earlier in this book, Lacanian ethics is often seen as an ethics of the self, not of the other. In keeping with this, for Zupančič, suicide is the 'act' *par excellence* because 'it is always auto ... it is radically beyond the pleasure principle, and it rests on what Freud designated "the death-drive"'.[9] An ethics based on suicide as the ur-act is not, however, without philosophical problems. For Zupančič, it is problematic because it is difficult to see how it would live up to Kant's criterion of 'universality' that is necessary for a truly ethical act. For me, it is problematic primarily because it would appear to be an ethics that negates any possibility of a resistant future by founding itself in a single moment of self-loss that gets reified (Symbolized) as meaning, rather than remaining beyond signification. Thus, as an ethical act, suicide is peculiarly static.

Futurity and temporality are complex ethical concepts in post-Lacanian discourse. In *Psychoanalysis and the Future of Theory* (1993), Malcolm Bowie undertook a series of studies of the strange and tortuous ways in which psychoanalysis conceives of the future, and asked what may be the future of a discipline that conceives futurity in such a problematic way. Lacan's model of temporality is particularly ambivalent and schismatic. When considering the function of the mirror stage in his very early work, notes Bowie, Lacan 'replaces a unilinear time-scale, generated from the relation "earlier than" by a temporal dialectic, a backward and forwards scansion. Beware, he is already saying, of any metaphor that promises a steady movement from earlier to later'.[10] The mirror stage, then, in which the child glimpses that illusory wholeness which might one day be his or hers, promises a future moment of unity and self-sufficiency, but in reality this will always be subject to the threat of rupture, regression, dissolution. The subject takes one step forward, but two steps back; the Lacanian future is not a clear pathway down which we may confidently stride forward, but a trajectory riven with the very schisms that threaten to split the subject. And the ego is our illusory friend in so far as it encourages us to shore up our Imaginary identifications with wholeness, rather than give ourselves over to the truth of the emptiness, rivenness and destitution that continue to haunt us.[11]

This counter-intuitive model of futurity is not surprising given Lacan's affiliation to Freud, and Freud's complex model of the workings of Eros and Thanatos. It is in imagining the death drive that Lacan maps movement forward in the most contradictory terms, but in terms that develop and follow on from his thinking regarding how the mirror stage will shape human temporality. The Freudian death drive is a mechanism which not only pulls against the life-drive's desire for the pleasure principle but also, as the title of Freud's essay 'Beyond the Pleasure Principle' of 1920 suggests, moves in excess of it. Reaching beyond the principle of pleasure (the reduction of tension in the system to a lack of excitation), death drive reaches for nirvana (the reduction of tension to zero). It seeks absolute negation, then, but this negation is merely an exaggeration of – in excess of – the movement of the life drive. It does not oppose it, pull against it, or pull backwards; rather it *outstrips* it. Moving forward in order to achieve the abyss, it is not negation of the future; rather it is beyond – and in excess of – simple linear ideas of futurity.

In the Lacanian system, the death drive is given motility in the desire of the subject structurally incapable of satisfaction. In the always forward-flung chain of signification punctuated by gaps, which is the form desire takes for Lacan, there is no possibility of my desire in the now touching the object of my desire in its remote temporal, geographical or metaphysical location; rather desire propels me *away from* that which I seek. Desire seeks, then, its own extinction as a concomitant aim, as a result of the frustration of its aims. It is the eternally forward-flung, and always inaccessible, nature of desire that makes desire deathly. As well as embodying a force of nihilism, however, the Lacanian concept of death drive, borrowed directly from Freud, also betokens – crucially – the possibility of creativity. In *The Ethics of Psychoanalysis* (*Seminar VII, L'Ethique de la psychanalyse*, 1959–60), Lacan states: 'Freud's thought in this matter requires that what is involved be articulated as a destruction drive, given that it challenges everything that exists. But it is also a will to create from zero, a will to begin again.'[12] This is an understanding of the death drive as productive of creativity and potentiality – but distinct from a linear narrative of progress and history. In this, it has affinities with Deleuze and Guattari's notion of becoming or 'creative involution' – a movement towards something, that does not reproduce *à la* Oedipus but invents *ex nihilo* and without end point.

The complex and paradoxical Lacanian understanding of temporality can be particularly fruitful for a study of film and filmic discourse. In many ways film is a particularly pertinent medium to consider in any discussion of a complexified psychoanalytic concept of futurity in and through art. Firstly, as the technologically most complex and the historically latest of the art forms, originating at approximately the same time as psychoanalysis, discourses of progress and technological advancement cluster around discussions of cinema. To illustrate this, we may remember Sartre's infamous metaphorical critique of Foucault's *The Order of Things*. Sartre claimed that in looking at history as a constellation rather than a chronology, Foucault was guilty of replacing cinema with the magic lantern.[13] Cinema here, then, stands for progress. Secondly, as a medium that moves temporally – as a medium whose form is intimately bound up with movement and with duration – cinema, like music and performance (and *unlike* a painting), engages problematically with questions of time in its very substance. For Jean Epstein in the 1940s, film marked 'the transmutation of the discontinuous into the continuous'.[14] Film, then, may be figured as bearing the problematic weight of representing the future of the arts – and, paradoxically and relevantly, in conservative discourses of artistic values – of spelling the dumbing-down or the death of high art. It stands in both for future as creative potentiality and the future as doom. The problematic concept of futurity and its relationship with death-driven ethics in psychoanalytic theory, in cinematic representation, and in discourses about the nature of the cinema, will be discussed in more detail in the rest of this chapter via a reading of Lee Edelman's *No Future: Queer Theory and the Death Drive* (2004) and a consideration of some of the Hitchcock films that psychoanalytic theorists of cinema – Žižek, Zupančič and Edelman – prize so highly as embodiments of Lacanian ethics.

Ethics without a future?

If the idea of 'the future' offers the possibility of critical inventiveness and doom both, certain recent Lacanian critics have focused on what happens when 'futurity' becomes reified as a normative ideology. Edelman's book argues that contemporary culture (by which he really means Anglo-American rather than Continental European or Eastern cultures) operates under the sway of the tyranny of 'reproductive futurity' – a normalizing discourse according to which we must postpone our pursuit of desire in the present for the sake of a putative future embodied in the institution of reproduction and the figure of the Child. Edelman posits the principles of 'queer' and 'the death drive' as on the side of a radical ethics, in opposition to reproductive futurity. However, rather than tarrying with a model of the death drive as that which instates the possibility of creative and unforeseen outcomes at the price of social norms, Edelman's is a radically nihilistic refutation of the future – any future – in the name of an anti-social refusal to engage in reproductive dynamics.

The figure that Edelman evokes to embody this position of radical anti-social refusal is the *sinthom*osexual. '*Sinthom*osexual' is a neologism, punning on Lacan's figure of the *sinthome* (homophonically 'symptom' and 'saint man'), a subject constituted through the individualized negotiation of the orders of the Symbolic, Imaginary and Real, but resisting total translation into Symbolic meaning. It is a subject fixated by its own *jouissance*, where *jouissance* designates an excess of pleasure akin to the death drive rather than any tame concept of 'enjoyment'.[15] The *sinthome* is fused with the homosexual in Edelman's pun, in the interests of harnessing for politically recuperative purposes, the homophobic accusations of sterility and antisociality levelled by right-wing commentators at non-normative sexualities and subjectivities.

The ethical status of *sinthom*osexuality is best illustrated for Edelman (after Žižek) by the cinema of Hitchcock. Edelman uses the example of a sequence in *North by Northwest* (1959), in which Leonard (Martin Landau), rather than saving Roger Thornhill (a hapless Cary Grant), who is dangling from a carved face on Mount Rushmore, allows him to plunge into the abyss. Leonard refuses the lure of the external or social humanitarian imperative, marked for us by the faciality of the Mount Rushmore physiognomies. He negates the futurity promised by the heterosexual couple Cary Grant and Eva Marie Saint, in thrall to the Real of his desire. This moment, explains Edelman, is properly ethical in the Lacanian sense, since guilt for Lacan in Seminar VII is not explained by the anxiety of a person having failed to obey the rules of morality, sociality or the law, but by a subject refusing to obey the command of their (unconscious) desire (a deliberate and strategic response to, and rejection of, the Christian – especially Catholic – ethics of guilt). Psychoanalysis is not in the service of social 'good', but in pursuit of the zero degree of truth. Only obedience to the law of desire, whose nature remains occluded to us (that is in the unconscious and the Real), constitutes an ethical act. That ethics in this extreme sense is construed to stand in determined opposition to the Levinasian ethics of the other is hinted at by the over-determined faciality of Mount Rushmore.

Indeed, such extreme refusals of the future in the name of an anti-humanist ethics may move us into the post-psychological or the posthuman (about which more in the next chapter). It is in Hitchcock's *The Birds* (1963) that the figure of impossibly ethical *sinthom*osexuality is found for Edelman outside of a human subject and in that avian collective that terrorizes the small community of Bodega Bay, preying particularly on children, those prized ciphers of the values of the future. Žižek has already discussed *The Birds* at some length as a film that is concerned with the disruption of phallic logic and heterosexual coupledom. The birds who attack are 'the stain [that] materializes the *maternal superego*',[16] as Mitch Brenner's mother seems to stand between the young couple (Rod Taylor and Tippi Hedren) and prevent their patriarchally sanctioned heterosexual union. The all-too-live avians of *The Birds* echo an earlier Hitchcockian reference to birds that are dead and stuffed – the output of mother-obsessed Norman Bates's taxidermic hobby in *Psycho* (1960), rhyming with a mother who is also dead and stuffed, but whose influence is none the less strong for that. For Žižek, then, birds mark the trace of the Real and its disruption of well-behaved social organization. They are 'the incarnation of a fundamental disorder in family relationships – the father is absent, the function of the pacifying law … is suspended and that vacuum is filled by the "irrational" maternal superego, arbitrary, wicked, blocking "normal" sexual relationship'.[17]

Edelman's critique pursues a very similar logic along slightly different conceptual lines. *The Birds* for Edelman is neither about the return of the maternal superego, nor about the importance of leaving nature alone (as Hitchcock glibly claimed on the occasion of the film's release). Rather, the birds are embodiments of queerness (or *sinthom*osexuality), where this stands (in the same place as Žižek's maternal superego) as a guardian of death-driven perversity against the ordered tyranny of 'family values' and the father's law. Edelman writes,

> *The Birds* comes to roost with a skittish and volatile energy, on a perch from which it seems to brood – dispassionately, inhumanly – on the gap opened up within nature by something inherently contra naturam: the death drive that haunts the Symbolic with its excess of jouissance and finds its figural expression in *sinthom*osexuality.[18]

The Birds, Edelman claims, has nothing to do with nature. Rather it is a meditation on the mediation of the unnatural – the technological mediation of cinema and an inhuman, machine-like principle of vengeance that visits upon heterosexual coupledom (represented by Mitch Brenner and Melanie Daniels), and upon reproductive figurality.

Edelman argues that Hitchcock is a director particularly attuned to the mechanistic nature of cinema and desire. He writes: 'the machinery of cinema envisioned here turns audience members into machines themselves, receptacles for stimuli' and 'Hitchcock's fantasy speaks less to his futuristic anticipation of what cinema might become than to his actual understanding of what cinema always already is.'[19] Hitchcock's cinema, then, taps into the Real of desire that programmes anti-humanistic outcomes in place of endorsement of the future. It is significant that in the seminar of 12 January 1955, *Freud, Hegel and the Machine*, Lacan insisted on the consummately modern nature of Freud's revelation/conception of death drive. 'Energy is a notion that could only appear at the moment when there are machines', says Lacan.[20] It was necessary for the locomotive engine to have been invented for Freud to characterize the principle of the death drive, which is impersonal, machine-like, and figured in a language of hydraulic pressure and energetic releases. The fact that, as has already been stated, cinema is the art form that has most embraced and harnessed the power of technology may make it susceptible to create the most mechanical and machine-like responses in the viewer. Cinema may force us to negotiate between impersonal and subjective responses, drawing attention to the constant oscillation between the two – Lacan's essential subjective misrecognition. This argument does not appear in Edelman's book, but can be adduced and developed from his analyses of Hitchcock's anti-humanistic ethical scenarios. The characteristic of impersonality so key to Lacan's idiosyncratic concept of desire and the drive, however, also forms the cornerstone of a serious critique of Edelman's project.

While admiring the power of Edelman's anti-normative ethical polemic, I would argue that his absolute refusal of any concept of the future in the name of death-driven *sinthom*osexuality betokens a misreading of Lacan's concept of the drive and of time. As we have seen, the future does not speak of a simple teleology of progress in Lacan – it is infinitely more riven with doubling, returns, regression and interruptions. It is hard to map this seamlessly onto the (undeniably prevalent and troublingly seldom-deconstructed) contemporary political discourse of reproductive futurity that Edelman describes. For political ideology is famously good – in its discursive and cinematic modes both – at suturing over its contradictions and appearing as a truth. Rather than attempting to unpick the stitches holding together reproductive futurity in an illusory wholeness, Edelman takes on an equally totalizing attack in the name of *sinthom*osexuality and the death drive.

This criticism of Edelman's use of death-drive theory is parallel to that made by Tim Dean in his essay 'An Impossible Embrace: Queerness, Futurity and the Death Drive' (2008). Dean takes Edelman to task here for making the death drive into something that we can consciously embrace or reject – a principle with which we can identify. (This is a particularly serious lapse in a work that is profoundly anti-identitarian and anti-identificatory in so many ways. For, as we have seen, Edelman counsels against the lure of compassion and argues that Hitchcock's cinema resists spectatorial identification and programmes machine-like responses in the viewer.) Dean rightly points out that Freudian 'drive' (*Trieb*) is characterized by never becoming conscious and by having no proper object, as Freud shows in 'Instincts and their Vicissitudes' (1915). Dean asserts that:

> if a drive can never become an object of consciousness, it follows that it can never be embraced or deployed for political purposes. This does not mean that drives have nothing to do with political processes. It does mean, however, that any proposal about strategically embracing the death drive must be based on a fundamental misprision or a sleight of hand.[21]

The nature of Freudian drive, Dean points out, is both to be constant and partial. Drives operate by exerting pressure over wishes and attachments, but cannot be seen to operate monolithically since all drives are partial drives (inaccurately translated by Strachey as 'component instincts'). 'The drive's partiality also makes clear why it cannot be embodied, identified with or embraced', Dean says.[22] He reformulates the value of Lacanian insights for Edelman's desire to disrupt reproductive futurity differently:

> What makes the psychoanalytic, as opposed to psychological – notion of the unconscious so challenging and yet so fruitful is its suggestion that this dimension of subjectivity possesses a virtually limitless capacity for displacement and condensation, but no capacity for synthesis or any grasp of finitude.[23]

It is the unconscious's refusal of totalizing narratives – such as Freud's passionate fiction of Oedipus, or the ideology of reproductive futurity – that precisely ensures their impossibility as totalitarian. Resistance will be contained within them rather than coming from an external point of resistance that may be characterized 'death drive'. The ideology of reproductive futurity, then, should be analyzed as carrying within it its own points of disruption, its own death drive.

The death drive which so fascinates Edelman, after Žižek and others, has been analyzed as operating within the mechanism of cinematic narrative as both the driving force, and the rupturing principle, of 'the social' that film models. Following Žižek and Edelman down through the Hitchcockian corpus in search of examples, one thinks obviously of the well-documented eruption of the birds in Bodega Bay, but equally, we can draw on other figures that function similarly, but problematize Edelman's assumption that the ethical real, embodied in a *sinthom*osexual, manages to negate the future entirely in Hitchcock's cinema. In *Rope* (1948), the murderous homoerotic pair (Farley Granger and John Dall) intervene directly in reproductive futurity; preventing a marriage by strangling the fiancé and then hosting a party around the trunk in which the corpse is hidden. This innovatively shot film, famously filmed with only two visible cuts in the 80-minute spectacle and the action unfolding in real time, enacts the idea of time having been meddled with, slowed down; the future put on hold by the workings of the death-driven pair. However, the film's ending does not allow for the triumph of the antisocial. Order is restored, along with the sense of an impending future punishment as the shots of the apartment are illuminated by a flashing red light, which we assume to come from a patrol car outside, while the confession of the murderous pair to their former idol and schoolmaster, Rupert Cadell (James Stewart) is masked by the sound of a police siren that progressively becomes louder, time speeding up again as their period of freedom runs out.

Similarly, *Shadow of a Doubt* (1943), stages the arrival of beloved 'Uncle Charlie' (Joseph Cotten) into the home of a family so perfect as to be nauseating (as ironically referenced in the script, when the mother says smugly to the detective on the trail of Uncle Charlie, who is posing as a census taker to gain access to the house, 'this *is* a nice family'). Charlie is the 'Merry Widow Murderer', a psychopathic strangler of rich women, wanted in several states and taking refuge with his gullible sister's family in their small town home. That the threat of the antisocial lurks in the bosom of the social, that the all-American family is almost destroyed by the avuncular presence that it welcomes in, is beyond doubt. Yet Uncle Charlie is ultimately unmasked and betrayed by his most devoted fan, young Charlie, the niece who has been named after him (Teresa Wright) and whose visit she predicts in the opening sequence. The potent affective, and almost incestuous, bond between them is manipulated such that Uncle Charlie must be the agent of young Charlie's loss of innocence, while young Charlie will inadvertently cause her uncle's death. In their struggle, on a speeding train, as the escaping murderer tries to push his niece out of the door and onto the rails, it is he who will tumble onto the tracks and die; while young Charlie, embodiment of hope for the future, is shown at the film's close in happy coupledom with the handsome young detective (Macdonald Carey).

In my third and final example, *Rebecca* (1940), the *sinthom*osexual figure is a dual feminine force. The obsessive housekeeper, Mrs Danvers (Judith Anderson), refuses to allow the ghost of her perverse and wilful same-sex love-object to be laid to rest by the demure and well-behaved 'new' Mrs De Winter (Joan Fontaine); while the eponymous Rebecca, a character already dead when the narrative begins, exerts a disruptive power from beyond the grave on the new couple. When her body is washed up on the shore, and what was assumed to be an accidental death or a suicide appears to be murder, Rebecca functions as a R/real threat to the new couple's marital happiness. When Rebecca fails to have her posthumous revenge on de Winter (Laurence Olivier), in the form of his conviction for her murder (a murder that remains a textual possibility in du Maurier's more morally ambiguous novel, but that is absolutely negated in the film adaptation, which demonizes Rebecca and ascribes virtue to de Winter, perhaps owing to the demands of Olivier's star persona), Danvers will act as retributive force. Her punishment on de Winter comes in the form of destruction of his patriarchal, aristocratic power: she burns down his ancestral home of Manderley. The closing shots of the film are of the house ablaze, with the silhouetted figure of Danvers flitting from room to room, being consumed by the flames fanned into life by her *sinthom*osexual thanatic passion.

In each of the films briefly discussed above, the agents of the ethical death drive – all sexually ambiguous, dissident characters – do not negate the future entirely. Rather, they fall prey to capture, accidental death while attempting murder, and self-inflicted death in the burning of Manderley. However, the power of the disruptive force of the Real embodied by a dissident social subject fractures ideology and propels us to question the status quo of social structures in all of the films cited. And in each case the agent of the Real wreaks visible and lasting Symbolic damage – the chaos in Bodega Bay in *The Birds*, the murder of a young man in *Rope*, the death of innocence and filial love in *Shadow of a Doubt*, and the gutted, flame-destroyed remains of Manderley in *Rebecca*. In each case, then, a change has been wrought, but the death drive has been activated from within the socially sanctioned sphere: the family, the home, the marital bedchamber. The trajectory of the narrative future is radically altered by the force of the anti-social ethical in Hitchcock, but the social structures modelled do not shatter and give, leaving only the gaping abyss of the Real. An application of psychoanalytic ethical death-drive theory for film, then, may be one that illustrates for us how certain cinematic narratives allow, at certain moments in their diegesis, for 'other' energies (other futures?) to emerge from the transformation or deformation of normative ideologies when their dark dialectical underbelly, to use a Žižekian metaphor, is temporarily exposed.

Some concluding remarks

Some filmmaking practices may enact the idea of future as partial, fractured and without having a fixed aim or being in service to a normalizing narrative in less violent ways than in the Hitchcock films to which I have referred above. Towards the close of Rossellini's *Journey to Italy* (1953), the heterosexual couple, Alex and Katherine, are reunited after a series of perilous adventures involving near death (metaphorically occupying the position of the dangling couple of Cary Grant and Eva Marie Saint in *North by Northwest*), and their survival is celebrated in a classic cinematic kiss. However, this is not allowed by Rossellini to have the status of closure. The camera does not fix or move for a close-up. It is not more interested in this tableau than in the crowds moving through the streets, and the film continues to meander, panning over them. Having evaded danger, the couple are not allowed a fixed ending that would mark either happiness or death as stasis. As Rossellini himself puts it in an interview cited by Žižek:

> There is a turning point in every human experience in life which isn't the end of the experience or of the man, but a turning point. My finales are turning points. Then it begins again. But as for what it is that begins, I don't know.[24]

This example of the inconclusive conclusion of *Journey to Italy* is taken from Laura Mulvey's latest book, *Death 24x a Second: Stillness and the Moving Image* (2006). Here Mulvey argues that film, particularly in its most recent, digitalized form, does something significant with our understanding of time. The disruption of linearity effectuated in editing processes and in new viewing practices (such as pausing a video during a home viewing), draw our attention to the at once static and moving, at once stilled and forward-flung nature of the filmic (and we may be aware here of a parallel with the model of Lacan's death drive that underpinned the logic of Mulvey's book). And just as the death drive's jarring properties may be ethically creative as well as death-bound, this interrupted watching, what Mulvey calls 'delayed cinema', creates new meanings regarding the relationship between recording time, viewing time and narrative time. Where the relationship between photographic art and cinema has commonly been described as the giving of life and movement to dead things, so Mulvey argues that a fresh awareness of death as a new form of creativity is filtering into cinematic production through digital and video technology, enhancing the qualities that editing have always possessed to still as well as to move, and to insist on the perpetual and unresolvable relationship between mobility and stasis.

If 'the future' can be imagined through a psychoanalytic lens as plural, disruptive and creative, rather than linear, normative and reproductive, then film and Lacanian psychoanalysis may well be the future of ethical thinking. Edelman challenges us to say 'no' to 'the future' by saying 'yes' to the death drive. However, we have seen that if he had attended more closely to the Freudian and Lacanian texts of the death drive which constitute it as on the side of a futurity that is never recuperable for single-minded or totalitarian aims, in a model in which temporality is anything but simple, that opposition would not appear so clear-cut – indeed, it would appear as a tautology. Tension is internal, not external to the unconscious drives that move us through time and space. Psychoanalytic theory's and film's ethical futures may well be understood as modes of resistance to, and re-imaginings of, simple conceptions of temporality and the too-simple modes of subjectivity and relationality that appear to accompany them.

Notes

1 Žižek, 'Looking Awry', 530.
2 Copjec, 'The Orthopsychic Subject', 437–55.
3 Žižek, *Looking Awry: An Introduction to Jacques Lacan Through Popular Culture*, 62.
4 Žižek, *Looking Awry: An Introduction to Jacques Lacan Through Popular Culture*, 63.
5 Žižek, *Looking Awry: An Introduction to Jacques Lacan Through Popular Culture*, 64.
6 Žižek, *Looking Awry: An Introduction to Jacques Lacan Through Popular Culture*, 63.
7 Žižek, *Looking Awry: An Introduction to Jacques Lacan Through Popular Culture*, 64.
8 Zupančič, 'A Perfect Place to Die', 92.
9 Zupančič, 'A Perfect Place to Die', 93.
10 Bowie, *Psychoanalysis and the Future of Theory*, 25.
11 It is to this extent that 'getting well' in a Lacanian analysis is marked by the very opposite of the strengthening of the ego-defences that would mark the success of an analysis carried out in ego psychology. For a Lacanian, the ego must be progressively stripped away to allow the subject access to unconscious desire (the Real) without slipping wholly into the realm of psychosis, which the Real presages.
12 Lacan, *The Seminar of Jacques Lacan, Book VII: The Ethics of Psychoanalysis*, 212–13.
13 Sartre, 'Jean-Paul Sartre répond', 87 (my own translation).
14 Epstein, 'Magnification and Other Writings', 23.
15 Edelman, *No Future: Queer Theory and The Death Drive*, 35–36.
16 Žižek, *Looking Awry: An Introduction to Jacques Lacan Through Popular Culture*, 97.
17 Žižek, *Looking Awry: An Introduction to Jacques Lacan Through Popular Culture*, 99.
18 Edelman, *No Future: Queer Theory and The Death Drive*, 119.
19 Edelman, *No Future: Queer Theory and The Death Drive*, 81.
20 Lacan, 'Freud, Hegel and the Machine', 69.
21 Dean, 'An Impossible Embrace', 31.
22 Dean, 'An Impossible Embrace' 134.
23 Dean, 'An Impossible Embrace' 134.
24 Žižek, *Enjoy Your Symptom!*, 42–43.

Chapter 10

What if we are post-ethical?
Postmodernism's ethics and aesthetics

Lisa Downing

Postmodernism

Much debate surrounding postmodernism focuses on the question of whether this aesthetic and philosophical mode is capable of having an ethical dimension. Does postmodern thinking, producing, reading, viewing (etc.) presuppose an attitude that encourages ethical indifference, apathy and a concern with the 'superficial' rather than the 'profound'? Does it, in short, usher in 'the demise of the ethical'?[1] In an essay on the history of the ethics of cultural studies, Slack and Whitt argue along just these lines, as they see the turn to postmodernism as 'the loss of criteria for moral judgement'[2] and as having 'serious and disturbing implications for a politics and ethics'.[3] Such assessments follow Jean Baudrillard's speculations on the postmodern condition, which are often accused of a spirit of apathy and indifference. For Baudrillard, in *America* (1986), the Californian desert is the best metaphor with which to describe postmodernism. It is, he claims, a cultural 'monument valley', a place where nature and *simulacra* exist side by side. The desert represents the site of the same, the elimination of difference and texture. Baudrillard states that: 'culture has to be a desert so that everything can be equal and shine out in the same supernatural form.'[4] For Baudrillard,

Figure 10   Kill Bill vol. 2

postmodernity is that cultural state in which nothing is real; instead everything is hyper-real. In such a climate, it has been argued, catastrophe can become banal. Television, film and the internet proliferate a non-stop stream of scenes of atrocity, alternating footage of massacre, nuclear warfare and genocide with the designer violence endemic to popular entertainment. Images of violence no longer ring the warning bell of any second coming, but create instead the effect of the numbing repetition of the same. One cannot but lack all conviction. This has been termed 'the atrocity of the consensual'.[5]

It is, however, also possible to argue the very opposite. We might propose instead that postmodernism, with its commitment to a questioning of authority, hierarchy and the official 'meta narratives' or 'grand narratives' of history (as Jean-François Lyotard calls them in *The Postmodern Condition*, 1979), is in fact the site of tantalizing and plural ethical alternatives to the universalizing (straight, white, masculine, middle-class and hetero-patriarchal) discourses of modernism. A book-length work devoted to the thorny question of postmodern ethics is Zygmunt Bauman's study of that name. By bringing currents of postmodern thought to bear on ethical philosophy, Bauman has contributed to the possibility of rethinking postmodernism in ethical terms, and vice versa. He argues that rather than *abandoning* all interest in 'modern' moral questions (human rights, social justice, balancing the needs of the individual and the collective), as a radical antihumanist thinker such as Alain Badiou would propose, a postmodern ethics may instead approach these very same questions in a new way. Postmodern ethics, according to Bauman, should show how 'modern societies practise moral parochialism under the mask of promoting universal ethics'.[6] Modernism, rather than postmodernism, becomes ethically suspect as an epistemology in Bauman's reading, and he suggests that an ethics *and* a moral code proper to our age might emerge as a result of a properly postmodern questioning of assumptions.

Taking our cue from Bauman's notion that postmodernism might be a properly ethical phenomenon if it involves interrogating the potentially altericidal absolutes of universalism, this chapter will consider both the ethics of postmodern filmmaking on the one hand, and ways of thinking about postmodernism in a way that is ethical, on the other. It will ask whether postmodern thought, in combination with the postmodern filmic aesthetic, can suggest ways of transcending the ethical *impasse* of more positivistic moral theories and didactic images. The mobilization of ideology in postmodernism may go hand in hand with the coming-into-being of an ethical mode of viewing appropriate to our *Zeitgeist*.

Killing modernism: Tarantino's *Kill Bill* Vols 1 and 2

Tarantino is one of the first names to come to mind when considering postmodernism and cinema, given that his aesthetic is often felt to exemplify postmodern filmmaking. Writing in *The Guardian*, one critic claimed that:

Tarantino represents the final triumph of postmodernism, which is to empty the artwork of all content, thus avoiding its capacity to do anything except helplessly represent our agonies ... Only in this age could a writer as talented as Tarantino produce artworks so vacuous, so entirely stripped of any politics, metaphysics, or moral interest.[7]

Yet, as suggested above, the association of the postmodern aesthetic with moral vacuity is by no means obvious or uncontested. Indeed, Fred Botting and Scott Wilson's *The Tarantinian Ethics* (2001) – one of the few full-length works dedicated to film and ethics – argues for Tarantino as an ethical director par excellence. The book claims, via a primarily psychoanalytic model of radical ethics as pure desire (as described in my previous chapter), that Tarantino 'put desire back into the process of movie-making ... where that desire is the desire of an Other that can be configured as a "data base of thousands of movies"'.[8] The ethical desire of a Tarantino film for Botting and Wilson lies in its going '[b]eyond the pleasures offered by the familiarity of cinema's generic conventions, themes, tropes and thrills' and aiming for 'something more'.[9] An artwork 'emptied of content' – the marker of the amoral in the *Guardian* journalist's account – is the space of the postmodern ethic for Botting and Wilson. The idea that a Tarantino film is an archive or database of references may remind us of Baudrillard's 'monument valley', as well as the concept of 'archive' in Derrida's sense, as introduced in *Archive Fever* (1995). Botting and Wilson remind us that, for Derrida, every act of archivization (memorialization; preservation for posterity) necessitates the 'violence' of leaving something out, 'some excision, repression or omission on which it is founded'.[10] On the basis of this, the linguistic pun found in the fact that Tarantino indulged his cinephilia and enlarged his bank of cinematic references not at film school, but by working in a video store named 'Video Archives' gain significance. The idea of *plural* archives excludes the strictly Derridean meaning of the archive as an exclusive *singularity*. This allusion thereby draws attention to the fact of Tarantino's foundational principle of the democratization of generic borrowing across filmic codes. Tarantino's ethical archive of codes and images in fact becomes the opposite of the Derridean archive in its refusal to privilege high art over any other form of representation; to exclude certain images on the grounds of elitism or in thrall to Western traditions. Botting and Wilson continue – drawing on and paraphrasing an interview with Gerald Martinez, that:

Tarantino refused to judge or classify films according to some external criteria of taste, aesthetics, moral or utilitarian value, but instead valued them according to what he perceived as their intrinsic singularity: a film need only be 'true to itself'. That does not mean 'true to its genre' or true to its 'time' or its 'purpose' or its stated 'aims and objectives'. It means, simply, 'true to itself'.[11]

As Tarantino's films are deliberately, perversely, generic collages, we might term this aesthetic principle a postmodern ethic of filmmaking, where 'true to itself' would mean the very opposite of true to 'meta-narratives' such as genre or history. Botting and Wilson argue that it means, in a strictly Lacanian sense, 'true to its desire in relation to the Other',[12] however, I would contend that the postmodern work of interrogation, as spelled out by Bauman, is at least as much a part of Tarantino's project as that of expressing the radical ethics of the real of desire as theorized by post-Lacanians. Tarantino's works strive to be true to the principle of shattering modern discursive certainties. Botting and Wilson's book was published before Tarantino made his pair of films *Kill Bill* Vols 1 and 2, in 2003 and 2004, respectively. *Kill Bill* employs an exaggerated postmodern strategy, borrowing from a series of representational modes including the cartoon aesthetic. The main character played by Uma Thurman is based on the eponymous comic strip character of *The Bride*, and the film moves into animated form in the sequence recounting the childhood of O-Ren Ishii (Lucy Liu); Samurai Japanese cinema (as referenced explicitly and comedically in the fact that The Bride's and Bill's young daughter's favourite film is the violent *Shogun Assassin*); the western; the revenge movie; and the kung fu film. In what follows, I will discuss *Kill Bill* Vols 1 and 2 in the light of Tarantino's ethical/aesthetic quest to make films that are 'true to themselves', rather than faithful to a generic model and give a critical account of both the richness and limitations of that project.

Much media attention focused on the violence portrayed in *Kill Bill* – such as the spectacularly bloody battle between The Bride and O-Ren Ishii's hoards of Samurai fighters or The Bride's plucking out of the one remaining eye of Elle Driver (Daryl Hannah) – and what the audience's reception of this violence might say about the culture that produces and consumes it. As Graham Barfield put it in an online review, 'The instant cult cachet of *Kill Bill* [can be] taken as an indicator of a sick society'.[13] He cites *Guardian* columnist Jonathan Freedland, who claimed that whereas the televized death of a soldier would repel us, 'when the victim wears lipstick and the killer is Uma Thurman, we pay just to get a look'.[14] Leaving aside the whole thorny issue (discussed in Chapter 5) that copycat violence as a result of viewing violent or sexual spectacles is unproven and highly contentious, such arguments that engage with the repercussions of the violence of *Kill Bill* on the viewer ignore the specific effects of the postmodern aesthetic. For *Kill Bill* does not represent real-world violence, rather it cites aesthetic codes of violence, drawing attention to the constructed nature of cinematic and other forms of representation. Tarantino does not aim in *Kill Bill* to be mimetic of real life, then, but to be self-consciously mimetic of traditions of representation in such a way as to tamper with, rather than elicit, the audience's pleasure and complicity.

Tarantino employs numerous techniques to break the audience's capacity to identify with the spectacle or understand it in a linear fashion. For example, the suspense we would expect in a revenge film is undercut by the non-chronological structure of the narrative. In the early sequence in Vol. 1, when The Bride, who has just killed Vernita Green (Vivica A. Fox), sits in her car consulting her hit list, we see that O-Ren Ishii's name is already struck off the list, suggesting that Liu's character is the first to be killed in the time of the diegesis. However, in the time of our viewing, we don't see this death until much later – at the end of Vol. 1. The very long (30-minute) fight scene with Ishii's army is thus not allowed to be about our wondering *what* will happen. By the time it comes, we already know the outcome as Ishii's death was inscribed on The Bride's list. This thwarting of our expectation of, and desire for, narrative suspense defuses the generic convention and wrong foots us, suggesting an ethical as well as purely aesthetic effect.

However, it is not clear that *Kill Bill* succeeds entirely in escaping traditional or conventional codes of spectatorship and audience engagement. Remembering the analyses undertaken in the previous chapter of the ethics of the death drive, and more particularly Edelman's refusal of reproductive futurity, we may argue that where Tarantino fails in his project of playing with and emptying out the codes of violence in a postmodern mode is in the centrality of the figure of the child and the emotional response this figure evokes as a symbol of redemption. Children effectively frame and give shape to the otherwise disjointed, temporally non-linear narrative of *Kill Bill*, from the opening sequence, shot in black and white, when we hear The Bride – bruised, supine and bleeding – gasp to Bill, on the point of shooting her, 'It's your ba-' (the second syllable '-by' cut off by the sound of gunshot). In the early scene of The Bride's encounter with Vernita Green, it is Vernita's daughter Nikki who is the catalyst for The Bride breaking off her attack on Vernita, stating that she has no wish to kill a mother in front of her child. This is a conceit that we will see echoed in a flashback towards the end of Vol. 2, when Uma Thurman's character, who has just found out that she is pregnant, persuades another hit-woman who comes to her hotel room not to kill her as she is carrying an unborn child. Finally, the meaning of the ending of *Kill Bill* is entirely dependent upon the idea of the redemptive power of motherhood. When The Bride arrives at Bill's house to do as the title suggests, it is the revelation that her daughter has survived after all, and has been raised by Bill, that 'elevates' The Bride from postmodern action-figure-made-flesh to psychologically recognizable and conventionally sympathetic archetype – the embodiment of maternal love. And in the closing credits, this idea is inscribed on the surface of the film as we see a list of the aliases of each of the 'Deadly Viper Assassination Squad'. Thurman's character's monikers are Beatrix Kiddo, The Bride, Black Mamba, and finally – and thereby definingly – 'Mommy'.

I would argue that when The Bride's revenge on the film's eponymous anti-hero is revealed as motivated principally by the need to safeguard and reclaim her child, the film becomes something other than a journey through a series of cultural filmic landscapes (a 'monument valley' or 'series of archives'). Tarantino risks undermining his project of postmodern pastiche by the prevalence of the sentimental discourse of maternity, which – unlike all the other gendered, ideological, aesthetic discourses presented in the films – does not seem to operate at the level of surface and to be immediately relativized by juxtaposition with other discourses. Instead, it is given the weight of a transcendental truth narrative. Uma Thurman's character's morality is restored – despite her having been a violent hit-woman – in this ending, because her (inappropriately 'masculine') violent agency is justified by her maternal love for her daughter (making her safely 'feminine' again, and therefore recognizable and traditional). What does this do to the ideas of Tarantino's cinema as a cinema of postmodern truth (in the sense discussed above)? Firstly, if the 'singular truth' of a Tarantino film lies in its authentic commitment to its own project of relativizing different codes and aesthetics by juxtaposing them at the surface of the film, then the theme of maternity in *Kill Bill* risks undoing this sense of 'truth'. The iconic mother-and-child image is not merely one in a series of references to grand narratives or generic traditions that cancel each other out, but rather it demands to be understood as bringing closure both to the narrative itself *and* to the game of citations that has previously offered an alternative to the modern morality stories such as are found in the original versions of the genres cited.

Secondly, it is possible to imagine the trajectory of Uma Thurman's character for much of *Kill Bill* as that of a subject of truth as discussed by Badiou in his version of an alternative to both modern and postmodern ethical philosophy. In her relentless search for those she must kill, and her patient, single-minded pursuit of the means to kill them (she waits 30 days for the Samurai sword that will decapitate O-Ren Ishii to be crafted by a master of the art, who had sworn never to make another sword), The Bride resembles that 'militant' of the truth described by Badiou whose motivating maxim is 'keep going!'.[15] The embodiment of ethics for Badiou is that subject whose truth is not grounded in a Levinasian ethics of the other, nor in a conception of 'human rights' more broadly, but in a subjective fidelity that strives 'through its own fidelity to truths to ward off Evil'.[16] If Badiou's conception of ethics – like Žižek's – lies in radical fidelity to the truth of one's own desire (though Badiou does not use 'desire' as a central concept), the capitulation to the lure of '"ethical" ideology', seen in 'the victimary conception of Man', 'shapeless "democratism"' and 'cultural relativism', spells the downfall of truth.[17] The discourse of maternity might well appear in a comprehensive list of modernity's 'ethical ideologies' or conceptions of ethics that rely, according to Badiou, on a humanitarian conservatism. Tarantino retains maternity as the one grand narrative that can pull his story back from being a meditation on surfaces. The film does not shatter the meaning-making system which associates female reproductive capacity with Madonna-esque virtue. If it did this, Tarantino's ending wouldn't work as redemptive any more, because it wouldn't tap into the shared cultural values which laud the maternal ethics of care. The very thing that, in conventional terms, might be thought to reveal – finally – a sense of an ethical (or at least moral) dimension to the film, can alternatively be read through the lens of postmodern ethics to *negate* the film's ethical project of expressing its desire to cite ad infinitum, taking no one position, shoring up no comforting modern narrative of morality. It sacrifices its drive towards 'truth' on the altar of sentimentality.

Posthumanism: *Alien(s)* and alterity

A related strand of thought to the postmodern, the posthuman designates the understanding that 'humanism' and 'the human', where these describe essential and unchanging qualities, are fictions; the greatest fictions, perhaps, of all the meta-narratives of modernism. According to Foucault in *The Order of Things*, the modern human sciences created the human being during the nineteenth century by taking 'man' as both the subject and the object of intellectual and epistemic investigation. Because of the nature of his precarious invention, his continued existence is equally arbitrary and dependent on certain cultural–historical reference points. 'If those arrangements were to disappear as they appeared,' states Foucault, 'man would be erased, like a face drawn in the sand at the edge of the sea'.[18] Badiou's criticism of ethical ideology, discussed above, takes up Foucault's position, and is similarly founded on the sense that moral codes deriving from a belief in the essential goodness, rights or value of 'Man' are perversions of the 'truth'. Man, argues Badiou, in terms that echo and transform Foucault's, 'is *the being who is capable of recognizing himself as a victim*'.[19] It is the modern obsession with protecting the other and the self from victimhood that gets in the way of the 'truth' for Badiou.

The notion that the human being has created itself as a particular and unique kind of entity can be traced back to historically earlier periods than the birth of the social sciences that Foucault cites as foundational. In the introduction to his edited reader, *Posthumanism*, Neil Badmington evokes Descartes's *Discourse on the Method* (1634) as a key moment in the construction of the idea of the human. Here Descartes argues that if we were to come face to face with a machine that had the exact appearance of a living organic monkey, we would be unable to tell them apart, as they would not differ in *essence*. We would not, however, he claims, be fooled by a human-shaped machine, for human beings possess as their essence something that sets them apart from both animals and machines: reason. Badmington contends that this idea of the privileged essence of humanity, expressed in the seventeenth century, is one that has continued to exert considerable force on our imaginations and to define our perception of ourselves as human. Postmodernism, and its offshoot posthumanism, may be the modes of thinking in which such certainties about the uniqueness of being human can be called into question and subjected to suspicion. Our tie with a fixed idea of the human essence can – and must – be profitably loosened.

A series of films that allow us to think productively through this set of ideas is the *Alien* quadrilogy (*Alien*, Ridley Scott, 1979; *Aliens*, James Cameron, 1986; *Alien 3*, David Fincher, 1992; *Alien: Resurrection*, Jean-Pierre Jeunet, 1997). Unlike *Kill Bill*, the form of the *Alien* films is not recognizably postmodern. They are structured around traditional modes of narrative suspense and three-dimensional characterization that are recognizably part of the science fiction/horror genres to which they (partially) belong. However, these films – especially *Aliens* and *Alien: Resurrection* – lend themselves thematically and philosophically to reflections on the meaning of becoming posthuman.

If the *Alien* films use suspense and audience identification in a relatively conventional formal manner, some of the kinds of identifications they ask that we make are challenging and unusual. In particular, they pivot around the idea of species loyalty and call into question the anthropocentrism that posthumanism too sets out to dethrone. The crews of the various ships that are launched into space in the four films contain a mixture of humans and androids (also called 'synthetics'), who are indistinguishable from humans to the eye. In *Alien*, the android Ash (Ian Holm) malfunctions and attempts to kill Sigourney Weaver's character Ripley in an odd sexualized attack, in which he/it tries to force a pornographic magazine down her throat until she chokes. In *Aliens*, this episode is recalled in Ridley's obvious unease and distaste at learning that a fellow crew member, Bishop (Lance Henriksen), is a synthetic. When she uses this word to describe him, Bishop replies 'I prefer the term "artificial person" myself.' This piece of dialogue very obviously reminds us of contemporary discourses about the use of non-pejorative language for minority social groups, but the distinction between same and other in this fictional example crosses the apparently absolute limit of the human/ artificial barrier. This barrier, however, is progressively troubled and broken down in the course of the four films. By the end of *Aliens*, Bishop has proved himself a loyal colleague, ultimately helping Ridley and the child Newt escape from the colonial planet on which the deadly alien life forms lurk. Ridley recognizes her debt to him in the words 'you did ok'; to which he in turn will respond, when she later helps to save them all from the alien creature that has stowed aboard their craft: 'not bad – for a human'. But this is not just a parable about tolerance of difference (a straightforward moral – or what Badiou would call 'ethical ideological' tale). Rather, the idea of difference itself progressively dissolves. The question of being able to tell the difference between 'essential' or 'real' (as opposed to inauthentic or robotic) human, around which the identificatory movement and narrative suspense of the first three films turn is radicalized in *Alien: Resurrection* as our female onscreen representative, Ridley, is no longer 'herself' but a clone of the earlier Ridley, a more physically powerful and less obviously 'moral' counterpart who is wholly posthuman. Having being placed in almost constant identification with Ridley throughout three films, we are forced to ask ourselves what it means to continue to identify with 'her' when she is not the 'same'; not 'natural'; not 'human'.

The other obviously ethical encounter that is staged in the *Alien* quadrilogy is that between the humans (and 'artificial persons' who resemble them) and the irreducibly and wholly other beings that are the eponymous aliens. Strong as machines, capable of bleeding or salivating acid that corrodes whatever it touches, and breeding by transmitting their eggs to the bodies of humans who then incubate the aliens to term, these creatures are the monsters of the sci-fi or horror genre par excellence and the battle against them at first appears to be structured straightforwardly as an us-against-them; good-against-evil conflict. However, at moments, and more so as the four films progress, this conflict is complexified.

In *Aliens*, the planet LV-426 – home of the aliens discovered in the first film – has been colonized and, of the colonist population, only a little girl, Newt, has survived decimation by the aliens. Scenes of Ridley's caretaking of the small child are central to this narrative, and the thematic of a tough or non-traditionally feminine woman who shows a sudden capacity for mothering is foregrounded, as in *Kill Bill*. However, the relationship between Ridley and Newt has a function that surpasses the Edelmanian dynamic of the redemptive child figure. On LV-426 Ridley and the crew discover that an Alien queen capable of laying thousands of eggs to repopulate the species has a fresh batch of about-to-hatch offspring. And so the theme of generation and birth is foregrounded, echoing the iconic scene from *Alien* in which Executive Officer Kane (John Hurt) 'gives birth' to the alien he has unknowingly incubated, when it bursts horrifically through his stomach. Moreover, the figure of mothering is used for a very particular effect in *Aliens*. Ripley comes face-to-face with the Alien queen twice. The first encounter comprises a memorable scene constructed in shot-reverse-shot between the close-up inhuman face of the alien queen with her protruding jaw and shiny metallic eyes, and Ridley, who is clutching the small body of Newt protectively. The image of the woman with the child immediately appeals to the sentimental codes discussed before and encourages the most traditional sort of identificatory response. However, this is immediately troubled when Ridley opens fire and torches the queen's eggs. The alien's cries of distress are piercing and disturbing and we become aware that Ridley's protection of Newt visually rhymes with the queen's attempts to save the eggs that Ridley has destroyed. Their face-to-face, shot-reverse-shot framing suggests a more intimate sort of mirroring than a mere face-off or confrontation. When we realize the parallel between the situation of the two, we are torn for a moment between identifying with (and championing) the 'non-human' against the 'human'. This is a moment of rupture within a broad-based genre of sci-fi that has traditionally drawn on fears of uncontrollable otherness that threaten our sense of communal (often national) identity. Kupfer has discussed the ethical import of *Aliens* in terms of offering a model of virtue in the figure of Ridley and her protection of Newt. He writes: 'the movie narratively uses Newt as [both] a prop toward which Ripley can display her virtues of compassion, care and nurturance [and] we can see in Newt a miniature Ripley'.[20] The assumption that Ridley is a character who provokes ethical reflection only because she shows the (stereotypically feminine) values of the ethics of care risks a reading of the film that falls into the same gender-blind traps from which Tarantino's *Kill Bill* does not quite escape, and also risks avoiding the bigger ethical question of why we are capable of identifying with, investing in, or caring about only our species group. The mirroring pair of maternal figures sets up fundamental questions for us about the relationships between living beings and the values we call on to distinguish between them that very deliberately go beyond the 'virtue' model.

The ethical import of the way in which Ripley and the Alien queen are visually pitted against each other in *Aliens* is underlined by the fact that it ultimately becomes clear that Ridley has been lied to, and that she and the queen are, in fact, both pawns in The Company's grand scheme. Rather than being a mission to annihilate the destructive alien forms, as Carter Burke (Paul Reiser) had promised Ridley before she agreed to join the crew as an advisor, the real aim of the trip is to take the aliens back to Earth as fighting machines for The Company's Bioweapons Division. Transplanetary capitalism, exploited by Burke, emerges in *Aliens* as the real political enemy. Ripley's battle for 'good' is subtly refigured by the end, then, not as a fight against the aliens but as an attempt to thwart the greed and treachery of The Company. In her attempt to scupper Burke, however, Ripley is forced to destroy another female body – the body that would have become the colonized commodity of the humans. Questions about the power and permeability of gender, solidarity, domination and humanity come to the fore here. When, in their second encounter, the queen stalks Newt as retribution for Ripley's incineration of her eggs, Ripley mounts the forklift loader to present as half-machine, half-woman; a cyborg, to fight a non-human opponent. Significantly, in this moment, Sigourney Weaver's character is not wholly human either and our anchoring points of identification are again loosened (prefiguring the consternation we will feel in *Alien: Resurrection*, when Ripley is not only a clone of herself, but an incubator for another Alien queen). How do we draw ethical lessons about the human and the non-human? By looking with extra attention at those moments when our certainties about human identity are most tested.

The deliberate and multiple (and increasingly experimental) play with cinematic modes of identification throughout the *Alien* quadrilogy results in the spectator losing sense of the familiar staging posts of identity. The radically ethical question that the *Alien* series poses concerns the extent to which our allegiance should always be to the same. To put it more forcefully, it hints at how an ethics based only on protection of the ideals of the human is inevitably altericidal. The dialogue of *Aliens* hints at an understanding of this form of altericide. When the ship is plunged into darkness, Ripley realizes that it is because the aliens have cut the power from the source. Hudson (Bill Paxton), a marine, responds that this cannot be the case because 'they're animals' and therefore incapable of reasoning or responding in a way that could challenge, outsmart or engage on the same level as 'us'. In this way, it seems justified to the likes of Burke to use the aliens as tools of destruction; to instrumentalize them, rather than seeing them as ends in themselves (to evoke a Kantian ethical paradigm that is, in its original context, applied only to humans).

The kind of posthuman ethical questioning modelled in *Aliens* offers a fantastical analogy with current debates in eco-criticism that look at the anthropocentric ideology which has sacrificed the long-term future of the planet with its millions of life forms, in the interests of short-term human gains (aping, however unconsciously, the logic of Descartes, that because humans have 'reason' and animals don't, we have the unquestioning right to take decisions that effect their survival). The set of assumptions that leads us to accord a higher status to whatever in animal-kind we perceive to be most 'human' or 'human-like' has been dubbed by Alice Kuzniar as 'anthronormativity'.[21] Derrida has also alluded to the problem of ethical relationality with the non-human, a relation that is difficult to formulate within existing philosophical presuppositions, but that must not be overlooked, when he asks: 'how can an animal look you in the face?'[22] And Noreen Giffney and Myra J. Hird's edited collection *Queering the Non-Human* (2008) has as its cover image *Axolotl*, Karl Grime's dead salamander preserved in alcohol, whose uncanny, strangely winning smile prompts them to reflect on the question of what knowledge, suppositions and cultural resonances inform our reaction to the depicted creature when gauging its status as 'human' or 'non-human'.[23]

Significantly, in their essay about the dangers of the turn to postmodernism in cultural studies, from which I quoted earlier, Slack and Whitt posit that it is in environmentalism, that is a perspective in which 'the ecosystem replaces the individual as the fundamental moral datum or unit of moral analysis, in terms of which we do our thinking about what is morally right or wrong',[24] that ethics must now be located. I would disagree that this is the *only* enduringly relevant ethical concern for our time, and would also be aware that such a concern is easily recuperable as an 'ethical' ideology or didactic imperative, if we lean towards a radical Badiousian ethics of the self and its critique of politically correct discourse. However, it is ironic that Slack and Witt reach their conclusion about the need to decentre the individual by means of a *rejection* of postmodernism and its cousin post-humanism, rather than by embracing their interrogative energies, as Derrida, Kuzniar, Giffney and Hird attempt to do. For it is precisely in its capacity to relativize the small concerns of humans – writ disproportionately large in modernity – that the kinds of questions asked under the umbrella term of posthumanism offers profoundly ethical insights into our contemporary global, humanistic and ecological dilemmas.

Some concluding remarks

In this chapter, I have argued explicitly against the notion that post-modernism, and posthumanism, in their filmic and theoretical incarnations, are so dissociated from questions of ethics and morality, are so 'over it all' in their consummate posteriority, as to be useless for ethical purposes (or, worse, to render ethics redundant in their all-encompassing indifference). The postmodern untying of narratives – of identity, of humanness – from fixed posts of meaning can conversely be seen to constitute nothing so much as a mobilization of the power of questioning, where questioning takes on the force of an ethical interrogation along the lines of an unravelling thread. Bauman has expressed this eloquently:

> Modernity has the uncanny capacity for thwarting self-examination; it wrapped the mechanisms of self-reproduction with a veil of illusions without which those mechanisms ... could not function properly. ... The 'postmodern perspective' ... means above all the tearing off of the mask of illusions; the recognition of certain pretensions as false and certain objectives as neither attainable nor, for that matter, desirable.[25]

Where postmodern film succeeds is in rendering visible the previously hidden threads that sutured generic – and gendered – narratives together and shored up naturalistic ideas about the inevitability of their logic. Some-times, as my reading of *Kill Bill* shows, grand narratives are imbued with so much meaningful authority that even a consummately postmodern decon-structive agenda does not wholly erase them, as in the troublingly persistent myth of The Bride's 'natural' maternal instinct and 'appropriate' femininity. It is, therefore, in the work of critical ethico-political reading and viewing, in the subjecting of filmic production to demystifying energies, that postmodern insights may appear most powerfully.

Joanna Zylinska, in *The Ethics of Cultural Studies* has made a similar point about the ethically imbued task of criticism for the twenty-first-century cultural theorist:

> We must [not] forget that ethics does not amount to a closed system of morals, and that any such system in existence at any moment in time is

always a result of a hegemonic struggle. Our task, cultural studies' task, consists thus in responding to the congealed system of values – through 'argumentative moments' and interventions – while remembering that there can be no closed ethical system that will be permanently filled with universal content.[26]

A properly critical interrogation of our investments, our belief systems and our identifications may ultimately be the most ethical academic and political gesture we can make. The analyses in this chapter have borrowed deliberately from a large range of ethical philosophical perspectives, often producing two or more opposing interpretations of the same image or representation, which have been allowed to remain unresolved, in play, in uneasy tension with each other (without being reified as binaries). This strategy has permitted a – however modest – relativization of the kinds of 'congealed' meanings and morals that Zylinska alludes to. Postmodern filmmaking and viewing films through the lens of plural postmodern ideas thus reappear in this light, not as vacuous or superficial endeavours, but as a valid ethical project proper to our contemporary moment.

Notes

1 Bauman, *Postmodern Ethics*, 2.
2 Slack and Whitt, 'Ethics and Cultural Studies', 581.
3 Slack and Whitt, 'Ethics and Cultural Studies', 582.
4 Baudrillard, *America*, 121.
5 Ames, 'Millenary Anamorphosis', 79.
6 Bauman, *Postmodern Ethics*, 14.
7 James Wood, *Guardian*, November 12, 1994.
8 Botting and Wilson, *The Tarantinian Ethics*, 6.
9 Botting and Wilson, *The Tarantinian Ethics*, 7.
10 Botting and Wilson, *The Tarantinian Ethics*, 7.
11 Botting and Wilson, *The Tarantinian Ethics*, 8.
12 Botting and Wilson, *The Tarantinian Ethics*, 8.
13 Barnfield, 'Killing *Kill Bill*' (accessed 29/01/09).
14 Freedland, 'The Power of the Gory' (accessed 29/01/09).
15 Badiou, *Ethics*, 91.
16 Badiou, *Ethics*, 91.
17 Badiou, *Ethics*, 90.
18 Foucault, *The Order of Things*, 422.
19 Badiou, *Ethics*, 10 (the italics are Badiou's).
20 Kupfer, *Visions of Virtue*, 217.
21 Kuzniar, 'Melancholia's Dog'.
22 Derrida, 'The Animal That Therefore I am (More to Follow)', 377.
23 Giffney and Hird, 'Introduction', *Queering the Non-Human*, 1.
24 Slack and Whitt, 'Ethics and Cultural Studies', 572.
25 Bauman, *Postmodern Ethics*, 3.
26 Zylinska, *The Ethics of Cultural Studies*, 22.

Bibliography

Aaron, Michele, '"Til Death Us Do Part": Cinema's Queer Couples Who Kill', in *The Body's Perilous Pleasures*, ed. Michele Aaron (Edinburgh: Edinburgh University Press, 1999), 67–84.
——, *Spectatorship: The Power of Looking On* (London: Wallflower, 2007).
Aitken, Ian, *European Film Theory and Cinema: A Critical Introduction* (Edinburgh: Edinburgh University Press, 2001).
Ames, Sandford S., 'Millenary Anamorphosis: French Map, American Dream', *L'Esprit créateur*, 32, 1992, 75–82.
Antelme, Robert, *The Human Race*, trans. Jeffrey Haight and Annie Mahler [1947] (Evanston, IL: Northwestern University Press, 1998).
Appiah, Kwame Anthony, *The Ethics of Identity* (Princeton, NJ; Woodstock: Princeton University Press, 2005).
——, *Cosmopolitanism: Ethics in a World of Strangers* (London: Allen Lane, 2006).
Appignanesi, Josh and Devorah Baum, '*Ex Memoria*: Filming the Face – Memorialisation, Dementia and the Ethics of Representation', *Third Text*, 21, 1, 2006, 85–97.
Arendt, Hannah, *On Revolution* (London: Faber & Faber, 1963).
Aristotle, *The Nicomachean Ethics*, trans. J. A. K. Thomson (London: George Allen & Unwin, 1953).
Armengaud, Françoise, 'Faire ou ne pas faire d'images. Emmanuel Levinas et l'art d'oblitération', *Noesis*, 3, 2005 http://revel.unice.fr/noesis/document.html?id=11#ftn13.
Assiter, Alison and Carol Avedon (eds), *Bad Girls and Dirty Pictures: The Challenge to Reclaim Feminism* (Pluto: London, 1993).
Atkinson, Michael, 'Michael Winterbottom: Cinema as Heart Attack', *Film Comment*, 34, 1, 1998, 44–47.
Aumont, Jacques, *Du visage au cinéma* (Paris: Cahiers du cinéma, 1992).
Avedon, Carol, 'Snuff: Believing the Worst', in *Bad Girls and Dirty Pictures: The Challenge to Reclaim Feminism*, ed. Assiter and Avedon, 126–30.
Badiou, Jean, *Ethics: An Essay on the Understanding of Evil*, trans. Peter Hallward [1998] (London; New York: Verso, 2001).
Badmington, Neil (ed.), *Posthumanism* (Basingstoke: Palgrave Macmillan, 2000).
Baecque, Antoine de, *La Cinéphilie: invention d'un regard, histoire d'une culture 1944–1968* (Paris: Fayard, 2003).
Barnfield, Graham, *Killing Kill Bill*, www.spiked-online.com/Articles/00000006DF88.htm.
Baudrillard, Jean, *De la séduction* (Paris: Galilée, 1979).
——, *America*, trans. Chris Turner (New York: Verso, 1988).
Bauman, Zygmunt, *Postmodern Ethics* (Oxford: Blackwell, 1993).

Bennington, Geoffrey, 'Deconstruction and Ethics', in *Deconstructions: A User's Guide*, ed. Nicholas Royle (Basingstoke: Palgrave Macmillan, 2000), 64–82.

Beugnet, Martine, *Claire Denis* (Manchester: Manchester University Press, 2004).

Boltanski, Luc, *Distant Suffering: Morality, Media and Politics*, trans. Graham D. Burchell [1993] (Cambridge: Cambridge University Press, 1999).

Boos, Stephen, 'Rethinking the Aesthetic: Kant, Schiller, and Hegel', in *Between Ethics and Aesthetics: Crossing the Boundaries*, ed. Dorota Glowacka and Stephen Boos (Albany, NY: State University of New York Press, 2002), 15–27.

Bordwell, David, *The Films of Carl-Theodor Dreyer* (Berkeley, CA; London: University of California Press, 1981).

Botting, Fred, *Gothic* (London; New York: Routledge, 1995).

Botting, Fred and Scott Wilson, *The Tarantinian Ethics* (London: Sage, 2001).

Bowie, Malcolm, *Psychoanalysis and the Future of Theory* (Oxford: Blackwell, 1993).

Bristow, Joseph, *Sexuality* (London; New York: Routledge, 1997).

Brunette, Peter and David Wills, *Screen/Play: Derrida and Film Theory* (Princeton, NJ: Princeton University Press, 1989).

Bukatman, Scott, 'Zooming Out: The End of Off-Screen Space', in *The New American Cinema*, ed. Jon Lewis (Durham, NC; London: Duke University Press, 1998), 248–72.

Butler, Judith, *Precarious Life: The Power of Mourning and Violence* (London: Verso, 2004).

Calhoun, Dave, 'White Guides, Black Pain', *Sight and Sound*, 17, 2, 2007, 32–35.

Caputi, Mary, *Voluptuous Yearnings: A Feminist Theory of The Obscene* (London: Rowman and Littlefield, 1994).

Cavell, Stanley, *Cities of Words: Pedagogical Letters on a Register of the Moral Life* (Cambridge, MA: Harvard University Press, 2004).

Celeste, Reni, 'The Frozen Screen: Levinas and the Action Film', *Film-Philosophy*, 11, 2, 2007, 15–36.

Chion, Michel, 'Le détail qui tue la critique de cinéma', *Libération*, 22 April 1994.

Chouliaraki, Lilie, *The Spectatorship of Suffering* (London: Sage, 2006).

Cook, Bernie (ed.), *Thelma and Louise Live! The Cultural Afterlife of an American Film* (Austin: University of Texas Press, 2008).

Cooper, Sarah, *Selfless Cinema?: Ethics and French Documentary* (Oxford: Legenda, 2006).

——, 'Introduction – The Occluded Relation: Levinas and Cinema', *Film-Philosophy*, 11, 2, 2007, i–vii.

Copjec, Joan, 'The Orthopsychic Subject: Film Theory and the Reception of Lacan' in *Film and Theory: An Anthology*, ed. Robert Stam and Toby Miller (Oxford: Blackwell, 2000), 437–55.

Crignon, Philippe, 'Figuration: Emmanuel Levinas and the Image', *Yale French Studies*, 104, 2004, 100–125.

Critchley, Simon, *The Ethics of Deconstruction: Derrida and Levinas* (Oxford: Blackwell, 1992).

Daney, Serge, *Devant la recrudescence des vols de sacs à main: cinéma, télévision, information, 1988–1991* (Lyon: Aléas, 1991).

——, 'Le Travelling de *Kapo*', *Trafic*, 4, 1992, 5–19.

Dardenne, Luc, *Au dos de nos images* (Paris: Seuil, 2005).

Davis, Colin, *Ethical Issues in Twentieth-Century French Fiction: Killing the Other* (Basingstoke: Palgrave Macmillan, 2000).

——, 'Levinas at 100', *Paragraph*, 29, 3, 2006, 95–104.

De, Esha Niyogi, 'Decolonizing Universality: Postcolonial Theory and the Quandary of Ethical Agency', *Diacritics*, 32, 2, 2002, 42–59.

Dean, Tim, 'An Impossible Embrace: Queerness, Futurity and the Death Drive', in *A Time for the Humanities: Futurity and the Limits of Autonomy*, ed. James Bono, Tim Dean and Eva Plonowska Ziarek (New York: Fordham University Press, 2008), 112–40.

Deleuze, Gilles and Félix Guattari, *Anti-Oedipus: Capitalism and Schizophrenia*, trans. Robert Hurley, Mark Seem and Helen R. Lane [1972] (Minneapolis, MN: University of Minnesota Press, 1983).

——, *A Thousand Plateaus: Capitalism and Schizophrenia*, trans. Brian Massumi [1980] (Minneapolis, MN: University of Minnesota Press, 1987).

Derrida, Jacques, *Memoirs of the Blind: The Self-Portrait and Other Ruins*, trans. Pascale-Anne Brault and Michael Naas [1990] (Chicago; London: University of Chicago Press, 1993).

——, *Spectres of Marx: The State of the Debt, the Work of Mourning, and the New International*, trans. Peggy Kamuf [1993] (New York; London: Routledge, 1994).

——, 'The Deconstruction of Actuality: An Interview with Jacques Derrida', *Radical Philosophy*, 68, 1994, 28–41.

——, 'The Spatial Arts: An Interview with Jacques Derrida', trans. Laurie Volpe, in *Deconstruction and the Visual Arts: Art, Media, Architecture*, ed. Peter Brunette and David Wills (Cambridge: Cambridge University Press, 1994), 9–33.

——, *Archive Fever: A Freudian Impression*, trans. Eric Prenowitz [1996] (London; Chicago, IL: University of Chicago Press, 1996).

——, *Adieu to Emmanuel Levinas*, trans. Pascale-Anne Brault and Michael Naas [1997] (Stanford, CA: Stanford University Press, 1999).

——, *Of Hospitality*, trans. Rachel Bowlby [1997] (Stanford, CA: Stanford University Press, 2000).

——, *On Cosmopolitanism and Forgiveness*, trans. Mark Dooley and Michael Hughes [1997] (London: Routledge, 2001).

——, *The Gift of Death; and, Literature in Secret*, trans. David Wills [1999] (Chicago, IL; London: University of Chicago Press, 2nd edition 2008).

——, 'Le Cinéma et ses fantômes', *Cahiers du cinéma*, 556, 2001, 74–85.

——, 'The Animal That Therefore I Am (More to Follow)', *Critical Inquiry*, 28, 2, 2002, 369–418.

Derrida, Jacques and Safaa Fathy, *Tourner les mots: au bord d'un film* (Paris: Galilée, 2000).

Derrida, Jacques and Bernard Stiegler, *Echographies of Television: Filmed Interviews*, trans. Jennifer Bajorek [1996] (Cambridge: Polity Press, 2002).

Desilets, Sean, 'The Rhetoric of Passion', *Camera Obscura* 53, 18, 2, 2003, 57–90.

Devi, Mahasweta, *Imaginary Maps: Three Stories*, trans. and intro. Gayatri Chakravorty Spivak (New York; London: Routledge, 1995).

Doane, Mary Ann, 'Film and the Masquerade: Theorizing the Female Spectator' [1982], in *Issues in Feminist Film Criticism*, ed. Patricia Erens (Bloomington and Indianapolis, IN: Indiana University Press, 1990), 41–57.

——, 'The Close-Up: Scale and Detail in the Cinema', *differences: A Journal of Feminist Cultural Studies*, 14, 3, 2003, 89–111.

Domarchi, Jean, Jacques Doniol-Valcroze, Jean-Luc Godard, Pierre Kast, Jacques Rivette and Eric Rohmer, 'Hiroshima, notre amour', *Cahiers du cinéma*, 97, 1959, 1–18.

Downing, Lisa, 'Between Men and Women; Beyond Heterosexuality: Limits and Possibilities of the Erotic in Lynne Stopkewich's *Kissed* and Patrice Leconte's *La Fille sur le pont*', *Romance Studies*, 20, 1, 2002, 29–40.

——, *Patrice Leconte* (Manchester: Manchester University Press, 2004).

Duffy, Jean, 'Message versus Mystery and Film Noir Borrowings in Patrice Leconte's *Monsieur Hire*', *French Cultural Studies*, 13, 38, 2002, 209–24.

Dworkin, Andrea, *Pornography: Men Possessing Women* (New York: Perigee Books, 1981).

——, *Intercourse* (London: Secker and Warburg, 1987).

Eaglestone, Robert, 'Inexhaustible Meaning, Inextinguishable Voices: Levinas and the Holocaust,' in *The Holocaust and the Postmodern* (Oxford: Oxford University Press, 2004), 249–78.

Easthope, Anthony, 'Derrida and British Film Theory', in *Applying: To Derrida*, ed. John Brannigan, Ruth Robbins and Julia Wolfreys (Basingstoke: Palgrave MacMillan, 1996), 184–94.

Edelman, Lee, *No Future: Queer Theory and the Death Drive* (Durham, NC; London: Duke University Press, 2004).

Epstein, Jean, 'Magnification and Other Writings', trans. Stuart Liebman, *October*, 3, 1977, 9–25.

Fabe, Marilyn, *Closely Watched Films: An Introduction to the Art of Narrative Film Technique* (Berkeley; Los Angeles, CA: University of California Press, 2004).

Feminists Against Censorship, *Pornography and Feminism: The Case Against Censorship*, ed. Gillian Rodgerson and Elizabeth Wilson (London: Lawrence and Wishart, 1991).

Foucault, Michel, *History of Madness*, trans. Jonathan Murphy and Jean Khalfa [1961] (London and New York: Routledge, 2006).

——, *The Order of Things*, trans. Alan Sheridan [1966] (London; New York: Routledge, 1989).

——, *Discipline and Punish*, trans. Alan Sheridan [1975] (Harmondsworth: Penguin, 1991).

——, *The Will to Knowledge, The History of Sexuality 1*, trans. Robert Hurley [1976] (Harmondsworth: Penguin, 1990).

——, *The Care of the Self, The History of Sexuality 3*, trans. Robert Hurley [1984] (Harmondsworth: Penguin, 1990).

——, *The Use of Pleasure, The History of Sexuality 2*, trans. Robert Hurley [1984] (Harmondsworth: Penguin, 1990).

——, *Technologies of the Self: A Seminar with Michel Foucault*, ed. Luther H. Martin, Huck Gutman and Patrick H. Hutton (Amherst, MA: The University of Massachusetts Press, 1988).

——, *Essential Works of Michel Foucault 1954–1988, vol. 1, Ethics: Subjectivity and Truth*, ed. Paul Rabinow, trans. Robert Hurley et. al. (Harmondsworth: Penguin, 1997).

——, *Essential Works of Michel Foucault 1954–1988, vol. 2, Aesthetics, Method and Epistemology*, ed. James D. Faubion, trans. Robert Hurley et al. (Harmondsworth: Penguin, 1998).

Freedland, Jonathan, 'The Power of the Gory', *Guardian*, 15 October 2003, www.guardian.co.uk/film/2003/oct/15/comment.features.

French, Peter, *Cowboy Metaphysics: Ethics and Death in Westerns* (Maryland: Rowman and Littlefield, 1997).

Freud, Sigmund, *The Standard Edition of the Complete Psychological Works*, trans. and ed. James Strachey, 24 vols., (London: Hogarth Press and the Institute of Psycho-Analysis, 1953–74).

Frodon, Jean-Michel (ed.), *Le Cinéma et la Shoah: un art à l'épreuve de la tragédie du 20e siècle* (Paris: Cahiers du cinema, 2007).

Garber, Marjorie B., Beatrice Hanssen and Rebecca L. Walkowitz (eds), *The Turn to Ethics* (London; New York: Routledge, 2000).

Giffney, Noreen and Myra J. Hird (eds), *Queering the Non-Human* (Aldershot: Ashgate, 2008).

Hartman, Geoffrey, 'Memory.com: Tele-Suffering and Testimony in the Dot Com Era', *Raritan*, 19, 3, 2000, 1–18.

Haskell, Molly, *From Reverence to Rape: The Treatment of Women in the Movies* (Chicago, IL: University of Chicago Press, 1973).

Heath, Stephen, 'God, Faith and Film: *Breaking the Waves*', *Literature and Theology*, 12, 1, 1998, 93–107.

Hegel, Georg Wilhelm Friedrich, *Introductory Lectures on Aesthetics*, trans. Bernard Bosanquet [1835] (London: Penguin, 1993).

Hiddleston, Jane, *Understanding Postcolonialism* (Stocksfield: Acumen, 2009).

Höyng, Peter, 'Schiller Goes to the Movies: Locating the Sublime in *Thelma and Louise*', *Die Unterrichtspraxis / Teaching German*, 30, 1, 1997, 40–49.

Jay, Martin, *Downcast Eyes: The Denigration of Vision in Twentieth-Century Thought* (Berkeley, CA; London: University of California Press, 1993).

Kabir, Shameem, *Daughters of Desire: Lesbian Representations in Film* (London; Washington, DC: Cassell, 1998).

Kant, Immanuel, *Groundwork of the Metaphysics of Morals*, trans. and ed. Mary Gregor [1785] (Cambridge: Cambridge University Press, 1998).

——, *Critique of Judgement*, trans. Werner S. Pluhar [1790] (Indianapolis, IN; Cambridge: Hackett Publishing Company, 1987).

——, *Religion Within the Limits of Reason Alone*, trans. Theodore M. Greene and Hoyt H. Hudson [1793] (New York: Harper & Bros, 1960).

Kierkegaard, Søren, *Fear and Trembling*, ed. C. Stephen Evans and Sylvia Walsh, trans. Walsh [1843] (Cambridge: Cambridge University Press, 2006).

King, Geoff (ed.), *The Spectacle of the Real: From Hollywood to 'Reality' TV and Beyond* (Bristol; Portland, OR: Intellect, 2005).

Kupfer, Joseph, *Visions of Virtue in Popular Film* (Boulder, CO: Westview Press, 1999).

Kuzniar, Alice, *Melancholia's Dog: Reflections on our Animal Kinship* (Chicago, IL; London: University of Chicago Press, 2006).

Lacan, Jacques, *Écrits: The First Complete Translation in English*, trans. Bruce Fink (New York: Norton, 1992).

——, *The Seminar of Jacques Lacan, Book VII: The Ethics of Psychoanalysis, 1959–1960*, ed. Jacques-Alain Miller, trans. Dennis Porter (New York: Norton 1992).

——, 'Freud, Hegel and the Machine', *The Seminar of Jacques Lacan, Book II: The Ego in Freud's Theory and in the Technique of Psychoanalysis, 1954–1955*, ed. Jacques-Alain Miller, trans. Sylvana Tomaselli (New York: Norton, 1988), 64–76.

LaCapra, Dominick, *History and Memory after Auschwitz* (Ithaca, NY: Cornell University Press, 1998), 95–138.

Lanzmann, Claude, 'Holocauste, la représentation impossible', *Le Monde* (*Supplément Arts–Spectacles*), 3 March 1994, i, vii.

——, 'Parler pour les morts', *Le Monde des débats*, 14, 2000, 14–16.

Lapsley, Robert and Michael Westlake, *Film Theory: An Introduction* (Manchester: Manchester University Press, 1988).

Lemire, Elise, 'Voyeurism and the Post-War Crisis of Masculinity in *Rear Window*', in *Alfred Hitchcock's Rear Window*, ed. John Belton (Cambridge: Cambridge University Press, 2000).

Levi, Primo, *If This Is a Man*, trans. Stuart Woolf [1947/1958] (London: Bodley Head, 1966).

Levinas, Emmanuel, 'Reality and its Shadow', trans. Alphonso Lingis [1948], in *The Levinas Reader*, ed. Sean Hand (Oxford: Blackwell, 1989) 129–43.

——, *Totality and Infinity: An Essay on Exteriority*, trans. Alphonso Lingis [1961] (Pittsburgh: Duquesne University Press, 1969)

——, 'The Servant and her Master', trans. Michael Holland [1966], in *The Levinas Reader*, ed. Sean Hand (Oxford: Blackwell, 1989), 150–59.

——, *Otherwise than Being or Beyond Essence*, trans. Alphonso Lingis [1974] (Pittsburgh: Duquesne University Press, 1981).

——, *Ethics and Infinity. Conversations with Philippe Nemo*, trans. Richard A. Cohen [1982] (Pittsburgh: Duquesne University Press, 1985).

——, 'Ethics and Politics', trans. Jonathan Romney [1982–83], in *The Levinas Reader*, ed. Sean Hand (Oxford: Blackwell, 1989), 289–97.

——, 'Peace and Proximity' [1984], in *Emmanuel Levinas: Basic Philosophical Writings*, ed. Robert Bernasconi, Simon Critchley and Adriaan T. Peperzak, trans. Peter Atterton and Critchley (Bloomington; Indianapolis, IN: Indiana University Press, 1996), 161–69.

——, 'Interdit de la représentation et "Droits de l'homme"', in *L'Interdit de la représentation. Colloque de Montpellier, 1981*, ed. Adélie and Jean-Jacques Rassial (Paris: Seuil, 1984), 107–13.

——, *Entre Nous: On Thinking-of-the-Other*, trans. Michael B. Smith and Barbara Harshav [1991] (London: Athlone, 1998).

Lyotard, Jean-François *The Postmodern Condition: A Report on Knowledge*, trans. Geoff Bennington and Brian Massumi [1979] (Minneapolis, MN: University of Minnesota Press, 1984).

M.G., 'Réactions: Questions sur la liberté de création', *L'Humanité*, 29 October 2003.

McGinn, Colin, *Ethics, Evil and Fiction* (Oxford: Oxford University Press, 1997).

McGowan, Todd, 'The Temporality of the Real: The Path to Politics in *The Constant Gardener*', *Film-Philosophy*, 11, 3, 2007, 52–73.

MacIntyre, Alasdair, *After Virtue: A Study in Moral Theory* (London: Duckworth, 1981).

Mackinnon, Catherine, *Feminism Unmodified: Discourses on Life and Law* (Cambridge, MA: Harvard University Press, 1987).

Malausa, Vincent, 'Histoires de fantômes', *Cahiers du cinéma*, 570, 2002, 78–80.

Maynard, Richard A. (ed.), *African on Film: Myth and Reality* (Rochelle Park, NJ: Hayden Book Co., 1974).

Mayne, Judith, *Claire Denis* (Urbana, IL: University of Illinois Press, 2005).

Moran, Dominic, 'Decisions, Decisions: Derrida on Kierkegaard and Abraham', *Telos*, 123, 2002, 107–30.

Morrey, Douglas, 'Textures of Terror: Claire Denis's *Trouble Every Day*', *Belphegor: Littérature populaire et culture médiatique*, 3, 2, 2004, http://etc.dal.ca/belphegor/vol3_no2/articles/03_02_Morrey_textur_en_cont.html.

Moullet, Luc, 'Sam Fuller sur les brisées de Marlowe', *Cahiers du cinéma*, 93, 1959, 11–19.

Mulvey, Laura, 'Visual Pleasure and Narrative Cinema', *Screen*, 16, 3, 1975, 6–18.

——, 'Afterthoughts on "Visual Pleasure and Narrative Cinema" inspired by King Vidor's *Duel in the Sun*, *Framework*, 15/16/17, 1981, 12–15.

——, *Death 24x a Second: Stillness and the Moving Image* (London: Reaktion Books, 2006).

Murray, Abigail, 'Voyeurism in *Monsieur Hire*', *Modern and Contemporary France*, 3, 1993, 287–95.

Nancy, Jean-Luc, 'La Représentation interdite' [2001], in *Au fond des images* (Paris: Galilée, 2003), 57–99.

Nash, Mark, 'Notes on the Dreyer-Text', in *Screen Theory Culture* (Basingstoke: Palgrave Macmillan, 2008), 70–111.

Nezick, Nathalie, 'Le Travelling de *Kapo* ou le paradoxe de la morale', *Vertigo*, 17, 1998, 160–64.

Nichols, Bill, *Representing Reality: Issues and Concepts in Documentary* (Bloomington, IN: Indiana University Press, 1991).

——, *Introduction to Documentary* (Bloomington; Indianapolis, IN: Indiana University Press, 2001).

Nobus, Dany, 'The Politics of Gift-Giving and the Provocation of Lars von Trier's *Dogville*', *Film-Philosophy*, 11, 3, 2007, 23–37.

Nussbaum, Martha, *Love's Knowledge: Essays on Philosophy and Literature* (Oxford; New York: Oxford University Press, 1990).

——, 'Non-Relative Virtues: An Aristotelian Approach,' in *The Quality of Life*, ed. Martha C. Nussbaum and Amartya Sen (Oxford; New York: Oxford University Press, 1993), 1–6.

Ohlin, Peter, 'The Holocaust in Ingmar Bergman's *Persona*: The Instability of Imagery', *Scandinavian Studies*, 77, 2, 2005, 241–74.

Philibert, Nicolas, 'J'ai choisi l'instituteur, une sorte de double', *Cahiers du cinéma*, 570, 2002, 80–81.

Plato, *Philebus*, trans. Robin Waterfield (London; Harmondsworth: Penguin, 1982).

——, *Phaedrus*, trans. Christopher Rowe (London; Harmondsworth: Penguin, 2005).

——, *Symposium*, trans. Robin Waterfield (Oxford: Oxford University Press, 1994).

Powrie, Phil, 'Unfamiliar Places: "Heterospection" and Recent French Films on Children', *Screen*, 46, 3, 2005, 341–52.

Pryluck, Calvin, 'Ultimately We are All Outsiders: The Ethics of Documentary Filming', *Journal of the University Film Association*, 28, 1, 1976, 21–29.

Rajchman, John, *Truth and Eros: Foucault, Lacan and the Question of Ethics* (London; New York: Routledge, 1991).

Raskin, Richard, *A Child at Gunpoint: A Case Study in the Life of a Photo* (Aarhus: Aarhus University Press, 2004).

Renov, Michael, *The Subject of Documentary* (New York; London: Routledge, 2004).

Rhodes, John David, *Stupendous, Miserable City: Pasolini's Rome* (Minneapolis: University of Minnesota Press, 2007).

Rivette, Jacques, 'De l'abjection', *Cahiers du cinéma*, 120, 1961, 54–55.

Robbins, Jill, *Altered Reading* (Chicago: Chicago University Press, 1999).

Rosario, Vernon, *The Erotic Imagination: French Histories of Perversity* (Oxford; New York: Oxford University Press, 1997).

Rosen, Marjorie, *Popcorn Venus: Women, Movies and the American Dream* (New York: Avon, 1973).

Rousseau, Jean-Jacques, *Discourse on the Origins of Inequality (Second Discourse)*, in *The Collected Writings of Rousseau*, vol. 3, ed. Roger D. Masters and Christopher Kelly, trans. Judith R. Bush, Roger D. Masters, Christopher Kelly and Terence Marshall [1755] (Hanover, NH: University Press of New England, 1993), 1–95.

Russo, Vito, *The Celluloid Closet: Homosexuality in the Movies* [1981] (New York: Harper and Row, 1987).

Samuels, Robert, *Hitchcock's Bi-textuality: Lacan, Feminisms and Queer Theory* (Albany, NY: State University of New York Press, 1998).

Sartre, Jean-Paul, 'Jean-Paul Sartre répond', *L'Arc*, 30 October 1966, 87–96.

Saxton, Libby, *Haunted Images: Film, Ethics, Testimony and the Holocaust* (London: Wallflower, 2008).

Schamus, James, 'Dreyer's Textual Realism', in *Rites of Realism: Essays on Corporeal Cinema*, ed. Ivone Margulies (Durham, NC; London: Duke University Press, 2003), 315–24.

Schellekens, Elisabeth, *Aesthetics and Morality* (London; New York: Continuum, 2007).

Scher, Lucy, 'Road Movies with a Map', *The Script Factory*, 15 March 2005, www.scriptfactory. co.uk./go/News/Articles/Article_18.html.

Schiller, Friedrich, *On the Aesthetic Education of Man*, trans. Elizabeth M. Wilkinson and L. A. Willoughby [1794–95] (Oxford: Clarendon Press, 1967).

Sedgwick, Eve Kosofsky, *Between Men: English Literature and Homosexual Desire* (New York: Columbia University Press, 1985).

Segal, Lynne and Mary McIntosh (eds), *Sex Exposed: Sexuality and the Pornography Debate* (London: Virago, 1992).

Sicinski, Michael, 'A Fragmented Epistemology: The Films of Abderrahmane Sissako', *Cinema Scope*, 29, 2007, 16–19.

Sissako, Abderrahmane, 'Interview: Abderrahmane Sissako', in Thackway, *Africa Shoots Back* (Bloomington, IN: Indiana University Press; Oxford: James Currey, 2003), 199–200.

——, 'La Conscience que l'Afrique n'est pas dupe', *Positif*, 548, 2006, 17–21.

——, 'Finding Our Own Voices', *Sight and Sound*, 17, 2, 2007, 30–31.

Sklar, Robert, 'A Woman's Vision of Shame and Desire: An Interview with Catherine Breillat', *Cinéaste*, 25, 1, 1999, 24–26.

Slack, Jennifer Daryl and Laurie Ann Whitt, 'Ethics and Cultural Studies', in *Cultural Studies*, ed. Lawrence Grossberg, Cary Nelson and Paula Treichler (London; New York: Routledge, 1992), 571–92.

Smart, Barry, 'Foucault, Levinas and the Subject of Responsibility', in *The Later Foucault*, ed. Jeremy Moss (London: Sage, 1998), 78–92.

Smelik, Anneke, 'Art Cinema and Murderous Lesbians', in *New Queer Cinema: A Critical Reader*, ed. Michele Aaron (New Brunswick, NJ: Rutgers University Press, 2004), 68–79.

Smith, Robert, 'Deconstruction and Film', in *Deconstructions: A User's Guide*, ed. Nicholas Royle (Basingstoke: Palgrave Macmillan, 2000), 119–36.

Sobchack, Vivian, 'Inscribing Ethical Space: Ten Propositions on Death, Representation, and Documentary', in *Carnal Thoughts: Embodiment and Moving Image Culture* (Berkeley; London: University of California Press, 2004), 226–57 (original version of essay published in 1984 in *Quarterly Review of Film Studies*, 9, 4, 283–300).

Sontag, Susan, *Regarding the Pain of Others* [2003] (London: Penguin, 2004).

Stacey, Jackie, 'Desperately Seeking Difference' [1987], in *Issues in Feminist Film Criticism*, ed. Patricia Erens (Bloomington; Indianapolis: Indiana University Press, 1990), 365–79.

Stam, Robert and Ella Shohat, 'Stereotype, Realism and the Struggle over Representation', in *Unthinking Eurocentrism: Multiculturalism and the Media* (London; New York: Routledge, 1994), 178–219.

Stam, Robert and Louise Spence, 'Colonialism, Racism and Representation' [1983], in *Film Theory and Criticism: Introductory Readings*, ed. Leo Braudy and Marshall Cohen (Oxford: Oxford University Press, 6th edition 2004), 877–91.

Sturken, Marita, *Thelma and Louise* (London: BFI, 2000).

Thackway, Melissa, *Africa Shoots Back: Alternative Perspectives in Sub-Saharan Francophone African Film* (Bloomington; Indianapolis, IN: Indiana University Press; Oxford: James Currey, 2003).

Todorov, Tzvetan, *Facing the Extreme: Moral Life in the Concentration Camps*, trans. Arthur Denner and Abigail Pollak [1991] (New York: Henry Holt, 1996).

Ukadike, N. Frank, 'Calling to Account', *Sight and Sound*, 17, 2, 2007, 38–39.

Vincendeau, Ginette, '*Baise-moi*', *Sight and Sound*, May 2002, 38.

Wayne, Mike, *Political Film: The Dialectics of Third Cinema* (London: Pluto, 2001).

Weiss, Andrea, *Vampires and Violets: Lesbians in Film* (Harmondsworth: Penguin, 1993).

Wild, Floriane, '*L'Histoire resuscitée*: Jewishness and Scapegoating in Julien Duvivier's *Panique*', in *Identity Papers: Contested Nationhood in Twentieth-Century France*, ed. Steven Ungar and Tom Conley (Minneapolis: University of Minnesota Press, 1996).

Williams, Linda, *Hardcore: Power, Pleasure and the Frenzy of the Visible* (Berkeley; Los Angeles, CA: University of California Press, 1989).

Williams, Linda Ruth, 'Sick Sisters', *Sight and Sound*, July 2001, 28–29.

Wood, James, 'Kill Bill', *Guardian*, November 12, 1994, 12.

Young, Robert J. C., *Postcolonialism: An Historical Introduction* (Oxford: Blackwell, 2001).

Žižek, Slavoj, *Looking Awry: An Introduction to Jacques Lacan Through Popular Culture* (Cambridge, MA: MIT Press, 1991).

——, *Enjoy Your Symptom!: Jaques Lacan in Hollywood and Out* (New York; London: Routledge, 1992).

——, *Everything You Always Wanted to Know about Lacan (But Were Afraid to ask Hitchcock)* (London; New York: Verso, 1992).

——, 'Looking Awry', in *Film and Theory: An Anthology*, ed. Robert Stam and Toby Miller (Oxford: Blackwell, 2000), 524–38.

——, *The Ticklish Subject: The Absent Centre of Political Ontology* (London; New York: Verso, 2000).

——, *Welcome to the Desert of the Real! Five Essays on September 11 and Related Dates* (London; New York: Verso, 2002).

Zola, Emile, *La Bête humaine* [1890] (Paris: Gallimard, 1977).

Zupančič, Alenka, 'A Perfect Place to Die: Theatre in Hitchcock's Films' in *Everything You Always Wanted to Know about Lacan (But Were Afraid to ask Hitchcock)*, ed. Žižek (London; New York: Verso, 1992), 73–105.

——, *Ethics of the Real: Kant, Lacan* (London; New York: Verso, 2000).

Zylinska, Joanna, *The Ethics of Cultural Studies* (London: Continuum, 2005).

Index